THE LABOR POLICY
OF
THE FREE SOCIETY

by

SYLVESTER PETRO
PROFESSOR OF LAW
NEW YORK UNIVERSITY SCHOOL OF LAW

THE RONALD PRESS COMPANY · NEW YORK

81160
331.1
P497L

Library of Congress Catalog Card Number: 57-6822

To
LUDWIG VON MISES
and
WILLIAM WINSLOW CROSSKEY

Since that moment when man first looked upon himself and saw the image of God, he has struggled against all the powers of nature and the supernatural, and against all the tyrannies of his fellow man, to fulfill the promise in that image. He has lived to the full, in pleasure and pain, the gregarious life to which half of his instincts and appetites committed him. And in response to the other half, he has striven in every element on earth, in the skies above the earth and in the waters under the earth, to express himself as an individual.

—Whitney Griswold

PREFACE

I have two objectives in offering this book to the public. I wish to define the essential features of the free society, and to advance certain proposals in the field of labor relations. These two objectives have, as it seems to me, many things in common, not the least of which is their common relevance to those prominent current problems which set our era apart in history. While we speak frequently of the free society, there is reason to believe that its essential nature is not clearly perceived by all its proponents. Yet we ought to know what it is that we proclaim and espouse when we oppose communism, fascism, and totalitarianism. I have, therefore, attempted here to restate and to reaffirm in the modern context the structural elements of the free society. As it happens, such a restatement also serves well as a standard with which to measure the labor policy of the United States. For I assume that our labor policy, like all our policies, should be the policy appropriate to a free society.

No part of the world of action or ideas lies closer to the central issues of our times than do the problems and conflicts in labor relations. It does not matter how one describes the great current issues. One may say that the heart of the matter lies in the conflict between individual freedom and the increasing activity of the state; or in the autarchic tendencies of so many nations; or in the struggle between limited government and totalitarianism; or in the subordination of the rule of law to executive authority. Others may think that the foremost problem of our age is posed by the poorer citizens and peoples who wish to share the wealth of the richer citizens and peoples through forcible means when others fail. There are those who insist that the most pressing problem of the times is that of creating an effective and enduring international order, the great society of nations.

Regardless of the manner of statement, labor relations affect or are a more or less intimate part of the great world problems. I have tried here to provide a means of understanding the relationship between some of the key problems in labor relations and the forces in the world which have brought about the present state of affairs. For labor relations are the world of today in small.

Studying this field, we shall see all the distortions of truth and history so characteristic of the modern world. Thus the common version of our labor law history casts the labor union in the role of the victim of enterprisers and their alleged servitors, the federal and state judiciaries. We hear repeatedly that for most of American history the working man committed a crime in joining a union; that the law discriminated against labor unions; that, until very recently, scarcely a strike could be called without having a court issue an injunction against it; that without unions the individual working man is a mere pawn and always treated as such by employers; that the courage of union officials is the only force which stands between workers and exploitation.

Some of these allegations of the current orthodoxy cannot be dealt with by resort to historical fact. That workers are absolutely dependent upon union representation; that only union leaders stand between workers and exploitation—these are theoretical, hypothetical arguments which cannot be either proved or disproved solely on the basis of fact or history. Since they are theoretical assertions, they can be dealt with only in terms of logic and theory. And so the first part of this book attempts to establish a set of standards against which arguments on the question may be judged in a more satisfactory way.

A straightforward account of the facts of our labor law history will suffice to dispel the factual inaccuracies in the remainder of these allegations. As we shall see in the following pages, there is little or no authority for the proposition that it was at any time illegal for workers to form and join unions. On the contrary, the best and most reliable authority has recognized the legal right to form unions for more than a hundred years. We shall see that, far from discriminating against unions, the law has struggled ineffectively—up to the very present—merely in the attempt to bring trade unions within the juridical structure, so that the same rules could be applied to them which apply to all other persons and entities in society. We shall see that the peaceful strike for higher wages or better working conditions has always been privileged in the United States; and that here, too, the legal situation has been exactly the opposite of what our history says it was. Unions have always had a specially privileged status. Finally, we shall see that, not unions, but nonunion men and employers have been denied adequate legal protection against coercion and violence. Correction of the historical record is one of the main objectives of the second part of this book, where an attempt is made to present as briefly as possible the major features of current labor law and policy in the United States in an accurate historical perspective.

The author shares the convictions that a free-market, private-enterprise, private-property civilization is the best guarantor of the well-being of every man, including workingmen; that well-run unions can help the operation of a free-market economy and in this way can add to the well-being of workers; that badly operated unions, while they cannot by themselves destroy the free market, may make it function poorly enough, or by ill-advised propaganda bring it into such disrepute as to provoke its gradual and unconscious abandonment, piece by piece.

Holding these convictions, the author urges the correction of the antisocial practices of trade unions. Fortunately this is a thing which can be done—it is a job for legal institutions already in being and for laws which are well understood. No great new administrative agencies, no complicated new codes, are necessary. It is necessary only to apply to unions, with adaptations made necessary by certain of their special characteristics, the same laws and legal institutions which apply to everyone else in a well-run, free society. Today, the progress of civilization requires that unions, with their capacity for good, be brought fully within the family of constructive, law-abiding citizens. The third part of this book offers proposals for a code of labor laws consistent with the goals and methods of a free and productive society.

*   *   *

This book is dedicated to the two most remarkable contemporary thinkers of my acquaintance, William Winslow Crosskey, Professor of Law at the University of Chicago, and Ludwig von Mises, Professor of Economics at New York University. The greatest product of the tradition which Crosskey symbolizes is the Constitution of the United States. The product of the tradition Mises represents is the market economy. From these two men and their antecedents, from the Constitution of the United States, and from the market economy have come the ideas which I have attempted to put together in elaborating the theory of the free society and in making the labor policy proposals which are to be found in Part III of this book. To these sources I must add those countless judges in England and America, living and dead, who, in writing reasoned opinions in the cases they have decided over the centuries, have been developing the most extraordinary instrument of reason that the world has ever known—the common law.

Sylvester Petro

New York
January, 1957

CONTENTS

Part I

The Free Society

Part II

Evolution of Labor Law and
Policy in the United States

Part III

A Labor Policy for the United States

Part I

THE FREE SOCIETY

Society is something temporary and ephemeral; man, however, is always man.

—Albert Schweitzer

. . . the movement in the progressive societies has hitherto been a movement from status to contract.

—Sir Henry Maine

Chapter 1

SOCIETY AND THE GOALS OF MEN

i repeat the definition of a primitive society given before. It has for its units, not individuals, but groups of men.
—Sir Henry Maine

The fundamental goals and problems in labor relations are the goals and problems of life in society. Well-being, stability, security, leisure, opportunity, rewards, freedom to do what one wishes to do and to try to be what one hopes to be—these represent the goals and raise the problems in labor relations, as they do in life generally. It could not be otherwise. For labor relations are human relations, an aspect of the single, complex category of human action. This being so, sound techniques of social relations must necessarily apply also in labor relations. A few may need to be adjusted and expanded for their most effective application in labor relations. But, aside from such adjustments, the problems in labor relations must be dealt with in largely the same way that problems in other areas of social life are met.

The Goals of Men

Much industry and some learning, as a great social scientist has said of another effort, have gone into analyzing the "worker." The findings and conclusions have not been startling. The worker turns out to be a human being, even as you and I, with largely the same instincts, desires, ideas, and habits. The worker wants more money, meaning more things, usually; but he would also like to work fewer hours and have better and longer vacations. He would like to have a secured income. He wants cleaner, safer, and, when he thinks about it, more attractive conditions of work.

3

Some workers feel more comfortable in group activity, and ill at ease and uncertain where group conflicts exist or the stability of their group's position or their individual position within the group is threatened. New methods, new tools, new techniques are often resisted where they involve an effort at adjustment, or where they threaten the going state of things. A group of unorganized workers once quit work because their employer asked them to use larger and more powerful machines even though the only difference, it later appeared, was that less physical effort was required to operate the new machines than the old. If new tools clearly make a job easier, can be readily handled, and do not threaten one's job or livelihood, workers usually welcome them or at least accept them ultimately. There should be nothing very revealing about these facts to anyone who has been around, anywhere.

Workers tend to prefer stability and security to instability and insecurity. They will often prefer a relatively low-paying job with higher security to a relatively high-paying job with lower security. Still, not all workers are trying to be mail carriers. Many workers give up "secure" jobs in order to take more insecure work at higher wages or to go into business for themselves.

For the truth is that the opportunity to improve one's position represents at least as fundamental and widespread a desire as the wish for security and stability. And an equally pertinent truth is that these concurrent desires, like so many others, tend to rub against each other at certain points. The security of the corner grocer, as such, can sometimes be bought only at the expense of stifling the opportunity of the laborer who wishes to open up a store himself. Often, too, the security of the corner grocer is at odds with the universal desire to have one's money go further, to get more of the goods of life per unit of expenditure. Where the corner grocer's security depends upon preventing the growth of chain stores, the conflict is clear.

In the current state of the world the desires of all workers, of all men, women, and children, for material things may be taken as infinite. The problem in satisfying these desires is one of production. There is a great and as yet unsatisfied *desire* for new automobiles. If they could be produced and sold at costs and prices substantially lower than those now prevailing, many more buyers would enter the market. Production is adequately meeting the actual demand at current prices; but there can be no doubt of the existence of a vast reservoir of unsatisfied desire. The problem is one of producing more cars at lower costs, to be sold at lower prices.

One way or another, real costs and prices must be reduced if production is to be increased. Unit costs and prices can be brought down in various ways: through harder work by everyone engaged in production (probably the least promising as well as least appealing method); through more efficient arrangement of the production unit (substituting more efficient working arrangements for less efficient ones); by replacing men with machines, where machines are more efficient and more economical; or by building up demand for the product to the point where the economies of larger-scale production come into play.

Each of these methods of reducing costs, and every other method ever described, involves change—change which at one point or another, in one way or another conflicts with the universally shared desire for security and stability. And this is true even of the method of reducing costs by larger-scale production. An immediate result of an increase in the production and purchase of automobiles is a reduction in the production and purchase of something else. Some other person or firm will feel the effects.

There will be resistance if the automobile manufacturer asks for faster and harder work. His workers, and their union, will complain if the manufacturer gives to a more efficient producer work which was formerly performed in his own plant, or if he revises job assignments and production teams. As illustrated by the controversy over "automation," a large-scale effort to increase mechanization, this method of reducing costs likewise does not by any means meet with universal acceptance.

Yet here we are, all of us, wishing material goods, plus freedom, plus opportunity; and at the same time strongly desiring personal security and stability. These concurrent desires, pervading all of individual and social life, pose the central problems in labor relations also. The social structure must resolve these problems and harmonize the ineradicable, sometimes competing interests, in labor relations as in every other aspect of the infinite variety of human action.

The General Features of an Enduring Society

The most successful social structure is the one which promotes all these interests most satisfactorily, the one which, in doing so, sacrifices to the least possible extent any of the great, central, human desires for well-being, freedom, and security. An enduring society may be described, then, as one which provides the environment for a maximum fulfillment of human desires and a minimum of frustrations—a system in which the means of achieving the deepest wishes of men are in smooth, effective working order. For societies which do not serve the abiding interests of their members are failures, and are rejected as soon as conditions are propitious.

The enduring society will not deal in exactly the same way with, or give equal emphasis to, every human desire. Desires differ; they fall into different categories and orders of importance; they find their fulfillment in different ways. Therefore there is no reason in the nature of things which dictates that society should deal with every desire in precisely the same way.

An institution or a method well designed for the achievement of one end is not necessarily well designed for reaching all ends. An army and a police force subject to political controls may be the best available means of maintaining the physical security of persons. But other forms of human activity may be more serviceable in the creation, testing, and propagation of ideas and other human productions. The great society will accordingly develop many institutions of varying character, and the method of natural selection will determine the success of each. Arbitrary compulsion to certain modes of operation will be eschewed for the single reason that such compulsion is unintelligent and unserviceable in determining the best available method of reaching an objective. Institutions and methods of operation, well adapted either singly or in combination to the promotion of fundamental objectives, will be permitted a free and natural course of development. There will be church and state, and areas in which neither institution is appropriate.

In order to endure, a society must attend effectively and in due proportion to *all* the central, vital desires of mankind. It must order itself coherently and intelligently, and it must maintain inherent integrity. The enduring society will accept or reject proposals and institutions in accordance with their usefulness to the fundamentally important human objectives. Such a society will have no taboos, no irrational, arbitrary delimitations on human action; it will maintain integrity by refusing to sanction or to condone inherently inconsistent means and programs.

Thus the great society will make a fetish of neither "freedom" nor "security." It will be aware that the interests of society, being the interests of persons, are exceedingly complicated; that societies, like persons, must order their internal complexities into coherence; that societies, like persons, must be well balanced if they are to be healthy and vigorous. It will, in short, refuse to sacrifice freedom for security, or security for freedom, but will look for and ultimately find a method of promoting both.

There can be no specially privileged persons or groups in the great society. As the mechanism for the maximum achievement of human desires, the great society has no alternative to the view that each person is of equal significance. All persons differ to some degree, in capacities as well as desires; and no one proposes that society erase these differences. But both intelligence and humanity require that society regard the person as its basis of calculation: intelligence, because society *is* for persons, because society depends upon the willing acquiescence of all in its measures, and because there is no telling in advance whence the great people who carry us forward will come; humanity, because of our common nature, because we are one species, and because, consequently, the subjugation of one leaves all potentially exposed to the same fate.

And so, in the good society, individual, undifferentiated persons count—not "farmers" or "workers" or "businessmen," but persons—each and every person. A farmer today may be a businessman or an industrial laborer tomorrow; and if not he, almost certainly his sons or his sons' sons. But always they will remain persons. That being the case, only greed or lack of intelligence can induce men who are currently farmers to seek a special advantage over men who are currently engaged in other kinds of activity. And if farmers nonetheless seek such advantage, the great society will deny it; for it cannot do otherwise and remain great.

The great society will, then, exhibit certain marked, central characteristics. Its fundamental rules will be equally applicable to all men. It will give appropriate attention to *all* the profound desires and drives of its members so as to realize all to the fullest possible extent. It will have a nonarbitrary method of selecting from available rules, methods, and institutions those best designed to achieve the desired ends.

The Unity and Harmony of General Human Goals

If the job of society is to serve the desires of its members, there must be some more or less generally accepted conception and ordering of the human desires which are to direct the society. These desires may all be comprehended within the elemental want: the desire for life. But we may go further and define the ramifications of the life-want. We desire material well-being, including security and stability; and we desire freedom, including opportunity to better ourselves in every way that appeals to us. We ask society to help us achieve these aims.

There is a magic unity in the central human objectives. If, desiring both material well-being and personal freedom, we give ourselves personal freedom how shall we use it? The probability, of course, is that we shall use it to promote our well-being—something which has proved to be historically true as well as logically probable.

And there is another kind of unity. Between well-being and security there is a relationship so close as to bespeak a virtual identity: "well-off" people are insulated against more kinds of insecurity than poor people; indeed, well-being might properly be defined in terms of security against various hazards. Substantially the same relationship exists between psychological security and freedom. The saying, "Ye shall know the truth and the truth shall make ye free," is an accurate formulation of the fact that no one is so insecure as the person imprisoned by ignorance in a cage of fears and phantoms. "The horrible dread of unknown evil hangs like a thick cloud over savage life, and embitters every pleasure."[1] The saying, "Ignorance is bliss," we know to be true in only a very narrow and special sense.

Enduring societies are those which have apprehended these unities and identities; they are those which have known that freedom, well-being, and security are one, and that the neglect of one means the frustration of all. Ephemeral societies are those which have not been built in accordance with these insights. If we are to understand the proper excellence of the free society, careful analysis of the unity and harmony of the concepts of freedom, well-being, and security is indispensable. To such a study we now turn, our aim being to demonstrate that a due proportion must be maintained among these concepts if they are to be realized.

Chapter 2

FREEDOM, WELL-BEING, AND SECURITY

> . . . but the only unfailing and permanent source of improvement is liberty, since by it there are as many possible independent centres of improvement as there are individuals.
> —John Stuart Mill

Well-being without personal freedom, security without well-being, and freedom in society without security—these are all meaningless concepts, both inherently contradictory and unrealizable in life. Freedom, well-being, and security are integral elements of a single reality: the goal of men in society. If men fail in the achievement of but one, they fail in all.

Freedom and Well-Being

For any man, a state of well-being means a condition in which his own conception of what is desirable prevails. Well-being, if it is to be meaningful, therefore, signifies a situation of persons which accords with their own opinion of what they want and of what serves their wants. If a community should produce two hundred million tons of steel in a year, it has certainly produced a considerable amount of steel in terms of present conceptions. But if the community has done so only in obedience to the directive of central governmental authorities whose commands cannot be effectively disobeyed, and if in the process the desires of the individual members of the community have either been violated or given no opportunity of expression, no one may correctly say that the well-being of the community has been served by the considerable steel production—especially when there is evidence that, given a free choice, the community would have directed itself to greater production of shoes, radios, and beefsteaks.

Well-being thus appears to be a subjective matter; as such, its existence or nonexistence can be detected only in circumstances of prevailing personal freedom. The only way to be at all sure that a society is on the right path to well-being is to establish that all persons shall have a right to act largely as they wish: to think, work, buy, and sell in accordance with their own desires. With such rules in effect there is a secure basis for the belief that the activity of the society is in accordance with the wishes of its members. The universal interests in freedom and in material well-being will both have been served.

A society which organizes production on any basis other than the freely expressed and acted-upon demands of its members may, it is true, be engaged in a considerable amount of productive activity. That is to say, its members may be going through many motions, may be able to demonstrate a substantial physical product for their efforts; such a society may even spend most of its effort on the production of consumer goods. Still, unless production is responsive directly to the consumer, the material well-being of the people is not being served. The machine serves, instead, the conception of material well-being held by its monopolistic masters, whoever they may be—commissioners or commissars.

The best method known of insuring the responsiveness of production to the demand of the members of a society is that of permitting the people as a whole to reward responsive production and to penalize unresponsive production. In an advanced and well-run society the procedure of reward and penalty will be simple, direct, and accurate—as much so as possible in an imperfect world. Some nations have reached the ultimate through the process of the continuous economic vote of consumers. By their free purchases, the people in such nations engage daily in rewarding responsive production and penalizing the less responsive.

It goes without saying that rewards or penalties in accordance with service to the people cannot be satisfactorily distributed unless the people are in a position to make a real judgment of the performance in question. If there is only one shoemaker, and if the desire for protecting and adorning the feet can be satisfied only by dealing with that shoemaker, the fact that one has patronized him does not tell as much as it would if one had patronized him in spite of the existence of a number of other shoemakers. Where I have a choice among competing methods of satisfying the same desire, there is a much greater probability that the choice I actually make has been responsive to my individual desires than if there have been no competing methods.

But this does not mean that there must necessarily always be *in existence* at any given time competing alternative methods of satisfying the same desire. It will suffice if *the opportunity* is open for anyone to produce anything. When such opportunity exists, one may be sure that, if there is in fact only one producer of a given good, he is alone in the field because of universal agreement that he is under all the circumstances doing the best possible job of serving the consumers in that area. It being open to anyone to offer competition to that producer, the fact that no competition is forthcoming can have no other meaning.

On the other hand it equally frustrates the desires of all if, contrary to the freely expressed will of the people, certain persons are specially privileged to remain in the production effort even though their service is not satisfactory. Such a situation exists, for example, where a retail distributor is permitted by law to limit the freedom of his competitors. Discriminatory taxation of large-scale distributors, or general prohibition by law of selling at anything lower than fixed prices, as under the deceptively named "fair-trade" laws, are both measures inconsistent with the fundamental principles of the free society. In both cases the effect on the material well-being of all the people is harmful. Freedom and well-being are both impaired, for the special benefit of a few.

It thus seems evident that freedom and general personal well-being are indispensable to each other. No one should be surprised that bread and meat, as well as personal freedom, are scarce in Russia today. If the right to produce for general consumption is restricted to one man, to one integrated group of men, or to one agency, social well-being in the sense of the greatest possible satisfaction of individual desires is impossible. Social well-being in that sense is open to realization only when the opportunities available to all who wish to serve are equal and unlimited by the society. The liberty of the consumer to buy as he wishes is meaningful only when equal liberty is available to all who wish to try their hand at satisfying consumer demands under a free price and free production system.

The Anglo-American legal system and other great legal systems of the world incorporated this reasoning into their basic principles. They regarded as fundamental to civilized society the right of all people to buy and sell as they wished, to produce or not to produce as they wished. Departures from these principles by current societies provide a basis for evaluating the worth of those societies. It is not possible in every instance to prevent societies from modifying or qualifying these principles. Perhaps it is not even always desirable to do so. But when one is conscious of the intimate relationship of these principles to the concept of the good society, one is in a position more effectively to evaluate proposed modifications and qualifications of human freedom.

Security, Well-Being, and Freedom

The concept of security has been sinned against most grievously, and the transgressions have been of almost every conceivable kind. In many instances, perhaps in most, it is easy to forgive; for the concept itself is complicated and ambiguous in an elevated degree, and in such circumstances errors in good faith are to be expected. But in certain instances the transgressions seem to have been basely motivated.

The problem of eliminating human insecurity is as complicated as the sources and kinds of insecurity. There is the insecurity of the wilderness for even the best-equipped man; of the child's first day in school; of the woman in childbirth; of one in a position, social or economic, which strains one's capacities and experience; of a property-owner faced with the threat of expropriation by a thief or a government; of a man without means of support for himself and his family; of man before death and the other mysteries of his own being and of the universe.

Of their societies men ask security, as well as the conditions of maximum freedom and well-being. It could not be otherwise; for freedom, security, and well-being compose a unitary conception, each taking its value from the other, each despised where solitarily enjoyed. The person condemned to life imprisonment sets a minimum value upon his security, feels himself deprived of well-being, because his freedom of action is severely limited. Yet liberty itself will often be sold for a pittance by the victim of fatal misery and insecurity. In such circumstances a man does not consider himself free, and his opinion is not subject to challenge by even the most sophisticated analysis; for he is right. Profound misery and insecurity are incompatible with freedom. Security, well-being, and freedom are one, or they are nothing.[1]

To the fullest possible extent the good society must fulfill the human desires for security, well-being, and freedom; in order to do so, it must harmonize them. But to say that the enduring society must perform this function does not mean that it must use a single mechanism in approaching all the facets of insecurity, in striving to check all the various types of insecurity. We have already observed as a general proposition that the intelligently operated society will in all instances make use of the best available means of achieving its objectives, and that one of the primary considerations in settling upon the means will be the relationship of the means chosen to the other profound objectives of society. Means must be tailored to their objectives, and they must be rejected if they involve the sacrifice or destruction of other equally important objectives.

Society—the cooperation of persons to facilitate the achievement of common objectives—is itself the fundamental condition of a satisfactory approach to the elimination of the kinds of insecurity which confront men. Government, as commonly understood, must not be confused with society. Government is only one social institution; there are many others. And in original thinking upon the problem there is no reason to assume that the institution commonly thought of as government is necessarily best designed to deal with all phases of the problem of insecurity. Other social institutions have grown as naturally and organically from basic human desires as government has; and intelligent men are committed to only one choice in deciding upon the functions to be allocated to the various institutions already in being or to be created: the choice of the institution best adapted to the end in view, the one most harmonious with all other equally important ends.

The cooperative activity which we call society inherently involves the division of labor and the pooling of resources. Some men specialize in curing diseases and healing injuries, some in producing desired goods, some in clearing the wilderness, some in training and educating children, some in preventing and punishing violent expropriation, some in pursuing truth concerning man and nature. Each of these occupations is designed to serve one or another phase of the security and well-being of men. Each is indispensable to the freedom of men, as well. All, so far as history reveals, were natural products of the voluntary cooperation of men in society.

There is little point in rating these functions in any kind of order of importance; each is indispensable to the fullest realization of the others. Without efficient production of the basically desired goods—food, shelter, and clothing—the health of the body is prejudiced. Without health the production of desired goods is impaired. Without careful analysis of the facts concerning man and nature, and appropriate teaching, adequate health facilities are impossible, and the production of goods must also rest in a more primitive and inefficient state than it achieves in a society where research and education are more advanced. Without law and order, the means of settling disputes peaceably among members of the society and of deterring violent assaults and expropriations, the tranquility indispensable to the functioning of civilized society is severely threatened.

If good health is the objective, the peak performance of many phases of social cooperation is vital. All must be properly informed and habituated in regard to the techniques of healthful living; for superstition, ignorance, and slovenliness are enemies of health. The production machine must be working well; for food, shelter, clothing, expensive sanitation methods and facilities, and equally costly diagnostic, preventive, and therapeutic devices—all being indispensable to the general good health of a society—must be produced efficiently enough to be available in the greatest possible quantities at the lowest possible costs. Scientific and educational activities must be proceeding in the environment most suitable to their functioning and progress; for they must produce and disseminate the ideas, theories, and information without which men remain exposed to the insecurities of disease and ill health. The measures best designed to secure able medical practitioners in sufficient numbers must be adopted, and arbitrary controls upon the preparation of such practitioners or upon their freedom to evolve the most useful forms of medical practice must be eliminated.

The role which freedom has to play throughout the quest for security from health hazards is central and dominating. In regard to education and research the role is as obvious as it is dominant. In regard to the business of production and in regard to medical practice it is not less dominant, only less obvious. The production and distribution of the life-goods, of the costly facilities indispensable to this security-objective, in the greatest possible quantities at the lowest possible prices, require maximum freedom for the producers and distributors. Free competition among them, with the spur of rewards in the form of profits to the ablest and most efficient, is the best technique ever evolved by mankind for the steady reductions in costs which make these goods available in ever greater quantities to ever more persons.

Freedom is likewise central in regard to medical practice. We can be sure that medical practice is at its peak of performance only if the conditions of freedom prevail as regards entrance into the practice and the evolution of medical practice itself. The only control upon entrance to medical practice which society can permit is that of proper qualification—proper training and ability. All other controls are socially arbitrary and tend to weaken the security of persons against the hazards of ill health. They tend to limit unduly the number of practitioners: a limitation which both violates the interest in promoting the freedom of persons to become what they want to be and can be, and at the same time tends to raise the fees and other prices of medical practitioners.

Medical practitioners themselves are the ones in the best position to determine which methods of practice are most effective. Every qualified medical practitioner must have the freedom to decide this issue for himself. If some physicians find it more advantageous to practice on an individual basis, they must be free to act accordingly. On the other hand, if some physicians freely decide to practice as a group, carrying out the division of labor which works so well in most phases of human life, they too must have equal freedom to implement their decision. No other system is consistent with the social interests in freedom, well-being, and security. Proponents of individual practice may not be allowed to frustrate the freedom of proponents of group practice—any more than the latter may be allowed to frustrate the former. Group practice in the form of highly complicated partnerships has been a feature in the practice of law in America for many years. No one has ever contended that this form of organization in a profession having many points in common with medicine has impaired the practice of law or the freedom of lawyers.

If we are seriously concerned with achieving maximum security against health hazards, it must be evident by now that maximum freedom in the relevant institutions is necessary. We must make a check list and go over it carefully, to discover whether we enjoy conditions of maximum freedom in research, education, production, and the practice of medicine. If we are dissatisfied with the present conditions in any field, we must abandon freedom as the dominant principle of improvement only if we are sure that freedom has been given a chance and that it has failed. The same is true of all other security matters, except those involving violence and expropriation—areas in which, as will be seen, compulsion has proved to be necessary, at least in the current state of human and scientific development.

"Social Security," Freedom, and Well-Being

The term "social security" would be inherently meaningful if it were used exclusively in reference to hazards which threaten a *society*, such as attempts at conquest by foreign powers or to individual conduct such as murdering, robbing, or cheating, which can, without stretching the truth at all, be characterized as essentially antisocial. As commonly used today, however, the term "social security" refers to the "security" of individual persons against the "hazards" of old age and unemployment.

The distinction between hazards which imperil a society as such and those concomitant to old age and unemployment is an important one. We shall deal with some phases of this matter at length in Chapter 6, where an attempt is made to demonstrate the undesirable consequences of failing to observe the distinction between voluntary action by individuals and the compulsory action of the state. At this point, however, it is desirable to elaborate the distinction between individual problems and the hazards which threaten a society, and to explicate some of the conclusions which follow naturally from a proper understanding of that distinction.

The person who will murder, rob, or cheat is quite literally an enemy of society. He refuses to abide by rules of conduct which any society needs to enforce if it is to survive *as a society*, as distinct from a mere aggregate of persons in an environment in which life is "nasty, brutish, and short." But effective enforcement of these rules against persons who repudiate them is possible only if the people in favor of the rules unite their power in order to create a force stronger than any other force. In civilized society that force is called the state; the state may, indeed, be defined as the greatest power aggregate in any society and the only agency which may legally use force and compulsion. As we shall see later in more detail (Chapter 6), the state by its very composition is coextensive with the society of which it is the common agent; every member of that society is a member of the state and subject to its rules. And this is necessary if the society is to preserve itself, for it must have an instrument more powerful than any possible combination of the persons who would murder, rob, or cheat.

The fact that states at times cannot or choose not to restrain some persons or groups from using violence for private ends should not be allowed to confuse the analysis. For it remains true, nevertheless, that if a society is to survive, its members must create an instrument strong enough to prevent violence. If they are not willing to create and support such an agency, they are apparently not in favor of civilization. If they do create and support such an agency, but the persons operating the agency refuse to suppress violence when it arises, then the decent members of the society must band together to replace the unfaithful agents. If there is no peaceful method of removing faithless political agents, violence has to be used. But it is much better to have a peaceful method, and the enduring society does of course work out such a method, the method of periodical election, under which state officers may be voted out when they fail to perform their job of preserving internal tranquility.

The safeguarding of a community against foreign conquest yields more or less the same analysis. Foreign conquest is a hazard equally disastrous to all, even though the actual impact may vary from one person or group to another. As it is equally disastrous to all loyal citizens, the job of safeguarding against conquest falls naturally to the common agent of all: the political government. Of course, no people or government can effectively provide alone against conquest by a stronger enemy. But the situation is not completely hopeless. There are always alliances. The quality of a people may still often be judged by their success in maintaining their political integrity, even though it must be realized that sometimes the best efforts will fail, as where a nation is invaded by a larger, more powerful one.

The kinds of "insecurity" ordinarily associated in our day with the term "social security" are as a matter of fact essentially different from the hazards thus far discussed. Old age, for example, is not, properly speaking, either a hazard or a catastrophe, although, in certain cases, it may be both. It is, instead, simply inevitable; it is a condition of the life cycle. Old age may as well be thought of as a good, a precious allotment of years which does not fall to everyone.

Whether or not old age proves to be preponderantly a period of satisfaction depends upon a large number of factors, some of which are subject to personal and societal control, and some of which are not. Like infancy, youth, and maturity, old age poses certain problems which are related specifically to the psychic, intellectual, and physiological conditions of the particular time of life involved. Old age takes on the appearance of a catastrophe, for example, if a society does not permit its members to prepare themselves for it. Consider a society which does not recognize private property rights and thus does not permit individual accumulations of liquid funds and other properties. In such a society an old person no longer able to support himself by current income-producing activity is in a difficult position. He must depend on charity or the support of his family, or starve. If a society is genuinely interested in the security and well-being of its superannuated members, therefore, it will take action designed to encourage and to promote saving.

Viewed in this light, inflation of the monetary unit is a great enemy of the security of the elderly. If a society pursues deliberately a policy of inflation, and at the same time professes to be seriously preoccupied with the problems of its old members, one must doubt either the good sense or the honesty of that society. Inflation of the monetary unit destroys, to the extent of the inflation, the savings of persons who have tried to provide for their old age. It amounts to expropriating old persons, or destroying their property rights, with the consequence that its victims face catastrophe when they are no longer able to produce current income. Those who find "nothing dangerous" in a program of "mild inflation," usually meaning an inflation of two to five per cent annually, surely are unconcerned with the problems of the old. If these same people protest that they are in favor of "social security," one may be pardoned for questioning their judgment.

One can scarcely provide adequately for his old age in a society in which opportunities of employment at good wages during one's youth are not available. The well-run society interested in its old people must therefore be concerned vitally in promoting the productivity of the economy. Only thus will job-opportunities be plentiful, the wages of workers high, and their ability to set apart some of current earnings toward future necessities be reasonably insured. Here again we meet in instructive form the reality of the unity of freedom, well-being, and security. For societies are most productive, and offer plentiful job-opportunities at good pay, where freedom prevails on every side to the greatest possible extent.

High productivity and plentiful job-opportunities at good pay are possible only in a society which has a great deal of capital in the form of productive plant and machinery. The more capital there is invested per man, the greater is the demand for labor and the higher the productivity of each working man and, therefore, his earnings. These are facts of economic life which no one disputes.

It is true that capital may be accumulated even in societies in which conditions of personal freedom do not obtain to the greatest possible extent. The administrators in a socialist economy are in a position to declare that a certain amount of current productive capacity is to be directed to the production of capital goods rather than consumption goods. Soviet Russia today is reported to be taking such action.

However, if the direction of the productive activity of a society is in the hands of its central political administration it becomes improper, as already noted, to speak of individual well-being as the driving force of that society. In such a society, the wishes and goals and ideas of the administrators are in control. These may or may not coincide with the wishes, goals, and ideas of the members of the society. There is no way of telling. One can be tolerably sure that individual desires are in control only if every man in society is free to try his hand at pleasing consumers. Such freedom presupposes that the basic resources of the nation are accessible to all who demonstrate skill in serving consumers. Where the basic resources of the nation—its wealth and capital— are commanded only by the political administrators, there is small scope for private initiative, and even less incentive. And where the conditions of maximum freedom do not prevail for private initiative it is futile to speak in terms of individual well-being.

Therefore, if one wishes to promote both freedom and well-being, as well as security for superannuated persons, he must think in terms of the operation of an individual-initiative, private-property (or "capitalist" or "private enterprise") society. The problem then becomes one of selecting from the various feasible alternatives the ones best designed to promote capital formation and consequent higher productivity. Careful students of the operation of a free economy have provided the solution to this problem. It is a simple and elegant one. A society need only concentrate upon encouraging work, savings, investment, and the greatest possible activity of the most able and astute producers and investors.

The conditions fundamentally necessary to the realization of the desire for old-age security, it will be noticed, are the same ones necessary to the realization of the desire for security from the hazards of ill health. Freedom, well being, and security again appear to be one thing; properly understood, they are integrating phases of a single indivisible concept. Like the valves, pistons, connecting-rods, spark plugs, and crankshaft of an internal combustion engine, they must all work together; and if the operation of any of the elements is faulty, the entire power output is affected.

In the United States, as elsewhere in the world today, a tendency prevails to abandon freedom-principles and to adopt principles of compulsion in the so-called social-security area. Employers and employees are compelled by law to put aside certain amounts for old-age retirement benefits. Employers are compelled by law to put into unemployment compensation funds a certain percentage of payrolls and to take out insurance against injuries to workers in the course of their employment. There is a persistent movement to extend these compulsory payroll-deduction principles in order to provide for medical care for everyone.

In analyzing these tendencies one of the first things to recognize is that they do not deal with the fundamental aspects of the problems with which they are concerned. Real security against all the hazards in question is the product only of a free society working at its peak of efficiency. This is as true in regard to unemployment hazards as it is in regard to medical and old-age hazards; for the best insurance against unemployment is provided by a society so productive and dynamic that there is work for everyone who wants it, when he wants it. But the tendencies under discussion now are characteristically uncreative and unprogressive. They do not concern themselves with creating greater social productivity and its consequent increased wealth, increased medical facilities, and expanded job opportunities.

The second thing to recognize about these tendencies is that they have, on the whole, contrary effects. Each puts a burden on payrolls. This frequently reflects itself in lower wages to employees than would otherwise prevail; but it also frequently means that it costs an employer more to hire a worker than he would otherwise have to pay. Higher costs of production and higher prices of products and lower profits are likewise predictable consequences. And decreased effective demand for the products involved, with, accordingly, less demand for workers, are further consequences. Furthermore, payroll deductions which go to the government do not result in the formation of the new capital and the greater productivity which are promoted by private investment in the production machine. The plain fact is that all compulsory payroll contributions have a directly dampening effect on the productive activity of the economy as a whole. Instead of promoting productivity, the only real method of increasing the well-being and security of a people, these measures depress productivity. Needless to say, in view of the preceding discussion, these inroads upon personal freedom work out as inroads upon well-being and security, as well.

Just how serious these inroads are cannot be determined in any quantitative way. What one can accurately say is that limitations on personal freedom and social productivity are the necessary consequences of compulsory payroll contributions. There is no telling just how much productivity is affected; but the greater the compulsory payroll costs, the greater the dampening effect on productivity.

Most students of society, even those who are strong advocates of maximum freedom, do not take an unequivocal stand against so-called social-security measures. The latter insist, however, that such measures be recognized for what they are: inhibitors of both personal freedom and a progressive, expanding economy. And they, the real progressives, attempt to warn against the adoption of measures which tend to destroy the very things which the advocates of "social security" and all men of good will seek.

Chapter 3

THE BASIC INSTITUTION OF THE FREE SOCIETY: PERSONAL FREEDOM

> The only freedom which deserves the name, is that of pursuing our own good in our own way, so long as we do not attempt to deprive others of theirs, or impede their efforts to obtain it.
>
> —John Stuart Mill

The basic institution of the free society is personal freedom. It is both end and means, desired in itself and for the social results it brings. The great society provides for its members the environment in which their personal freedom is at a maximum. It is a great society partly for this reason and partly for the reason that with personal freedom at a maximum, general well-being and security are realized in an elevated degree; and they, in turn, make possible an ever-growing scope of real personal freedom.

The Freedom to Act

By personal freedom in society is meant, not the actual physical or mental area of accomplishment of any particular person, but the scope of activity open generally to all. One person's natural endowment of will or talent or both may make possible for him activities and achievements not equally open to other, less well-endowed persons. Society can do nothing about this; cannot make a Shakespeare of a person who lacks the will and the talent to write supremely. Nevertheless it promotes human freedom if it permits no human agency to prevent any person from trying to write as well as he can.

Society can likewise not make a tool-and-die maker of a person who lacks the requisite will and capacity; yet once again, if it is interested in promoting maximum human freedom, it will prevent any person or organization from frustrating the desire of

24

persons who wish to try to become tool-and-die makers. The job of the free society is thus, in part, one of preventing human restrictions upon personal freedom.

Universal personal freedom must tend to set each person into the position which best compromises both his own wishes and the wishes of all other members of the community. The desires of any given person may be a chaos. Within the same psyche may be mingled longings of the most outrageously conflicting character. The free society does not arbitrarily simplify or order this chaos. It does not even command an irrevocable election. A man may strive to be a ditch-digger, a tramp, a lawyer, and a poet—successively or simultaneously. He may work as a physician for years, and then study hard to prepare himself for the life of a machinist. His friends and enemies may counsel against such a switch; but, in a free society, no person or institution is given the power to prevent his election. Instead, a vastly more wise and just and sensitive and social method operates; and it operates without prejudice to any one concerned, leaving all free.

The physician is free to try to become a machinist. His friends and enemies are free to counsel him concerning the project. And all other members of the community are free to exercise their own choice in the matter. If the community needs machinists, and if the erstwhile physician is qualified to do such work, the switch may be accomplished in a free society with no fuss. Of course the community may, if it wishes, offer less remuneration for the work of machinists than it does for the work of physicians. But the community's power to make such a decision in no way lessens the freedom of the physician. It merely represents the evaluation of the members of the community as to competing desiderata. Freedom would be diminished if some force external to the spontaneously expressed wishes of the members of the community in the free market should impose a scale of remuneration for machinists different from that which the community had decided upon.

The freedom of the physician remains unimpaired so long as no one—agency or person—may conclusively prevent him from attempting to make the change he contemplates. His freedom is not diminished by the fact that he will have to accept less remuneration for his work as a machinist—any more than it is diminished if by choosing one road he misses the beautiful scenery which lies along another road to the same destination. Every choice involves a sacrifice. When the members of society offer more compensation to physicians than they do to machinists, they are saying that the community's desire for physicians is more pressing. The man who nevertheless chooses to become a machinist is in a sense refusing to cooperate with society, and he cannot complain if his refusal costs him something.

Societies less intelligently operated, less flexible, and less humane than the free society, might be tempted to force the person who is qualified to do various jobs into the position for which the demand is at the moment greatest. Members of a free society need never fear, however, that their community will suffer in virtue of this difference. For the man who is *forced* to remain a physician when he has the capacity and would prefer to engage in some other occupation is in a constant state of frustration. He is less effective in his work. He represents a weakness in the social structure. If he is only one of great numbers in the same psychological difficulty, as would probably be the case in societies which act so arbitrarily, the social structure becomes very shaky.

The strength, the well-being, the enduring qualities of any social structure depend essentially upon the degree to which it reflects the wishes of all its cooperating members. The good society is the society in which persons have voluntarily fitted themselves into the productive, social process. It is fair to say, in fact, that civilization realizes itself to the highest degree when the various jobs of a society are distributed according to the will and capacities of its members. This most precious goal is frustrated no less when the society permits human institutions other than the state to control occupations, than when the state itself assumes command of the destinies of persons. In our day, trade unions have repeatedly sought to exert a proprietary control over various productive social functions. They, rather than the state directly, are for us the greatest threat to personal freedom at the moment. The state, however, is by no means free of responsibility in the premises. On the contrary, the state shirks its central responsibility when it allows any institution, whether it be a trade unon or any other aggregate, to frustrate that free intercourse between the community and the individual by means of which the individual fits himself into the social process of the division of labor.[1]

Freedom, Equality, and Taxation

All men are agreed today that the state should be concerned with the freedom of every person. This widely shared conviction has led in some cases to the identification of equality and freedom. Many say that it is idle to speak of general freedom where some persons are in a position of substantial material disadvantage. This attitude has created a certain amount of confusion concerning the role of the state in society; and it has led to the adoption of certain policies which must be examined here.

The children of rich men have certain apparent advantages over the children of poor men, in somewhat the same way that the children of talented persons have certain apparent advantages over the children of untalented parents. Whether or not these advantages will in fact obtain in any particular case is unpredictable. Instances are known in which the inheritance of riches, while generally an attractive prospect, has not produced a net advantage for the heir. Commonly enough, a child of poor parents achieves a position of greater artistic, financial, or intellectual eminence than a child of wealthy parents.[2]

The fact that many societies have adopted the principle of discriminatory, steeply progressive, income taxation cannot alter the fact just stated. It merely reflects one of the graver mistakes which have been made in some relatively free societies. Discriminatory income taxation puts at a disadvantage those born poor who earn high incomes; but the people who propose and support such taxation do not intend thereby to put the productive poor at a disadvantage. As a rule, indeed, they aim by such policies to promote equality. The trouble with them is not so much bad faith or bad motives as simply bad thinking. They have tried to gain an unattainable objective by an inappropriate means.

Progressive income taxation does not have much of an effect upon income inequalities. Essentially it puts the productive poor at a relative disadvantage—relative, that is, to the unproductive poor and to those who inherit great wealth; it reduces incentives of the able and productive and the otherwise willing workers, with, unavoidably, unfortunate social effects; and it tends finally to hamper the growth of new private capital. Thus, as we shall see in more detail presently, it insulates against the competition of the able poor those who previously acquired eminent positions. In sum, it impoverishes the society. Perhaps its most undesirable feature is that, by thwarting private capital accumulation, it reduces the productive functions possible to private persons and creates an apparent necessity for more and more positive governmental intervention in economic affairs.[3]

Such being the natural consequence of steeply progressive income taxation, that device can scarcely be viewed accurately as one which promotes human freedom generally. The greater the activity of government, the smaller, inevitably, is the positive area of freedom open to the immense majority of people who are not members of the government. Furthermore, there is no basis for considering steeply progressive income taxation a means well-adapted to equalizing the opportunities between the children of the rich and the children of the poor. One way or another, the children of the well-to-do are going to be better off, materially, than the children of less well-to-do parents. Progressive taxation may to some degree reduce the disparity, but long before it has done that it will have worked results damaging to all, rich and poor alike. By hitting hardest the best servants of society—those who are currently the best earners—it tends to induce them to spend a good deal of their productive energies in tax-avoidance schemes, rather than in their socially precious productive activities. It is an open question whether steeply progressive tax rates really produce more revenue for government than they lose by virtue of the reduced productivity they encourage. Here one needs only reflect upon the time, effort, and talent which go into tax-avoidance schemes rather than into production, let alone the loss in productivity which taxing away funds otherwise destined for investment involves.

To the degree that high-income producers absolutely cannot avoid taxes, they have less to spend and invest. But the normal person does not, in such circumstances, deny advantages to his children. He sees to it that they get the best available in terms of toys, teachers, schools, and clothes. The reduction in income

worked by steeply progressive taxation thus reflects itself primarily in reduced investment by the currently most productive
members of society, not in reduced expenditure for personal and
family consumption.

If continued seriously and effectively, steeply progressive
income taxation must eventually mean smaller opportunities and
less attractive incentives for everyone. No single measure would
do more to promote productivity, employment, general well-
being, and personal freedom in the United States than the abandonment of such taxation.

Many who now concede that discriminatory income taxation
cannot be seriously regarded as a socially proper equalitarian
device nevertheless contend that government functions cannot be
adequately financed without relatively heavy taxation of those
who earn the larger incomes. This contention is based upon two
assumptions: first, that the "social welfare" functions of the state
are indispensable, and second that high incomes must be virtually
expropriated if tax revenues are to be adequate. Both assumptions are erroneous.

One of the purposes of this book is to demonstrate the mistake
in the assumption that universally shared desires for personal
welfare are best served by positive, compulsory state action. It
has been emphasized herein that the greatest possible welfare
of any community is the inevitable consequence when men are
socially free to pursue their own interests in a peaceful, honest,
and noncoercive way. Positive action by the state always reduces
net social freedom and, therefore, net social productivity, because
the government in a market economy can take action only with
funds drawn from the persons who earned them.

If the state subsidizes farmers, it may increase production of
the subsidized commodities: but only at the expense of the
production which would have been evoked had the purchasing
power been left with those who earned it and had those farmers
encouraged by subsidies to produce unwanted commodities been
induced to cooperate with the rest of society by getting into
some line of production in which consumers were more interested. If the state sets up a Tennessee Valley Authority, it may
accord a special benefit to persons in the area served by that
agency, but only at the expense of the taxpayers of the country

who were denied the power to spend at will the income which the state took away from them.

A net loss accrues to society in both cases because state subsidies are always—and have to be—contrary to the will of the consumers. The political process never allows the people to register their choice in such matters as these. In the only popular referendum ever submitted to the people in regard to farm prices (that is, the referendum of the free market), the consumers unequivocally let their wishes be known. Had the consumers themselves been willing to pay higher prices for farm products, the government subsidies would not have been demanded. Had the people been willing to provide service below cost to the persons specially benefited by such governmentally owned and operated agencies as the TVA, it would not have been necessary to force them to do so through the coercive device of taxation.

Only the inherently inadequate political process accounts for the continuation of the subsidy programs of governments. No citizen has ever been given the political opportunity to vote directly and unequivocally on the question of whether there should be farm subsidies, uncomplicated by the simultaneous existence of numerous other planks in the platforms of the political parties. If the citizens of this nation were given such an opportunity, there can be no doubt that the program would be rejected. Let the party in power submit the "farm issue" to the voters one day in the form of an unequivocal referendum which reveals its costs.

It is a safe general rule that whenever the state engages in activities of the kind under discussion—tariffs are perhaps the best example of all—it harms the general welfare in order to accord benefits to a specially privileged few. The state may conceivably take such action, at rare intervals, on the assumption that it is serving the general welfare. More often the essential motivation is political advantage; everyone knows, for example, that the two great parties are continually worried about the "farmer vote," and that one of these parties tends to induce the other to agree to subsidize the farmers. But always social productivity suffers.

Were governments to restrict themselves to general rule-making functions, the burden of necessary taxation would be, in the United States, of no real economic significance to anyone. A flat ten per cent tax on *all* net incomes would be more than adequate, except during periods of national emergency. And during times of emergency a flat thirty per cent tax on all incomes would provide all the funds which the most ingenious officers could spend. Irrefutable calculations establish this fact even under current conditions, when expropriatory taxation and other political errors have greatly reduced our total productivity.[4] Under conditions encouraging productivity to the greatest possible extent—if, for example, employers were given the freedom to bring efficiency to a maximum during wartime—the probability is that a flat tax of twenty per cent on all incomes would provide more than ample funds.

The fact remains that children of poor or untalented parents begin life with a disadvantage, as compared with the children of rich or talented persons. Yet the disadvantage is at an absolute minimum where the children of poor or untalented parents are born into a free society which does not permit their modest birth to be held against them, and where the society provides in other respects the environment within which their native qualities may flower. In a free, well-run, prosperous society, the disadvantage of children born of poor parents is insignificant; it will not be an important factor in the achievement or the failure to achieve their ultimate ends, whatever those ends may be. Their will, their talent, accident, the breaks of the game will be determinative.[5]

When a society has done all it can to insure personal freedom and to promote production, it has done a great deal for the children of the poor; and it has done so without penalizing or impairing the freedom of anyone else—a fact of immense importance when one considers that the good, free society cannot exist where some persons are penalized or restricted solely for the advantage of other persons. Such a society will have wealth and productivity enough to permit leisure to all its children and to spare the human and physical resources for teachers and schools. It will not need to make ostentatious plans, promises, and boasts about "free education" (nothing is gratis in this world); the government, the single human agency of compulsion in a free society, will not need to take property from one person or class in order to subsidize another.

On the other hand, if the society is not free, well run, and prosperous, all the paper promises in the world will fail to bring the children of the poor to a point where they will even think about improving their bad condition, let alone actually do so. Study the Constitution of Italy, and then walk for a day among the towns clustered around ancient Pompeii. The Constitution of Italy guarantees every child an education, every person employment with income sufficient to insure "human dignity." These promises are unknown to the people who live in the towns inland from the beautiful Bay of Naples; and if they were known they would be regarded as meaningless, as indeed they are. Italy lacks the means of providing an education for all its children, and in consequence the children of the poor are strangers to the concept of human dignity, as well as strangers to soap, water, and the most elementary education. In such circumstances the great concept of society as, in the words of von Humboldt, the mechanism for promoting "human development in its richest diversity," blares forth as an ugly, blatant mockery. Let those who deplore the alleged "materialism" of the United States reconsider the relationship between material productivity and the dignity of man.

If Italy and other societies similarly depressed wish to improve their position, they must provide incentives for, and erase the restrictions upon, their ablest and most astute producers of material goods, instead of permitting freedom and power only to the agents of the state. In Italy all mineral resources are owned by the state; it is no wonder, therefore, that petroleum has been discovered there only recently, and then only by United States capitalists. The freedom and authority of businessmen are severely circumscribed in Italy, except in the case of businesses monopolized by the state; and it is not surprising, therefore, that private initiative is at a minimum. In Italy there is no real mobility of labor, and powerful labor unions insist upon this restriction. That this beautiful land, teeming with able, hardworking people, should be languishing, may be deplorable; but for one who understands the principles of social welfare, it is not mysterious. One needs to understand here that the wealth of businessmen is not gained at the expense of consumers or of workers. Businessmen do not force people to buy from or work for them. They offer goods and services and employment. Their wealth depends upon the attractiveness of the things they offer. Taking a narrow, vindictive attitude toward the wealth of businessmen is the best way possible to frustrate the operation of the principles of social welfare.

The poor and the untalented, like the rich and the talented, sometimes have children who are abnormally indolent or stupid, or both. As for abnormal indolence in the child of rich parents, one should note that while the child has an advantage, it is an advantage provided him by the wealth of his parents. Those who find it disagreeable that a lazy wastrel should have as much wealth as they have, or more, must remember that they probably had nothing to do with the accumulation of that wealth, and that the public was well served by the men who made fortunes; and they may take comfort from the fact that if the heir is absolutely indolent, he will not have his money very long. There is no reason to feel any more deeply for the poor and indolent than one feels for the rich and indolent.

In many countries large estates are heavily taxed at the death of the owner. This extreme form of expropriation is said to be justified by the social interest in equality. But the fact is, of course, as in the case of steeply progressive income taxation, that the heavy taxation of inheritances has had no appreciable effect on inequality.

Thus far it seems that in the United States of today the very rich are in an even more disparate position than ever. Fewer people, relatively, seem to be able to live on a gracious or luxurious level. But the relatively few who still can, stand out the more; while, owing to income and estate taxation, large numbers of people are less well off than they would otherwise be. This does not mean that equality has been promoted in any desirable way; it means only that everybody is somewhat worse off, except the *very* rich who have literally more money than they know what to do with, and who enjoy fantastic incomes merely from tax-exempt bonds.

As the great social scientist Mises has pointed out, discriminatory taxation actually entrenches the already rich and powerful against the currently able, who are prevented, by taxation, from ever building up enough capital to challenge the established powers:

> Today taxes often absorb the greater part of the newcomer's "excessive" profits. He cannot accumulate capital; he cannot expand his own business; he will never become big business and a match for the vested interests. The old firms do not need to fear his competition; they are sheltered by the tax collector. . . . It is true, the income tax prevents them, too, from accumulating new capital. But what is more important for them is that it prevents the dangerous newcomer from accumulating any capital. They are virtually privileged by the tax system. In this sense progressive taxation checks economic progress and makes for rigidity.
>
> The interventionists complain that big business is getting rigid and bureaucratic and that it is no longer possible for competent newcomers to challenge the vested interests of the old rich families. However, as far as their complaints are justified, they complain about things which are merely the result of their own policies.[6]

Perhaps the most significant effect of heavy estate taxation has been to create all sorts of complicated devices designed to reduce the amount of estates subject to death taxes. Although inheritance taxes do bring in a certain amount of governmental revenue, it is simply absurd to think of that revenue as being in any way effective to reduce inequalities as between the children of the rich and the children of the less rich. Even where not completely wasted by unwise and inefficient governmental action, the income from expropriatory estate taxation is neither used for erasing inequalities nor adequate, in any realistic sense, for achieving that objective. If all estates exceeding twenty-five thousand dollars were completely expropriated by the state and redistributed among families of less wealth, no one would be any richer. But some people would be much worse off, as would the society itself on the whole.

There may be more charitable foundations in existence today than there would have been in the absence of heavy inheritance taxation; they are one of the acknowledged techniques of avoiding such taxation. But whether or not the rich give more now to such charitable uses than they did prior to heavy taxation on incomes and estates is doubtful. Most people who think about the matter are of the opinion that private universities and private charities of all kinds have been harmed more than they have been helped by discriminatory taxation.

The most fruitful way of looking at inheritance taxation is in terms of the social utility of expropriating private property lawfully accumulated. Like all other forms of expropriation, it constitutes a serious infringement upon personal liberty. It hits hardest those people whose great earnings, where lawfully made, suggest the greatest socially productive activity; for no one can lawfully earn money in a free, well-run society unless he has produced something which people, acting freely, wish to purchase. Viewing the matter in this light, it is difficult to find any basis for approval of discriminatory inheritance taxation. Such taxation, penalizing as it does the socially productive, would seem to frustrate one of the greatest of all social objectives: the expansion of material well-being through the encouragement of the ablest and most industrious producers.[7]

It is indeed a fact that literally *no one* in the United States has ever suggested a complete leveling of incomes and properties; the equalitarian function of taxation, everyone knows, is a mischievous thing which remains a part of our policy only because we have never permitted free rein to its disastrous potentialities. About the only good thing that can be said concerning estate taxation is that in many instances its greatest impact can be avoided through various types of legal devices. Like steeply progressive income taxation, discriminatory estate taxation, if rigorously and effectively enforced over long periods as some college professors keep advocating, could help to destroy the free society.

It seems evident by now that governments do not promote either freedom or equality through taxation. More is lost than gained. Governments never use wealth as efficiently and economically as do the private persons immediately responsible for the creation of such wealth. There is an explanation of this fact, more cogent than charges of bribery and corruption as inherent attributes of bureaucratic activity. The explanation is that governments will not and cannot permit themselves to be subjected to the rigorous laws of the free market, the laws which make short shrift of inefficiency and waste and which carry the command of the people concerning what is to be produced.

All this is not to say, however, that governments do not have an important role in the promotion of personal freedom. On the contrary, the role of government in the promotion of personal freedom is crucial. Personal freedom cannot exist without strong and effective government. And this is true even though the positive aspects of personal freedom are owing, not to law or other compulsory features of government, but to nature and to man's understanding and control of nature. The positive aspects of personal freedom must be defined in terms of knowledge and power—the powers which nature has given men, and which men have used in turn to increase their understanding and consequently their control of themselves, nature, and events. The investigators who discovered the principles of electricity and the other secrets of nature, and the businessmen who translated this knowledge into real physical power, put humanity in a position to reach its present status of freedom.[8] The function of the state is to make sure that all men are free to use the powers which nature has given them and which they have improved. The methods perfected by free societies to fulfill this function are the principles of private property and freedom of contract—the basic and most important working principles of any free society.

Chapter 4

OPERATING PRINCIPLES:
PRIVATE PROPERTY AND FREEDOM
OF CONTRACT

Without a society in which life and property are to some extent secure, existence can continue only at the lowest levels—you cannot have a good life for those you love, nor can you devote your energies to activity on the higher level.
—Alfred North Whitehead

If personal freedom is the basic institution of the free society, then the principles of private property and freedom of contract must be the vital instruments of the free society; for personal freedom cannot even be conceived outside the environment provided by property and contract rights. And since all rights are meaningful only to the degree that they are secured against invasion, it follows that the role of the state, as the exclusive source of the legal sanctions which secure personal rights, is a critical one in the operation of the free society. We should no longer be surprised to find that freedom, well-being, and security are one: that the security of the rights necessary to freedom of action is essential to the personal well-being of all members of the community.

The founding fathers used to talk about the "security of our liberties." They knew what they were talking about. And they knew what they were doing, too, when they took the "life, liberty, and pursuit of happiness" of the Declaration of Independence, and substituted for it, in the Constitution, the phrase "life, liberty, and *property*."

The Indispensability of Property and Contract Rights

A secured freedom to act in the pursuit of personal ends prevails only in a social environment based on private property

37

and freedom of contract. Anyone inclined to doubt this proposition must try to visualize the condition of men in a community where these are not secured rights. The vast mass of persons in such a community have no freedom to follow their own will, no freedom to act; they have only the "freedom" to do what they are told or be killed. In the absence of secured rights of private property and contract, persons own and control nothing; no real or personal property, no tangible or intangible goods; the very food they eat—when and if they eat—is not, properly speaking, *theirs*; they are not the assured masters of the disposition of even their own bodies except in committing suicide; they have no secured recourse against anyone who invades their physical integrity, who abuses or injures them. They may think what they wish and what they are capable of thinking in such stultifying conditions. But they may speak and write only if their tongues and hands are left intact.[1]

Freedom of action in the absence of property and contract rights is open only transiently to the physically strongest persons. Under such circumstances, there is no scope for the productive, the talented, the men able in the gentle arts of peace. For those talented in the productive pursuits are not necessarily talented in the arts of war; and even when they are, the social conditions prerequisite to concentration upon productive pursuits do not exist during the war of all against all. Alfred North Whitehead spoke with his customary percipience when he said: "Responsibility for a social system is the groundwork of civilization." And he left no doubt as to what he meant by "social system" and "groundwork of civilization," for he immediately added that: "Without a society in which life and property are to some extent secure, existence can continue only at the lowest levels—you cannot have a good life for those you love, nor can you devote your energies to activity on the higher level."

The complicated and efficient production processes of a society characterized by a high degree of division of labor are a consequence, as we know them today, of the endurance of private property and contract rights in our society for an appreciable time. Take away private property and freedom of contract, and you may still have a division of labor; but you will no longer have a free society. For that, private property and freedom of contract are indispensable.

The Scope and Character of Property and Contract Rights

It is currently fashionable to pose a strong contrast between "human rights" and "property rights." One also frequently hears it said that property and contract rights necessarily conflict with social goals. Such statements reflect a misunderstanding of the principles of private property and freedom of contract. It must be a misunderstanding, for these principles by their very nature relate to human, personal right; and as such they have no claim upon consideration except to the degree that they are useful to men in society.

Individual and social goals are, in fact, unified *only* by property and contract rights. This point is most readily apprehended by noting how individual and social goals are merely two ways of expressing a single concept. Thus the most drastic deprivation which any person can suffer is that of the freedom to utilize and enjoy the faculties which nature has given him and which his will and desire have developed. Keep a man from exercising his mind, his body, his faculties in the pursuit of his own wishes and delights, keep him from enjoying the fruits of his efforts—and you have done everything evil to him that you can. The greatest desire of each person, in short, is to be free to get the most he can out of life. There is no other way objectively to define social goals than to call them the sum of those individual goals which can be harmonized in society.

Far from frustrating these essential interests of men and of society, the principles of private property and freedom of contract integrate them in a manner which tends to produce a harmoniously operating, enduring society. These principles make for interpersonal compatibility. More important, they are the *only* working social principles which make for such compatibility in a society dedicated to the simultaneous achievement of maximum personal freedom, well-being, and security.

The best way to demonstrate the validity of these statements is to set forth the scope and character of private property and freedom of contract, and the place to start is with the person. A society which makes any pretensions to freedom must accept and securely guarantee individual autonomy. Each member of society (children and other legal incompetents excepted) must be in control of his own person. All must be afforded protection against attempts by others to invade the integrity of their person. A property right in this sense means that everyone has a legally protected interest in his person, the invasion of which is interdicted by society. And each must control the disposition of his person—his person as established by nature and as developed by himself.

Every man, to use an alternative formulation, must have a socially protected right to live his life in his own way, to do with himself and his abilities, or to refrain from doing with them, such things as he wishes. We may recall here John Stuart Mill's statement: "The only freedom which deserves the name, is that of pursuing our own good in our own way." Does this mean that a man must be accorded the freedom to do *anything* he wishes? The answer, of course, is No. And Mill, it will be remembered, completed his statement by adding, "so long as we do not attempt to deprive others of theirs, or impede their efforts to obtain it." For if a man were allowed to do *anything*, he might choose to kill or maim his fellow men. And he certainly may not be allowed to do that; if he does, he violates the basic rule itself: he invades the physical integrity of others. And what is secured for one must be secured to all in the great, free society—the society, as we have noted, which is essentially characterized by the fact that its basic rules apply equally to all its members.

What has been said is sufficient to reveal the thinking which underlies the generalization that "each person must be free to follow his own desires up to the point at which his conduct negates the precisely equivalent freedom of others." It may be useful to add, however, that the analysis sketched here was largely influential in the production of the basic approach of Anglo-American common law to the problems of labor relations. Picketing and other devices of a similar character, when employed by unions to block the access of nonunion workers to places of employment, were often condemned by common-law judges. The basis of condemnation was the conclusion that the obstruction of access destroyed the balance of rights as between employers, organized employees, and unorganized employees. Each was thought of as having a socially protected interest in the nature of a property right: the employer, in having free access to all who might wish to take the jobs he was offering; the organized workers, in striking or otherwise withdrawing themselves from employment; and the unorganized workers, in applying for or remaining at work as they wished. The role of the law was conceived as that of giving full scope to each of these legally protected interests—of forbidding conduct which tended to impair any of them. When the organized workers tried to push their own basic and unquestioned personal right to the point where it impinged upon and tended effectively to erase the equivalent rights of the employer and the unorganized employees, as picketing very often plainly does, common-law judges prohibited their action.[2]

If the property concept secures the person and the free disposition of the person, it must also secure each person in the possession and enjoyment of that which his efforts have gained. Men give away or sell voluntarily the things they have produced. But a man who has had taken from him arbitrarily the things he alone has produced, is justified in concluding that he does not have an unassailable right to his own personal integrity. The case is different if the man agrees, either before or after he has produced a thing, that it is to be conveyed to, or is to be the possession of, another. There, although he may regret parting with his production, he must concede that he has himself disposed of it. He has availed himself of his property right to contract freely.

But the man who has his production wrenched from him against his will is not a free man with an unassailable property right in his own person. He is a slave, a being whose person and therefore whose product are the possession of someone else. However loathesome it may be, the fact that the products—even the children—of slaves were considered to be the possession of the slave-owner, resulted from a consistent application of the property principle. One should be careful to note, however, that the private-property principle itself is not to blame for slavery. Quite the contrary. Pushed all the way, that principle makes each person autonomous—makes every person free. The fault under slavery, therefore, lies not in the principle of private property or in the free society but in their imperfect realization.

The principle of private property involves more than personal autonomy and the exclusive right to the enjoyment of the fruits of one's personal efforts; it includes also the ultimate control of one's productions. If a man is entitled, in the legal phrase, to the quiet enjoyment of a machine he has made, he is necessarily entitled to use the machine, to control it, to give it or sell it to someone, or merely to sit and worship it. We err, if this is not true, in stating that the right of private property is the right of personal autonomy and the right to the fruits of personal effort. For the phrase "the right to the fruit of personal effort," if it be meaningful, means the right to use and control that which one has produced.

This point marks the outer limits of the principle of private property. Properly speaking, it comprehends also the principle of freedom of contract. Freedom of contract is not only conceptually implicit in the right of private property, but as a matter of history as well, it grew along with the gradual elaboration of the private-property principle. In technical legal discussions, it is true, "property law" and "contract law" are separately identified; and the two principles developed independently to some extent. Nevertheless, lawyers often refer to freedom of contract as a "property right." And it has been habitual among jurists to say that the free access of workers to employment opportunities is a property right. When they express themselves this way, they mean that employers and workers have mutual property rights to make employment contracts with each other.[3]

The fact that the right of private property inherently includes the right of control (the right, in other words, to contract freely in respect to the subjects of the property right) has created an enormous amount of trouble for students of society, including those unexcelled students of society, the common-law judges. Critics have continually asserted that the right of autonomous control is the feature which reveals the basically "antisocial" character of the principle of private property. As examples they cite cases in which judges have held that the "property rights" of one owner of land or a factory justified him in so using his land or factory as to impair considerably an adjacent landowner's enjoyment of his property.

There are some such cases in the law books. Yet the fact that some judges, or even all judges, handed down such decisions, does not necessarily mean that they correctly applied the *social* principle of private property; it does not even mean that they were correct applications of the *legal* principle. The social and the legal principle of private property have in common the formula: *sic utere tuo ut alienum non laedas* or "so use your own as not to injure that of another." Now this formula, like all legal formulae, does not solve disputes between persons automatically. It is a guide, a principle designed to provide orientation for the judge's thinking. It tells him, for example, that he must decide the case, not on the basis of the social status of the disputants or their race or their sex, but in the manner best calculated to reconcile their equal property rights. Thus if the President of the United States should use his private land in a manner which tends to destroy the property right of an adjacent landowner, the President's status should make no difference in the thinking of the judge.

As either a social or a legal principle, any person's right of private property may properly extend only to the point at which it coexists harmoniously with the equal property rights of all other members of society. One who uses his possessions in a manner destructive of the rights of others is not protected by the right of private property. He has invaded the rights of others. The law reports are full of cases which demonstrate the reconciliation of intersecting property rights along the lines of the principle here stated.

At times the reconciliation of property rights effected in a particular case may not suit the tastes of independent observers; but that, of course, has no bearing one way or another on the adequacy or social utility of the private-property principle. The reconciliation must in each case turn on the particular facts. The proper job of the judicial system is to provide the procedural techniques most appropriate to the establishment of the operative facts and to clarify the legal issues raised by those facts. A good legal system is one which fills the bill in these respects. If its rules of evidence and procedure are in order, and if the method of selecting judges is the best one that can be put into effect under all the circumstances, the legal system has done its job. Questionable decisions may still be handed down from time to time, but there is not much that anyone can do about that beyond the process of patient criticism carried on continuously by legal scholars and the slow elaboration of sound and coherent subordinate principles. Deficiencies in the structure of legal procedures—condemnable on independent grounds—should not be made the basis of condemnation of the substantive principles of the law, for confusion is the only result.

In a proper analysis, the private-property principle must therefore be measured only in terms of its social utility as a principle. It may properly be characterized as "antisocial" only if it can be shown to be inherently in conflict with the concept of the good and free society. This, no one has ever done, a fact which will become apparent as we consider the principles of property and contract in action in Chapter 5.

The Enforceable Contract

Like the private-property principle, freedom of contract is inherently limited by the necessity of making it a property of every member of society. Contract rights may not be conceived in terms which would involve the cancellation of equal rights for every one. The right of freedom of contract of any person, in short, may extend only to that point at which it remains harmonious with the equivalent property and contract rights of all other persons.

On the most basic level, the principle of freedom of contract accords to each person the right to enter into any agreement suitable to himself and to the other contracting party concerning the disposition of any act or thing subject to their respective property rights. A contract to commit murder or any other expropriatory act logically falls within the same ban as the expropriatory act itself. No act that is illegitimate when performed by an individual becomes legitimate when done by a combination pursuant to a contract.

On an equally elemental level, the principle of freedom of contract implies that no one may be compelled by means of force, fraud, or coercive intimidation to enter into or to refrain from entering into an "agreement." For the essence of the concept of contract lies in the element of assent; "contract" and "voluntary contract" mean the same thing. When one says he will do something because a gun has been held at his head, or because some other kind of equivalent human compulsion has been exerted, it is improper to describe his promise as contractual in nature. Similarly, a man who agrees to purchase an automobile on the basis of certain representations by the seller agrees only to purchase the machine as represented; he cannot properly be said to have agreed to purchase a car which does not meet the description.

Perhaps no problem in jurisprudence or in any of the other social sciences has been more difficult to solve than that posed by the lack of stability in the concepts of coercion and intimidation. We have just said that a promise exacted by coercive intimidation may not properly be viewed as an exercise of freedom of contract. Everyone agrees that a man who promises to pay a certain sum to one who threatens to kill him, or to abduct his wife or son, or to blow up his home, has not freely contracted and is therefore neither legally nor otherwise bound to pay as promised. But then consider the following case.

Fahed Haddad is in the middle of the Sahara Desert, suffering seriously from hunger and thirst. Just a few thousand feet away, over a low hill and out of sight, lies an oasis, the private property of one Izar Tabet who sells water and other refreshments there. Has Fahed been coerced in any, or some, or all of the following instances?

1. Yussef Shakir, related in no way to Izar Tabet, finds Fahed semiconscious and unable to move. He tells Fahed that food and everything else necessary to restore him are available nearby; that for a thousand dollars he will procure these things. Fahed agrees. Yussef scurries away, secures for ten dollars all the water and food necessary to save Fahed's life, and returns in less than a half-hour. He turns these over on the understanding that he is to be paid the thousand dollars.

2. Fahed is in bad shape but could just about make it to the oasis after a little rest. Yussef, well-mounted, comes upon him, estimates the situation accurately, informs him that there is no

food or water within thirty miles, a distance well beyond his capacity, and for a thousand dollars offers to get Fahed what he needs. Fahed accepts and promises to pay the money. Yussef then goes to the oasis, rests there for a good while, and then gets back with the food and water, again handing it over with the understanding that he is to receive the thousand dollars.

3. Fahed makes it to the oasis. Izar Tabet, who would have asked ten dollars of Yussef, will supply Fahed with adequate food and water only if he agrees to pay a thousand dollars.

Now there is no question in any of these instances about one thing: in the broad sense of the term, Fahed has been *coerced* in all three cases. But there is at least one distinction. In case one, he has been coerced by nature, inasmuch as his body by its very nature needs food and water if he is to survive and inasmuch as nature has been skimpy in the distribution of provender in the desert. In case two, while nature's coercion was still at work, it was not sufficient to induce him to promise the thousand dollars. He would not have agreed to pay that sum *except for* the fact that Yussef misled him. Had the latter said or done nothing, Fahed would have made it to the oasis. Case three is really case one over again, with two parties involved instead of three.

Nature's limitations and scarcities are always with us. Together with the fact that men have desires of various kinds, they are ultimate givens. Much can be done about natural scarcities and human desires; but they cannot be abolished. They form, in fact, the imperishable framework of human action. Since men act always within the structure of natural coercion and their own desires, it seems only confusing to regard freedom in society as either hampered or coerced when the source is merely one's own desires or nature.

The conclusion to be drawn from this analysis is that the promise to pay a thousand dollars was coerced only in case two. For in that case alone did one of the "contracting" parties coerce the others. In that case nature's coercion did not suffice to exact the promise to pay; Yussef *created* a coercive situation. In the other two cases, nature did the coercing. Yussef and Izar did not, properly speaking, coerce Fahed. Instead they performed a very important service for him. The value they attached to their service may seem exorbitant to some, but then it must be remembered that their service was an extraordinarily precious one to Fahed. It saved his life.

An extreme case has been chosen in order to illustrate sharply the most important point about coercion for an analysis such as this: only human coercion is significant in thinking about freedom in society. In the vast majority of cases which have caused trouble, the situation has not involved a matter of life or death at all. The cases which give trouble are usually those in which men complain because they are "compelled" to give more than they *like* to give in order to acquire from another the object or service of their desire. A worker complains that he does not receive high enough wages for his work. A tenant thinks he is "being forced" to pay more rent that he "should." A borrower talks of the "coercion" which compels him to pay rates of interest which seem "too high" to him. Our purpose at this point is to provide an objective basis for evaluation of the contention that contracts for wages, rent, and interest are "coerced"—that they are not, properly speaking, exercises of freedom of contract.

The proper evaluation, of course, is that every contract is an exercise of freedom of contract so long as there is *mutual assent;* that is to say, so long as it was not secured through misrepresentation, human coercion, or force. If freedom of contract were held not to exist in cases in which one party was induced by natural scarcity and his own desires to make a promise, it would cover very few, if any, cases which are now thought of as involving a contractual arrangement. For in practically every case, each party to a contract enters into that contract because he wants—he desires, he "needs"—what the other contracting party has. Indeed, contract is one of the basic operating principles of the free society precisely because it is so serviceable a method of integrating human action in a peaceful way, to the end that everyone is better off as a result of the voluntary pursuit of self-interest. The fact that persons—workers, tenants, and debtors—may later regret the agreement which their own desires have led them to make, cannot be a valid ground for vitiating such contracts; for the inevitable effect would be to abandon the whole concept of contract; and this is true even though such persons may argue that they were "victims" of natural scarcity and the "prisoners" of their own desires in making the agreement which they seek to avoid.

Whatever opinions to the contrary may have been voiced upon the subject, the common law has sanctioned contracts only when it has been satisfied that real assent was present among the parties. Fraud, misrepresentation, duress, coercion, even mistake or misapprehension upon some material matter—all these have served common-law judges as grounds for avoiding "contracts" which might otherwise have met the formal legal requirements. Brief reference to any of the treatises on the law of contracts will bear out these affirmations.

Contracts Contrary to Public Policy

In the theory of the free society all real agreements are enforceable except those which negate the fundamental property and contract concepts themselves. Thus contracts to commit murder, to defraud, or, in general, to destroy the fundamental property rights of another are inconsistent with the theory of the free society and should, therefore, in societies which aim at freedom be declared unlawful or "contrary to public policy."

The complexities of human action are such, however, that it would be impossible to identify for all time the precise types of agreements which should be held contrary to public policy by the free society intent upon safeguarding its members against contracts which tend to negate fundamental property rights.[4] In the free society, contracts contrary to public policy must constitute an open category. It is not a completely guideless category, however; for private property and freedom of contract, the basic principles of the free society, provide a definite and useful orientation. Intelligent analysis based upon all the insights afforded by both the natural and the social sciences must ultimately yield in each particular case a reasonably sensible rule, that is, one consistent with the great objectives of the free society. No other theory of society offers as much guidance.

Questions must therefore arise from time to time as to whether particular types of agreement are contrary to public policy. Thus, in the United States, "yellow-dog" contracts and closed-shop contracts have often been challenged; and in response to the frequent challenges, both types of agreements have at one time or another been held invalid by courts or declared positively unlawful by legislatures. Whether or not the courts and legislatures operated consistently with the goals and objectives of the free society in so ruling is a problem which can be satisfactorily solved only by a full understanding of the principles of the free society.

The "yellow-dog" contract involves a promise by an employee that for the duration of his employment he will not become a member of a labor union. The fact that the federal and state governments have prohibited such agreements does not necessarily mean that the fundamental principles of the free society have been compromised. It must be remembered that the right to join or not to join a union flows naturally from the private-property principle, and that a contract forbidding union membership forfeits that right. There is something to be said for enjoining contracts based upon the negation or cancellation of basic property rights of the parties to the contract. Thus, it could hardly be contended that a society would depart from the principles of freedom if it prohibited employment contracts under which employees agreed to vote in accordance with their employer's directions. And so, it might be argued, the "yellow-dog" contract should be suspect.[5]

But there is an aspect of the problem of "yellow-dog" contracts which has scarcely ever been satisfactorily explored. In many instances employers insisted upon such agreements because experience had taught them that acceptance of the unionization of their employees would amount to accepting the potential destruction of their businesses. Reference to the most famous of all cases involving this type of contract, the Hitchman Coal case,[6] reveals that the employer had originally not opposed unionization among his employees, and that his opposition, in the form of "yellow-dog" contracts, came only after the union had manifested its contempt for contracts generally and for the property rights of the employer in particular. Employers sharing such experiences can scarcely be censured for having resisted unionization by means of such relatively moderate devices as the "yellow-dog" contract. Even employers who had not directly shared such experiences might readily be pardoned for fearing that unionization of their employees would prove disastrous. For all such employers the "yellow-dog" contract might well have seemed more like a promise by employees not to sabotage than one forfeiting a basic property right.

It takes a society a long time to unscramble considerations as complicated as the foregoing, and the United States is only now on the right track to an enduring solution. The "yellow-dog" contract is unlawful today, as a corollary of the principle of free employee choice, which, as we shall see in Chapter 8, has come to dominate the labor relations policy of the United States. But the law today also prohibits coercion of employees by unions; it is on the way to insisting that unions become law-abiding institutions; and the principle is now well established that employers may defend their businesses against irresponsible conduct by either employees or unions. In Part II of this book we shall deal at much greater length with the pattern of labor policy in the United States and may therefore postpone further analysis till then. At this point it is necessary to add only that while the prohibition of "yellow-dog" contracts might have amounted to a substantial impairment of freedom of contract not justifiable in principle at a time when the law did not protect employees and employers against union coercion, and when other antisocial activities of unions were not curbed, a different analysis and evaluation are appropriate at the present time: The way is largely clear now to getting our legal house in order; and with a coherent code of laws restraining antisocial conduct by unions there will be no justification, and therefore no occasion, for anti-union contracts. The intelligently operated free society can very often solve its problem in this way: by removing causes, through sensible and comprehensive adjustment of all the relevant property rights, rather than by arbitrary rules which expand the privileges of some at the expense of the rights of others.

No one in the United States currently objects to the prohibition of "yellow-dog" contracts. Yet union officers and their supporters are today engaged in a campaign on all fronts to gain repeal of the state and federal laws which prohibit closed-shop contracts.[7] One who contended that "yellow-dog" contracts should be permitted and enforced by law, might rationally urge a similar status for closed-shop contracts.[8] For, just as the "yellow-dog" contract makes *nonmembership* in a union a condition of employment, the closed-shop contract makes *member-ship* in a union a condition of employment. The characteristic common to both types of agreement is the subordination of the property right of employees as regards joining or not joining a labor organization to the contractual arrangements insisted upon by unions and employers. If one takes the position that freedom of contract is more important than the free choice of employees in regard to unionization, he may insist that both the "yellow-dog" contract and the closed-shop contract be considered valid and enforceable under the law. But if it be argued, as the union officers and their supporters do, that the "yellow-dog" contract is properly prohibited while the closed-shop contract should be accepted, little attention need be paid to the argument; for it is really only a demand for a special privilege, not a rational argument for freedom of contract.

Despite the support which unionists receive from politicians for their demand that the closed shop be permitted, it is difficult to take the demand seriously. It is in all ways so patently unjustified. Unionists say that they must have the closed shop if unions are to survive. But this is the same as saying that unless unions are permitted to coerce membership they will have no members—scarcely a very persuasive way to argue the case. And the contention is manifestly not accurate. Unions can and do secure members by uncoercive means. Unions can and do serve useful purposes, and they have only barely scratched the surface of their potential utility to employees. When they really get to work on the job of serving employees instead of making such bad names for themselves as they do in coercing and abusing employees, they will have much less difficulty than they presently have in securing and keeping new members. As matters now stand, union insistence upon the closed shop amounts to an admission that unions are really not performing their functions very well.

There are other considerations relevant to analyzing the soundness of laws prohibiting compulsory-unionism "contracts." Perhaps the foremost of these considerations is whether such "contracts" should properly be called contracts at all. Trade unions customarily secure compulsory-unionism "contracts" either directly through violence and threats of violence, or indirectly through the exertion of power which rests fundamentally upon their coercive methods of building and maintaining their organizations and of preventing the access of nonunion employees to labor markets. Few indeed would be the compulsory-unionism "contracts" if the state had always performed its basic function of preventing trade unions from using violent and coercive methods in building up their organizations and in exercising their organized power in order to compel acquiescence by employers in closed-shop arrangements.[9]

A consideration equally important but far more subtle is whether acts of associations are properly regarded as identical with the superficially similar acts of individual persons. A single employee is exercising a basic contract right when he insists that he will work only for an employer who hires exclusively union personnel. Yet it does not necessarily follow that compulsory-unionism conditions imposed by unions either involve the same kind of thing factually or should be viewed legally in the same way. This matter is considered further in Chapter 6, pages 81-83.

*   *   *

The principles of private property and freedom of contract stand out as the basic, indispensable, operating principles of the free society. Unless they are preserved intact, it is useless to think in terms of freedom, well-being, and security as the animating objectives of a society. But private property and freedom of contract are complex principles, and the equilibrium they establish in society is dynamic rather than static. The structure of the free society will always and everywhere be much the same, and the outlines of the principles of private property and freedom of contract must probably remain fixed in the free society for as long as men remain the kind of beings they are now. Yet specific exercises of property and contract rights must be subjected to the test of whether their consequences are consistent with the maintenance of the dynamic equilibrium of all property and contract rights.

Chapter 5

PROPERTY RIGHTS, HUMAN RIGHTS, AND THE STATE

> For I have reason to conclude that he who would get me
> into his power without my consent, would use me as he
> pleased when he had got me there, and destroy me too, when
> he had a fancy to it; for nobody can desire to have me in his
> absolute power unless it be to compel me by force to that
> which is against the right of my freedom, *i.e.*, make me a
> slave.
>
> —John Locke

Denigration of the right of private property usually begins
with a sharp distinction between "human rights" and "property
rights." Those who habitually make this distinction normally go
on to contend that society—and by society such persons usually
mean government—may qualify property rights without seriously
affecting the "essential human freedoms." They argue, indeed,
that the restrictions on property rights which they favor will in
fact expand the "essential human freedoms."

There is no truth in any of these assertions. Property rights
are human rights, and nothing else. The various human rights
comprehended in the general right of private property cannot be
neatly distinguished, portioned out, and separated in the real
world of action; those are things which cannot be done satisfactorily even in analytical abstraction. Pruning and excisions,
divestitures and re-allocations of property rights, all necessarily
amount to arbitrary action which reduces human freedom and
social productivity.[1] Everyone now realizes that slavery is arbitrary; but few, apparently, know why it is arbitrary. For most
people who oppose slavery are in favor of discriminatory taxation,
in spite of the fact that such taxation is arbitrary in exactly the
same sense that slavery is arbitrary.

Property Rights, Interventionism, and Totalitarianism

Some objections to the right of private property are of a relatively superficial kind, easily cleared up by placing the right in its appropriate social context. The right of private property did not spring full-blown upon the world. Nor did the intimately related idea of the strictly enforceable contract have an easy time of it. Sir Henry Maine was of the opinion, indeed, that "the positive duty resulting from one man's reliance on the word of another is among the slowest conquests of advancing civilization." As defined in this book, property and contract rights are the end products of a long and fitful evolutionary process; they are understood and appreciated only by men in a relatively sophisticated stage of development.

The evolution to the final, symmetrical form was dictated by the necessities which presented themselves to our forebears who wished to live in free and productive societies. Private property in its broad form commended itself to those men because it worked. It offered both freedom and order. It set loose the constructive energies of men, and at the same time constituted a rational, social basis for the integration of the activities of all men. It was a great, central organizing principle that carried within itself the idea of the society which might be both free and harmonious. Private property in its comprehensive form is not merely indispensable to the free society; it is the free society itself. Once this is perceived, a good many of the objections disappear.

Yet there are still many who rebel against the comprehensive definition, who insist that the "good of society"—a concept which they never define—absolutely requires that the state be generally empowered at all times to expand or diminish or revise the right of private property. These are the people who see red when they hear the words "inalienable property rights," no matter how carefully those words may be used. The idea of property rights secured to all persons against invasion by the state or anyone else, seems hopelessly "dated," even "reactionary," to them. Rejecting both "totalitarianism" and comprehensive property rights as the central principles of social organization, they call themselves "liberals," "progressives," or some other such modest name, and announce that they have found a "middle way."

Beyond any question, application of the private-property principle does create difficult problems at times. Emotional and intellectual difficulties present themselves even when the general principle itself is rightly understood. The more complicated the society, moreover, the more frequently do difficulties of application arise. But this kind of thing is unavoidable. As a matter of fact, in the free society it really reflects the existence of a state of affairs which most find highly desirable. For property problems become the more complicated the more widely dispersed the property rights happen to be, and the more intensively human affairs are integrated. Restrict property rights narrowly, reduce personal autonomy to the minimum, and you will have a minimum of property problems. Take away private-property rights completely, destroy entirely the autonomy of the person, and you have no private-property problems at all. If no person *legally* owns or controls anything, including himself, the problem of control is solved quite simply by force. If all property rights are vested in the state (that is, in the strongest force in the community), problems of personal *right* likewise do not arise to complicate the social structure. A monolithic structure of this kind may appeal to some. But it is no way to achieve personal freedom, well-being, and security.

As to the so-called "middle way" in current usage, this is actually a misnomer. Personal private-property rights, in the sense of the common-law doctrines and old-fashioned liberal political theory, represent as meaningful a pursuit of the "middle way" between the political absolutes of anarchy and socialism as straight thinking has yet produced. One may, in short, make a respectable argument to the effect that the private-property way is the only meaningful "middle way," since totalitarianism and anarchy are the only other pure forms of social organization which may be meaningfully conceived.

But the "middle way" as used in current debate is only a semantically attractive synonym for the *interventionist* state. It defines a condition in which the state is at all times authorized to modify personal property rights at will: the state may expand or contract the rights of persons as political exigency may seem to dictate to those in public office. The perpetual dynamic equilibrium of personal rights as here defined is anathema to the interventionists.

Many interventionists insist, it is true, upon respect for the rights of free speech, free thought, and free press. But they are apparently not aware of the unity of all personal rights. They do not see that all personal rights have a common core in the autonomy of the person, that the so-called "human rights" are merely one surface manifestation of the elemental right of private property.

The interventionist state is actually a state moving intermittently toward the complete destruction of all the personal freedom which it can reach. As such, in terms of formal analysis it must be defined as a totalitarian state, since its own proponents insist that the state is the source of all rights. In empirical terms it might be called a potential totalitarian state.

How long will freedom of the press endure, if interventionism finally triumphs? Freedom of the press is nothing more nor less than the condition which exists when publishers have their property rights intact. Even in the United States today, when interventionism is still struggling to substitute political exigency for private property rights, interventionists have unconsciously shown what they genuinely think of freedom of the press. The term "captive press" gets a great deal of use from trade unionists and from politicians who consider themselves "moderates."

If interventionism finally triumphs, will its less moderate apostles limit themselves to this mere vilification of those who oppose them? Have interventionists, when they have come to full power and when political conditions have been propitious, ever so limited themselves? Is not vilification always the first step—and only the first step—of demagogues? When Juan Peron tired of freedom of the press in Buenos Aires, he expropriated the publishers. If "it" happens here, expropriation in one form or another will be the means used. The basis for such expropriation exists in the way that interventionists look at property rights, thinking of them as subject to revision whenever the "good of society" so requires. The Union of Soviet Socialist Republics may very well today have a law or a bill of rights which "guarantees" both freedom of speech and freedom of the press. But what good is such a guarantee when no private person or group may own a printing establishment?[2]

It is inaccurate to describe a press based on private property rights as "captive." Publishers under such conditions are limited in what they print only by their own personal views or interests and by the libel laws—and those laws are themselves an expression of the property right in the integrity of one's character. It is inaccurate also to say that the editorial policies of newspapers are determined by advertisers. Businessmen may be the greatest source of advertising revenue of one branch of the press, the dailies and the other periodicals. But advertising revenues rise and fall in accordance with the circulation of the particular newspaper or magazine, not with the secret or public ideology of the publisher.

The difference in advertising revenues of the New York City newspapers, the *Times,* the *Daily News,* and the *Post,* is determined by their readers, not by their varying political attitudes. The revenues of the *Post,* whether they be higher or lower than those of the others, are determined by the extent to which it has been successful in securing readers. And the political views of newspaper publishers apparently bear little relationship to the political attitudes of their readers, beyond, possibly, reflecting them. The newspapers with the largest circulation in the United States—the Chicago *Tribune* and the New York *Daily News*—are located in cities which are almost always carried by the political party which the *News* and the *Tribune* usually oppose. The contention that the press is the captive of its advertisers is absurd and ridiculous.

But the fact that a contention appears upon examination to be absurd and ridiculous has not always kept people from repeating it; moreover, it has not always succeeded in precluding widespread acceptance of the absurd contention as truth. Some of the things which demagogues repeat most frequently are pure fictions. When the repetition has been carried on long enough to induce some conviction, the demagogue stops talking. He begins to act. And the consequence of his action in every case is a more or less drastic revision of the right of private property, with the usual damage to personal freedom and the good society.

We in the United States compose a still largely free society, based on private property and freedom of contract. But, as a matter of history, the distortions of the principles of property and contract which mar our society trace to the demagoguery implicit in the characterization of our pioneering businessmen as "robber barons" and "malefactors of great wealth."

Robber barons were those physically and militarily powerful persons in the Middle Ages who expropriated and enslaved others, depriving them by the use of force of all property and contract rights, even the most elemental. Their minions and allies were famine, sword, and fire. They were destroyers. They alone enjoyed the fruits of their activity. Their conduct, if we are to believe the worst said of them by historians, resulted in the reduction of social productivity and the destruction of personal freedom.

The American businessmen who have been characterized as "robber barons" bore no resemblance whatsoever to the robber barons of the Middle Ages; and whether or not they were "malefactors" depends upon our evaluation of their essential product: the form of our productive organization and the standard of living of the American. Our pioneer capitalists and entrepreneurs—representative examples are Astor, Carnegie, Ford, Morgan, and Rockefeller—operated in an era when the principles of private property and freedom of contract enjoyed a status which compares favorably with the one they occupy in our own era. Violent and coercive conduct was as unlawful then as it is now. In those days one might no more expropriate or defraud another, legally, than he may now. Personal freedom and opportunity were at least as broadly diffused as they are now—probably more so among all men, not merely Astor, Carnegie, *et al.* Furthermore, justice was dispensed about as even-handedly by the courts then as it is now. In short, the basic human rights were the same, and they were at least equally vigorously enforced.

This being true, it is plain that the means used by the robber barons of the Middle Ages were not available to our early enterprisers. They might not then, as businessmen may not now, expropriate or enslave any one; they might not use force and violence, and they might not defraud. What they might do, and what they did do, was to work, save, and invest; and then as their investments proved profitable—as it appeared that they had invested in accordance with public demand for the products which their investments made possible—they invested more and more, increased the capital equipment of the nation fantastically, and thus raised to a point never before envisioned in human history, the productivity of their society.

The productivity of our economy today is in considerable degree the result of the astute, far-seeing exercise of property and contract rights by our early capitalists and enterprisers. They were men, of course; and as men it is probable that, besides violating the law upon occasion, they did not lead perfectly moral and blameless lives. But the extent to which character-assassination has gone in regard to these productive men, in the estimation of the generations which followed them and which reaped the benefits of their industry, has been a shameful thing.[3]

This would not have been so bad if it had produced only general scorn and contempt for the early entrepreneurs; their works have survived, as living, growing testimonials to their greatness, and even the historical record is in the process of correction.[4] But really significant harm has been done in terms of general understanding and appreciation of the principles of private property and freedom of contract, as well as to the principles themselves. For the personal attack became an attack upon the social principles and institutions within which the early entrepreneurs operated. When demagogues had succeeded in discrediting the men most clearly responsible for building the country, they found conditions propitious to the modification of the principles which have had more to do than has any man with bringing about a harmonious and productive society.

Part II of this book is largely concerned with tracing the career of interventionism in one large area of public policy, the labor-relations field. As is demonstrated in detail there, interventionism does not destroy property rights, mainly because property rights cannot be destroyed; the control of persons and things must rest somewhere in any society or in any aggregate of human beings. The difference between interventionism and the free society lies in the mode of distributing property rights. The free society distributes property rights equally among all persons so as to secure interpersonal compatibility; and, thus distributed, the rights are *secured* to persons, are *private*-property rights guaranteed by law, and immune to tampering. The interventionist society establishes ultimate control of all property rights, including the control of persons, in the state; and then redistributes fragmentary portions of the property right among the various members and groups of the society, according to the discretion of those operating the machinery of the state and with political expediency largely constituting the standard of distribution.

Under the rule of private-property rights, the person is all and the state is neutral in disputes among persons; the judges, to the best of their ability, give equal justice in accordance with law. Under interventionism, a person as an individual unit does not count. He is only one vote. Classes and groups count, for they are potentially many votes, a rich prize for any politician who can think up or promote some measure which will capture them all.

If debtors are numerous, and if their greed has conquered their judgment, so that they have gone further into debt than their productive abilities warrant, then let there be a universal moratorium on debts. If manufacturers in a given area or in a given line of production are relatively inefficient, so that the consumers are served better by foreign producers, why then let foreign imports be blocked by a tariff wall. If tenants are more numerous than landlords and would prefer to pay less than market rents, then let there be maximum rent controls. If some retailers cannot meet the competition of others, let there be laws fixing minimum retail prices. If a markedly identifiable voting group such as the farmers shows dissatisfaction with its income under free-market conditions, let the group be subsidized to the point which satisfies the most vocal of its members.

This catalogue could be extended further. But enough examples have been listed to demonstrate the nature of interventionism. In each instance cited, the state rearranged property and contract rights in a manner which favored one group over another, without regard to the real effects of the rearrangement on the general harmony of society, and even without regard to the specific consequences of the rearrangements in any particular case. Thus very wealthy debtors were often specially privileged at the expense of moderately circumstanced creditors, and similarly in regard to tenants and landlords. This interventionism—

government by pressure groups—is not a *social* system in any proper sense of the term. It does not bind people together by means of a harmonizing principle which will increase both their freedom and their productivity. It is another form of the war of all against all. The only organizing principle is that of maximizing votes. As Professor Hans Kelsen points out in *The Communist Theory of Law*,[5] such a view of the role of law and of government is indistinguishable from the view which prevails in Soviet Russia today. If we insist upon characterizing the Soviet system as totalitarian, we are compelled again to recognize the fundamentally totalitarian character of interventionism.

Those who read the literature in economics should note that the present discussion undercuts all the technical issues raised by the thinking of men like John Maynard Keynes. I myself think that Keynes was wrong on the technical level, that at the most his contribution amounted only to the putting of old mercantilist doctrines, the errors of which have been frequently exposed by both rational analysis and history, into more attractive modern idiom.[6] But, right or wrong, the Keynesian proposals assume a totally empowered, godlike state, a state with authority to intervene at will in the relationships among men and to adjust and readjust property and contract relationships in accordance with the judgment of government personnel. And it is at this level that the most serious and obvious weaknesses of the Keynesian proposals appear.

For government personnel simply are not godlike. They are not omniscient, not omnipotent—and above all can never be objective. Keynes himself was an individualist, distrusting the state. Before he died he showed recognition on his part that the essential weakness of his own proposals lay in the unlimited discretion which they vested in the state. He began to see that one could not keep political interventionism from declining into the institutionalizing of special privileges for politically potent pressure groups. Were Keynes alive today, he would very probably endorse these observations. His enthusiastic approval of Friedrich Hayek's *The Road to Serfdom* justifies this conjecture, for the central thesis of Hayek's valuable work is that the interventionist state is a machine headed toward totalitarianism, with the complete destruction of the basic human rights, private property and freedom of contract, in the end.

Property Rights and "Bargaining Power"

Even when it is realized that all precious human freedoms flow from the right of private property; that the right itself evolved organically from the desires of men in search of the principle best designed to build an enduring, free, and productive society; and that the only alternatives to broad private-property rights are chaos and the destruction of civilization, some still continue to insist that the principles of private property and freedom of contract are nothing more than "empty formalism" or even "pernicious abstractions."[7] These empty principles, it is said, serve only the "vested interests" and "big business," not the toiling masses of hard-working men. The rich get richer, we are told, and free-market capitalism leads inevitably to great concentrations of economic power, to monopoly.

Perhaps the attack against property and contract has most frequently and most effectively taken the form of the charge that in most instances of interpersonal relationships there is no real freedom of contract at all, because the "bargaining power" is all on one side. Thus, in the employer-employee relationship, all the bargaining power is with the employer, none with the employees; as between businessmen, the big businessmen overwhelm the small ones; and as between producers and consumers, the consumer must take what he is offered, at a price fixed beyond all deviation in some furtive meeting of exploiting capitalists.[8]

Now there can be no question at all about one thing: the principles of private property and freedom of contract *are* formal principles. But so, too, are all other basic rules of law or of society. Therefore, unless one wishes to live in a society devoid of rules, he may not rationally propose the abandonment of private property and free contract solely because they happen to be formal principles.[9] He is obliged, instead, to offer alternative principles, more attractive than those under attack. If he contends that he is a proponent of the free society, moreover, he is obliged to demonstrate that the substitutes he offers will more effectively secure and promote the free society than the principles of private property and freedom of contract do.[10]

We are in a position now to evaluate one of the chief deficiencies of those who rebel against the property and contract principles: they do not seem to be at all aware of the consequences of abandoning those principles as the basic methods of organizing both social and economic affairs. They irresponsibly— the word is not too strong, I think, considering the gravity of the subject—assume that *ad hoc* rearrangements of property and contract rights do not essentially impair the freedom or productivity of men in society. And they persist in this assumption notwithstanding that brief reflection must reveal that men cannot be free and productive in society unless property and contract rights are preserved largely intact.

History is full of the ruins of societies organized on the basis primarily of principles other than private property and freedom of contract. These relics of past societies are what Albert Schweitzer was thinking about when he said that "Society is something temporary and ephemeral; man, however, is always man." The contemporary world, too, contains a number of examples of societies in which private property and freedom of contract do not exist, or exist in only more or less drastically modified form. We therefore do not lack historical and contemporary material with which to check our thinking concerning the role of property and contract in society.

Any *society,* any human aggregate characterized by the division of functions among its members, must have some method of allocating those functions. All the methods revealed by history or the imagination tend toward one or the other of two categories. One involves the allocation of productive functions by direction of some central human authority. The other operates by way of volitional offer and acceptance among the persons involved in those functions, the method of free contract.

Both methods may exist side by side in the same family, tribe, or larger social aggregate. Custom or a tribal council may determine which men are to be hunters, for example, while the hunters may voluntarily agree among themselves as to the allocation of particular hunting functions, according to the adjustment of their desires that suits their respective skills and convenience.

Under the *patria potestas* known to ancient Roman law, the
father of the family had literally life-and-death powers over his
family and slaves—could, if he wished, lay down the most absolute and detailed rules for them—but there can be no doubt that
at a certain point functions were allocated among the family
upon the basis of voluntary cooperation. Beyond any question
today in Russia, many functions are allocated in accordance with
the orders of the ruling elite, while many other, perhaps more
modest, functions are allocated in accordance with the mutual
consent of the persons immediately involved.

The difference, the main difference, between a free and an
unfree social grouping lies precisely in the degree to which
mutual consent by the persons immediately involved determines
the allocation of functions within the group. The more functions
so allocated, the more does freedom prevail as the organizing
principle of the society; and, consequently, the closer does that
society approximate the conception of the free society.

According to this analysis, no society has ever been completely
free; and no society, including today's Russia, has ever been
completely unfree. But this fact does not mean that one may
restrict freedom of contract and private property with impunity;
for the extent to which those principles prevail is precisely the
determinant of the scope of individual and mutual consent as the
basis of the allocation of social functions. Every restriction of
those principles reduces accordingly the role of voluntary cooperation in the allocation of social functions. And it also amounts
to a restriction upon human freedom, well-being, and security.
Where it is understood that property and contract rights—the
formal principles which declare men free in society—are not the
unassailable possessions of all men, but may instead be adjusted
at will by the state, it is improper to call the society a free society
at all.

Not only is it improper to call the society free in a formal
sense. Everything which history and science teach, suggests that
in such a society, real, substantial, positive freedom will also be
lacking. Neither reason nor actual experience supports the
assertion that a society based on private-property and contract
rights will inevitably produce expropriated masses who live and
breathe and think only on sufferance of exploiting monopolists.

To be sure, Karl Marx said that this would happen. But as in the case of a good many other things he said, there was no rational or experiential basis for this prediction; and history has shown his error.

There is no rational basis for the prediction that in an unhampered, free, market economy, wealth and economic power inevitably gravitate into fewer and fewer hands. Quite the contrary. In such an economy, incomes are the production of those who provide the goods and services which people want. Higher incomes go to those who best satisfy, at the lowest costs, the most pressing demands of the consumers. As a sheer matter of biology, there is no basis for the assumption that productive ability follows any particular, predictable pattern.[11] Excellent, astute producers may crop up in any family, no matter how moderate the circumstances of that family. Anyone who knows anything at all about American history is in a position to demonstrate the fallacy in the Marxist notion.

The mistake made by the followers of Marx lies in assuming that the market society is one in which certain families are absolutely privileged to retain the fortunes which their productive ancestors made. But in the free society a person or family retains wealth and economic power only so long as they are astutely utilized in the continuous service of the consumers. The Du Ponts maintain their position by skillful investment policies—by policies, in other words, which serve the consumers. If the Du Ponts invest contrary to the wishes of the consumers, they, too, will find themselves broke, as has happened to other well-to-do families in America.

It is true that in the United States, perhaps the society which has come closest in history to the conception of the free society, there are numerous relatively large-scale business enterprises. It is also true that there are numerous relatively small-scale enterprises. Again, it is true that there are numerous relatively middle-scale enterprises. We have the one largest business enterprise in the United States, the two largest, the three largest, the three thousand largest, and, so far as I can tell, the three million largest enterprises. One may play this kind of game, too, I suppose, in terms of the material wealth of persons, saying that we have the one wealthiest person in the country, the two wealthiest, the three wealthiest, and so on.

But these relationships are so implicit in the natural order of things as to be meaningless. They have no tendency toward proving anything in regard to the question whether, in a free society, monopoly and the expropriation of the masses are inevitable.[12] We in the United States have a degree of up-and-down fluidity in every respect which far exceeds anything that has ever previously existed in human experience. The most recent researches show that there has been no tendency at all over the last fifty or sixty years toward increased concentration of wealth or economic power, except in the hands of the government.[13]

The fact that politicians and other uninformed persons continue to warn us of the "ever-increasing concentration of economic power" must not be allowed to obscure the really important facts of life. In the last fifty years some firms have increased their proportion of the production of certain commodities, other firms have decreased their proportion; some have gone out of business entirely, and others have come into existence. Some of the largest enterprises now operating are producing things unknown fifty years ago. Whether these firms will exist fifty years from now will depend, if we remain a tolerably free society, exclusively upon whether or not they continue to serve consumers. Their relative status will depend on the character of their performance.

The fluidity of this economy is the more remarkable in view of the fact that it has had to contend against the rigidifying tendencies of interventionism. We have already seen, in Chapter 3, how steeply progressive taxation tends to put at a disadvantage the productive poor, thus favoring the already rich persons and the established enterprises. All other forms of interventionism have the same effect of discouraging competition.

That interventionism has failed to rigidify American society is owing in a way to the inherent futility of interventionism. But it is essentially a consequence of the toughness, the resiliency, the dynamic character of a society in which all persons have the freedom which the principles of private property and freedom of contract secure to them. Interventionism thus far in the United States has been of a merely random, experimental, superficial, and largely duplicitous character; for example, people have been able, in large degree, to avoid paying expropriatory taxes. The state has not yet slashed away in any determined, thoroughgoing way at essential property rights; it has only hampered them. While those rights remain largely intact, the fluidity and the productivity of the society are insured.

The contention that a free, market society inevitably produces terrible inequalities of bargaining power is as fallacious as the prediction that it must necessarily end in monopoly and expropriation of the masses. The fact is that "bargaining power" is a loose and misleading way of describing a phenomenon which becomes intelligible only when one considers it in terms of property rights.

Assume life in a society where only one person or one agency has property rights in the means of production; in other words, assume the conditions of the ideal socialist community where the men in control of the machinery of the state also control all the means of production. It is fair to say that in such circumstances there is a self-perpetuating inequality of bargaining power, since only the one entity may ever have the kind of property rights which could disperse bargaining power. In such a system there is, one might say, absolute inequality of bargaining power, since one group has all of it, in virtue of its exclusive possession of all the most important property rights.[14]

Conditions in a private-property society are categorically different. Whereas inequality of bargaining power is an ineradicable feature of the socialist society, the natural tendency in the private-property society is always in the direction of equalizing bargaining power. Thus, if housing is relatively scarce and many persons are looking for shelter, those who provide housing are at first in a position to exact high prices; they are in a favorable bargaining position. But if they exploit this position and make profits which are high relative to profits elsewhere in the society, other men will, using their own property rights, engage in providing housing, until the preponderant bargaining power of the first builders will be reduced to the vanishing point. Tenants in a free society are always only temporarily at the mercy of landlords. But when the state intervenes to expropriate landlords, usually in the form of rent-fixing laws, tenants crouch permanently.

The same is true in the case of the butcher, the baker, and the automobile-maker. In the unhampered free society it is never very long before the sellers of goods are extending themselves, with all kinds of blandishments, to woo the consumers to their products. This proposition may be verified by the fair-minded simply by observing what goes on in the United States *in spite* of the many unwise, antisocial measures which interventionist pressure groups have induced us to accept to our grave detriment. In spite of such measures, our relatively free industries virtually embarrass us with their efforts to secure our patronage. It is a rank error to say that there is an inherent tendency in the free, private-property society to put consumers at any kind of a disadvantage relative to producers.

Error is equally egregious, though of a different kind, in the contention that workers are always at the mercy of employers in the private-property society. More accurately stated, workers and their employers *share* the same bargaining position *vis à vis* the consumers and other producers. Workers and their employer are usually on one side of the bargaining, the consumers on the other. When employers are making "high" profits, their workers are in a position to improve their own lot. When employers are working on thin margins or are incurring losses, their workers also must tighten their belts. These simple facts, properly understood, provide the key to understanding the really important aspects of the labor relations field.

A proper understanding of these basic facts suggests that workers interested in improving their position must focus their attention and effort primarily upon two things: first, improving their employer's position in the market and, second, increasing the significance of their own contribution to the total product. These are the fundamental prerequisites to real improvement of the bargaining power of workers.

The operating principles of the free society are in no sense prejudiced or impaired by worker organizations as such. Quite the contrary. The right of free, voluntary association is a right which derives clearly and directly from those principles. More than that, the right of workers to organize has a sound basis *only* in a society based on private property and freedom of contract; a rational or natural basis for the right of self-organization does not exist in a society which rejects those principles. If the latter grants such a right it does so arbitrarily, and the right should then be called a "special privilege," something which may be revoked at will without affecting the basic structural principles of the society. Only interventionists and other totalitarians may talk in terms of "abolishing labor unions." The adherent to the principles of the free society cannot engage in such talk deliberately; if he does so, he is not what he thinks he is.

There is thus no basis of any kind for the contention that inequality of bargaining power as between employer and employee is an ingrained feature of the free society. Accurate understanding reveals that the worker and his employer share bargaining power as against consumers; that their common interests greatly outweigh the points of conflict between them. Finally, as regards the relatively few conflicting interests, the free society's basic principles accord to workers the right to join together and to work in common as a means of inducing their employer to respect their position. No type of society, no structure of principle, could do more for the worker.

A great deal of unnecessary and unfortunate confusion has been created by the demands of some persons for special privileges for trade unions. Because free societies have sometimes been slow and reluctant to grant such special privileges, it has been contended that trade unions have been discriminated against. At this point in the discussion we need only repeat that the rights of private property and freedom of contract are exceeded when one person or group takes action which destroys the property and contract rights of other groups. To prohibit such action is not to discriminate against the person taking the action. Should the free society fail to protect against the destruction of property and contract rights it would be failing as a society in its fundamental objectives.

Most of the remainder of this book is devoted to a description of the sometimes fumbling, sometimes deceptive, sometimes courageous and straightforward efforts of the United States to apply the principles of the free society to the activities of trade unions. Adequate understanding and appraisal of the charge that the law has discriminated against unions are possible only after a great many other things are taken into consideration. We may conclude at this point with the observation that, whatever complaints trade unionists may address to the free society, their interest in preserving it is primary and absolute. They have no reason for being in any other kind of society. If they destroy the free society, they destroy themselves.

Chapter 6

VOLUNTARY ASSOCIATIONS AND THE STATE

The business of government is to see that no other organization is as strong as itself; to see that no group of men, no matter what their private business is, may come into competition with the authority of society.

—Woodrow Wilson

Free association is a property right of all men in the free society, and the voluntary associations which men form raise no insoluble problems of principle for such a society. Voluntary private associations create insoluble problems of principle only in unfree societies, or in free societies which are on the way to becoming unfree because they have lacked the intelligence or the courage to apply the principles of the free society.

In the free society voluntary associations differ categorically from the state as to function, composition, and authority. A tendency in the potentially unfree society is to confuse the attributes of private associations and the state. When this tendency drifts far, in accordance with the logic of its origins, a condition of minimum personal freedom prevails: private associations may continue to exist in form for a greater or less period, but in fact the compulsory attributes characteristic of the state alone, in the free society, extend to all associations. Really free trade unions, medical associations, bar associations, business associations, or other similar groups can exist only in the free society. In the unfree society they are administrative branches of the state, if they exist at all.

The long-run consequences of confusing the roles of voluntary associations with those of the state are to be expected from abandonment of any of the basic principles of the free society.

If the free society is the society proper to the goals of men, to abandon the principles of such a society involves abandonment of the goals of men: universal personal freedom, well-being, and security must tend to disappear. In the miserable interim before their reappearance, slavery, suffering, and insecurity must prevail. And there is no assurance that the free society must ultimately reappear, for great areas of the world have never produced free, well-ordered societies; in the world today the vast mass of people have never known the free society, its comforts, its securities. No known law dictates that men will ultimately find their way back to the free society if it is once abandoned. One may with some justification assume that a concept so inherently congruent with the nature of men, so rationally appealing, must ultimately reassert itself, and yet those cognizant of the happy accidents and the peculiarities of history which helped account for the growth of the free society in the United States must be appalled at the odds against a recurrence of the phenomenon.

The place of voluntary associations and the role of the state in the free society are thus matters as central to adequate understanding of the free society as are the principles of private property and freedom of contract. They weigh heavily, too, in the project of formulating the labor policy of the free society. For these reasons, analysis of the respective functions, compositions, and authorities of the state and voluntary associations in the theory of the free society seems indispensable.

Functions

A striking feature of the free society is the diversity of the voluntary associations it tends to breed. A voluntary association is potential whenever two or more members of the free society decide that it would be mutually advantageous to pool their efforts, or a part of their efforts, in the achievement of a mutually desirable objective. Even a relatively ungregarious member of the free society may find himself belonging to more voluntary associations than he can enumerate off-hand. His associations may include economic, professional, educational, health, good-fellowship, sporting, and religious societies or associations, to mention only the possibilities which come to mind instantly.

Nor is there anything in the theory of the free society which confines a voluntary organization to any particular function. The functions of an association may be as various as its members wish them to be and can agree upon. The mutual interests of the membership define the objectives of the voluntary association. If the membership can agree upon diverse objectives, their mutual activities in the voluntary association may be aimed at more than one objective. If, on the other hand, a given member of a voluntary association is unable to induce his comembers to join with him in an objective different from those currently pursued by that association, he is free to try to form or to join another association, one which will pursue the objective he has in mind. There are several bar associations in the City of New York. Some lawyers belong to one, some belong to another, some belong to more than one—and some belong to none.

The only limitation upon the voluntary association in the free society is the standard limitation placed upon the activities of all men in such a society: the voluntary association as a separate entity may not invade the property rights of persons; it may not engage in violent, coercive, or fraudulent conduct.

While the function of the voluntary association in the free society is to advance the interests of its members, whatever those interests may be, the function of the state in such a society is to preserve the peace: to prevent and remedy expropriations, to establish and maintain conditions which insure the freedom of persons to go tranquilly about their business. The state establishes the conditions of peace and freedom; within that environment men cooperating singly or in groups are free to exercise all their ability, ingenuity, power, and imagination to improve the lot of man on earth.

Preservation of the peace involves insuring domestic tranquility, providing for the common defense, and establishing an effective system of justice. These, in the free society, are the primary and essential functions of the state. They are the primary and essential functions because they are the things, desired by and necessary to free men, which an institution organized like a state can best do, which no other form of organization can do as well.

No other type of organization is in a position as naturally well adapted as the state to insure domestic tranquility by the prosecution of the criminals who would advance their own interests by expropriating others. The state is likewise the best designed of all organizations to promote domestic tranquility through the administration of justice in property and contract disputes between persons. The state alone may definitively resolve such disputes and put an end to them. To do so satisfactorily it must have a system of justice which works well. The legal system must be the most orderly and efficient one which can be conceived by the best professional minds. Judges must be selected in the manner most likely to secure disinterested, intelligent, and judicial minds and personalities. And there must be a sufficient number of judges to secure the reasonable dispatch of the business of the courts, for justice delayed is justice denied.

Securing the common defense is likewise a function which the state is naturally designed to perform well and which no other type of organization can perform as well. The requisite machinery is similar in general character to that just discussed. Just as the internal tranquility of a society requires police, so does the discouraging of invasions require armed forces. No organization other than the political agency of a society is in as good a position to understand the weight and nature of international threats to peace, and to command the necessary resources in defense.

Preserving the peace and establishing justice have been called here the primary and essential functions of the state in the free society. By this generalization it is not meant to imply that there is in the theory of the free society some implacable principle which forbids the state to do anything more. Thus the fact that some states assume the function of building and maintaining roads, railroads, postal systems, hospitals, and school systems does not necessarily mean that the principles of the free society are being violated, or that they are meaningless or "impractical." The free society has only one principle relevant to this problem: the principle that jobs be done by the persons or organizations which do them best, and most consistently with all the objectives of the free society.[1]

If the state's hospitals or railroads are the best, cheapest, and most convenient, the theory of the free society does not suggest that the state is doing something which it should not do. But the proponents of the free society will insist that in measuring the performance of the state, one should not discard one's intelligence or forget that there are other things to be considered as well as the fares charged by the state. One should not infer from the mere fact that the fares on a state transit system are fifteen cents while those on a private system are twenty cents that the state is doing a better job. One must know also whether, in such an unlikely situation, the cheaper fare charged by the state is covering the costs of the system and whether the state is consuming capital in maintaining its fare. If the fare is not covering costs, and if the state is consuming capital in the process of maintaining its fare—and both conditions are characteristic of state transit systems—it is erroneous to conclude that the state has proved its qualifications to operate a transit system. Furthermore, if the deficits are covered by other methods of taxation, the costs are merely hidden and transferred, in the normally duplicitous and expropriatory tradition of the interventionist state. Exactly the same analysis and intelligence must be applied in assessing the performance of the state wherever it undertakes to provide goods and services.[2]

It is always relevant, moreover, to consider what effects an indefinite proliferation of state activities may have upon the state's performance of its central, essential functions. One must ask whether there is something about the state which naturally equips it to do well infinitely diverse and absolutely unrelated things, while every other type of organization known to man performs well only relatively few functions, and closely related ones at that. One must also ask whether governments have performed their few essential functions so excellently as to give promise of generally excellent performance in all other fields.

Of all the insights afforded by the theory of the free society none perhaps is more significant than the teaching that by its very nature and inner structure the state is an organization well designed to secure the peace of society, but rather poorly designed

as regards the creative and productive functions. Appreciation
of this teaching is enhanced by a comparison of the constitution
and the authority of voluntary associations with those of the
state.

Composition

In the theory of the free society, a voluntary association is
composed of those who have freely chosen to form or join it,
whereas *every* citizen is a member of the state and *every* person
within the physical boundaries of the state is subject to its
jurisdiction.

Membership in a voluntary association must be volitional for
more than merely grammatical reasons. An association entitled
to compel membership by violent, coercive, or fraudulent means
would not only no longer be a *voluntary* association, it would
have the privilege of destroying property rights. A voluntary
association is a contractual arrangement among persons. To say
that a person may be compelled to participate in such an arrangement is to deny him the right to refuse to make a contract which,
in the exercise of his own choice, he would rather not make;
and that, in turn, amounts to a deprivation of a basic property
right.

As has appeared in connection with analysis of other corol-
laries of the theory of the free society, there is more than merely
logical strength in this one. The practical consequences of permitting private associations to compel membership also are undesirable, if maximum freedom, well-being, and security provide
the standards of measurement.

The strictly voluntary association prospers only if it performs
a needed function relatively well. And whether or not its
performance is good can best be judged by whether or not it
survives the test of the free market. It does not matter what
kind of private association we examine; whether it be a business
enterprise, an association of such enterprises, a bar or medical
association, a religious group, a charitable foundation—in every
instance the best test of the effectiveness of the organization is
whether or not it stands up in competition with other organizations engaged in like or competing functions, or with other
methods of attaining the ends which it seeks. As noted earlier

(Chapter 2, pages 10-13) the test is not necessarily absent merely because there does not happen to be another such organization in existence at any given time. The opportunity to compete is what really counts. There would be no test only if persons were not free to form competing organizations at will—only, that is, if "voluntary" organizations were permitted to practice compulsion, or if they were given a protected monopoly by the state.

Permitting compulsion by private associations would seem to presuppose that association is always superior to individual action. As a general proposition, however, such a presumption would certainly be inaccurate. Associations sometimes provide more effective methods of getting things done; but not always. One must bear in mind that society is itself an association designed for the common good. Within society, individual action is the only kind of action there can be. The question is whether individual action is always more effective within a private association. As is well known, some of the greatest products of mankind have been the creation of solitary workers, and could not have been otherwise.

Furthermore, on the probably valid assumption that some action is most effective within private associations, it still does not follow that any particular association should be allowed to practice compulsion; for the consequence would be to insulate that association from the selective and improving rigors of competition or to substitute competition in coercion for competition in excellence. In those instances in which associated efforts are more productive than individual effort, the ordinary effects of free competition between individual men and associations of men will make the point clear to all. Associations will be formed, for men well understand their own interests. But it serves no socially useful purpose, even in such circumstances, to give a private association the privilege to compel membership.

The fact must be recognized that in some parts of the United States "voluntary" associations are permitted to compel membership as a condition precedent to working in the occupations covered by those associations. Thus in many states trade unions are permitted to use coercive devices in order to compel employees to become members and to deny employment opportunities to nonmembers.[3] In some states, membership in a bar association is a prerequisite to the practice of law. But it goes without saying that the privileging of compulsion does not necessarily mean that compulsion is a good thing. Most people have probably learned through hard experience that there is no truth in the saying "everything that is, is right."

Furthermore, there is no evidence tending to prove that private associations which enjoy the special privilege of coercing membership perform more effectively than those which do not enjoy that privilege. Indeed, such evidence as we have suggests the contrary. It suggests that associations which may compel membership tend ultimately to lose sight of the objectives which originally had been sought in forming them, and that the interests of the membership become subordinated to the institutional interests of the bureaucracy of the association. There is reason to believe, as we shall see, that the defects of trade unions as we know them are largely a consequence of the privilege of coercing membership which unions have enjoyed.[4]

There can thus be no doubt of the validity of the proposition that compulsory membership in a private association is radically at odds with the theory of the free society. Furthermore, it would seem that rejection of this proposition leads to the same antisocial consequences which follow upon rejection of other principles of the free society.

But while compulsory membership in a private association conflicts with the theory of the free society, that theory holds it necessary for every person to be a member and subject to the rules of the state which has sovereign power in the territory in which he happens to be. This rule is dictated by the unavoidable necessities which confront a society intent upon establishing the conditions of maximum freedom for its members. George Washington left us, among other things, the insight that "the very idea of the right and power of the people to establish government presupposes the duty of every individual to obey the established government." A society determined to establish the conditions of freedom must have the means of suppressing or discouraging attempts by any individual, group, or group of groups to invade the property rights of others. Nothing less than the full power of the society will adequately serve this end. In consequence, the society's defender of property rights must be able to count upon the life and treasure of every member of the society; and the organization so constituted, the organization which is authorized to represent the greatest combination of power of the society, is called the state.

It is unrealistic to assume that the state can perform its basic functions without the power to compel the acquiescence of all in the measures designed to serve those functions. One may regret that violators of the peace and other invaders of property rights exist, or that superior force concentrated in that agency of society called the state is necessary in order to provide reasonable security against criminals. Yet political science must operate within the deficiencies of the other sciences; until biologists and other natural scientists demonstrate a better method of dealing with antisocial persons who would expropriate their fellow members of society, the compulsory powers associated with the state will continue to be necessary if the free society is to carry on. The state is not performing its proper functions when it practices expropriation, even if it does so in order to "forestall crime" or to "avoid revolution" through arbitrary redistribution of material wealth. Such action by the state is merely the consequence of gullible acceptance of the mistaken theory that private property is the cause of crime.

Compulsory and coercive powers are needed also if the state is to perform its function of settling definitively the civil disputes over property and contract rights which continually arise among members of a free society. The state does not fulfill this function merely by formulating and promulgating clear-cut rules of law concerning property and contract rights. A large job is left even if the rules are supplemented by the best judicial system that can be conceived. That job is the one of seeing to it that the decisions of the judges, in applying the rules to the disputes brought before them, are obeyed. If it became understood that no untoward consequences would flow from disregard of the judgments and decrees issued by courts, there can be little doubt that the judgments and decrees would not in all instances be respected. Men are not all angels. If they were, there would be no disputes in the first place. Without laboring this unfortunate point we may conclude by saying that unless men are aware that their liberty and property will be endangered more by disobeying the courts than by obeying them, the likelihood is that the peace of society will be precarious.

Force and compulsion are thus the characteristic instruments of the state. The state is the strong man, stronger than any other man or group of men in society, and it must be so constituted if it is to perform its basic function of preserving tranquility. These attributes of the state, however, as well as they may equip it for the performance of its essential functions, tend to limit its capacities in very much the same way that the features which contribute most to the effectiveness of a bull-dozer tend to make such a machine inappropriate on a pleasure trip or a race-course.

The compulsory, coercive characteristics of the state must be contrasted to the voluntary character of private associations in the free society. Compulsion and coercion are necessary to keeping the peace; but freedom is indispensable to the achievement of the great spiritual-material goals of men. To utilize an agency conceived in terms of compulsion and coercion in order directly to achieve those goals, rather than merely indirectly by establishing the conditions of freedom for individuals, is to choose the less intelligent way of doing things and to invite confusion and ineffectiveness, if not disaster. These observations gain in cogency when one considers also the nature of the authority and power of the state, as contrasted with the authority and power of voluntary associations.

Authority and Power

The authority and power of a voluntary association differ essentially from the authority and power of the state. Strictly speaking, a voluntary association is a contractual arrangement; but the state may be called a contractual arrangement only in loose terms. The membership of a voluntary association may not contract to do together that which the law would not allow to any member as an individual; but the state both *may* and *can* do anything which representatives of a large enough majority of the people will countenance (and this is true, as we shall see, even under the Constitution of the United States).

The voluntary association has only such authority as its members agree to give it and only such power to act as is consistent with the ruling principles of the free society. The members may join together, and from their association they may reap benefits which none could secure from individual action; but they may not, in the free society, create in their association the authority to act in a way forbidden to individuals. Scientists may find their researches benefited by the pooling of their efforts, just as investors may find their purposes best served by putting their savings together; but neither group, any more than an individual, may invade property rights in promoting its interest. The late Justice Jackson was relying upon a principle of the free society when in a famous decision he repudiated the contention of a trade union that "otherwise illegal action is made legal by concert."[5]

While it is plain that an association may *not* engage in conduct prohibited to individuals, it is not nearly so plain that an association *may* take every kind of action open to individuals. Many jurists have taken the position that persons may do in concert anything permissible to them as individuals.[6] While there is no reason to question this proposition in most cases, there are nevertheless certain troublesome features about it.

For it must be noted that, as a simple matter of fact, an association is not an individual, not a person; it is a group of persons. Thus, just as a group is more than, and different from, an individual, so too an association's acts may be more than and different from the acts of an individual, even though they seem superficially the same. Justice Holmes dealt briefly with this problem in one of his earliest and most famous dissenting opinions. Some judges, according to Holmes, had taken the position that "a combination of persons to do what any of them lawfully might do by himself will make the otherwise lawful conduct unlawful." Holmes thought "it would be rash to say that some as yet unformulated truth may not be hidden under this proposition." "But," he went on to say, "in the general form in which it has been presented and accepted by many courts, I think it plainly untrue, both on authority and on principle."[7]

Holmes was right. Neither reason nor authority supports the proposition that a lawful individual act *always* becomes unlawful *merely* because done by persons in concert. The trouble is, however, that at times the essential character of an act changes when done by many people concertedly.[8] One person rushing down a sidewalk probably does not hamper the passage of others, not very much, anyway; but if five or six persons rush abreast they will very probably materially affect the passage of others. One picket at the scene of a labor dispute will probably frighten no one, but multiply the pickets and the intimidatory potentialities increase. Where a single person refuses to work for an employer unless the employer agrees to hire only union members, the access of a nonunion worker to employment opportunities is probably not materially hampered; his chances of securing employment for which he is qualified are about as good as ever. But if a large enough group of men unites against an outsider, the effect may be to replace the competition which it is in the interest of the free society to foster with a genuinely monopolistic condition which involves essentially the vitiation of property rights. A man may find himself denied access to employment possibilities despite the fact that he is fully qualified to do the work involved, and indeed despite the fact that he is the best qualified man available in the judgment of persons offering employment.

These considerations suggest the "as yet unformulated truth" to which Holmes referred. The point is not that lawful individual acts become automatically unlawful when performed in concert; it is not even that the rules applicable to associations must somehow be more stringent than the ones applicable to individuals. The real point is that a superficial resemblance between the acts of a single person and the acts of many in concert must not induce us to conclude that the acts are necessarily identical, especially in terms of their effects upon the property rights which, in the free society, the state is committed to defend.[9]

The state must be preoccupied with rights, not with particular kinds of acts. Every free society must consider freedom of speech among the most important of property rights. Yet speech as such is of no particular significance at all. If one invades the property rights of another by means of the mechanism of speech—for example, in saying "shoot" to a felonious accomplice—the right of free speech does not immunize his conduct. What we really mean when we recognize free speech as a right is that the right to act vocally extends as far as the right to act generally extends in the free society; that is, it extends only short of the point where it violently, coercively, or fraudulently invades the property rights of others.[10]

So, in the intelligently operated free society, as contrasted to the primitive or superstitious society, the preoccupation is less with acts as such than it is with the consequences of acts upon property rights. An act unlawful under one set of facts may become lawful under another, depending upon objectives and consequences. Killing a man is not always an unlawful act.[11] No magic, talismanic fetish attaches to any particular act. Even a perfectly peaceful strike, with no overtones of violence whatsoever, may in certain circumstances involve an expropriation and therefore be prohibited in a sophisticated legal order, despite the fact that in the same legal order the right of an individual person to quit his job whenever he wishes may always be respected.[12] Unless these considerations are kept in mind it will be impossible to understand, not only the theory of the free society, but the actual course of development of labor law in the United States.

A precise formulation would have it, then, that in the free society the voluntary association has only such authority as its members may properly give it; and its members may not authorize their association to engage in conduct which invades the property rights of others, even though such conduct resembles that which, when done by an individual, does not invade property rights. Again, the rules lying within the authority of a voluntary association are rules applicable to and only binding upon members of the association; they cannot bind outsiders.

As a matter of history, the formation of some states has resembled in certain respects the methods of forming voluntary associations; and the fragmentary resemblance tends to lend color to the "contract theory" of the state. This theory holds that states generally are the product of a "social compact" among their members. Few careful students now accept the compact theory as a valid explanation of the actual genesis of states; there is therefore no need here to recount the historical researches and the analyses which have induced the virtually universal rejection of the compact theory. It does seem necessary, however, to establish the point that it can never be accurate to identify the kind of authority possessed by a state with that of voluntary, private associations.

In its origins, the government of the United States came about as close as any government in history to being the product of a deliberate contract among the men within its sovereign boundaries. Standard theory holds this government limited by the terms of the grant of power from the people expressed in the Constitution, and the Constitution did not take effect until approved by the people of the United States in the ratifying conventions.

Speaking loosely, one may call the United States a government by consent of the governed. One would speak entirely too loosely, however, if he should go on to say that the government of the United States is a contractual arrangement. The votes of a *majority* in the ratifying conventions determined the adoption of the Constitution in the first place; and a large enough majority can do just about what it wishes as regards amending the Constitution. Majority rule is the principle which governs in the United States in matters involving the action of the state. And it serves no useful purpose to confuse the principle of majority rule with the principle of contract. The two principles are distinct in all material points, and confusing distinct principles is never conducive to fruitful analysis and accurate conclusions.

Contract means that the parties mutually assent to the rule which is to govern their conduct for the duration of their agreement. Majority rule means that the conduct of some persons is governed entirely without regard to their desires. In recognition of the fact that majority rule does not necessarily insure the most desirable results in all cases, some societies have more or less explicitly adopted the so-called limiting principle of "minority rights." In the nature of things, however, such a principle cannot mean very much, and no society today is really governed by that principle in any ultimate sense. It is open to a large enough majority in the United States to pass any kind of law it wishes, and it can do so entirely in accord with due process by amending the Constitution first if it wishes to pass a law which the Constitution presently forbids.

Doubtlessly, therefore, the principle of majority rule, rather than the principle of contract, defines the authority of the state, even in a society such as that of the United States. The fact that both historically and contemporaneously, some societies have defined the authority of the state on the basis of some principle other than majority rule (i.e., "divine right of kings," or "dictatorship of the proletariat" as divined by such an agency as a politbureau) should not be allowed to obscure the central feature of the analysis: namely, that the contract principle does not define the authority of the state.

Nor should we allow ourselves to be confused by the fact that, even in the "western democracies," it is true only in principle that majority rule governs. In the real world of action, it must be recognized, an actual majority is rarely responsible for the enactment of any law, even in countries which have relatively enlightened and interested electorates. What actually happens is that a majority *of those voting* in an election select representatives; and then, influenced in one way or another by pressure groups or leaders, the representatives legislate. The people in rare and relatively unimportant instances may be given the opportunity to vote directly by way of referendum on some proposals. Usually, however, the majority's will regarding any specific item of legislation is unknown, unknowable, and, in fact, unsought.

Political parties offer the voters a congeries of related and unrelated policies. Even if elections turned upon reasoned understanding of the platforms of the various parties, such platforms never represent exactly what *any* voter wants. But it is doubtful that elections turn on any kind of reasoned understanding of real issues. Too many people vote for a particular party's nominees only because of family tradition, or because they are a part of that party's machine, or because they like the looks of the nominee, or for some other similar reason essentially unrelated to the issues. This is not to say that such motivations are senseless or irrational. It is only to insist upon recognition of the tolerably evident fact that the political process in even a relatively advanced representative government is inordinately complicated and ambiguous.

The theory of the free society does not clash with, nor does it even question the desirability of, the facts which have just been sketched; it merely accepts them as the established facts they are and accommodates itself accordingly. That majority rule, not contract, in principle defines the authority of the state, and that in the real world majority rule is more a principle than a fact are consciously taken into account in the theory of the free society. In fact, majority rule in matters concerning the state is a principle of the free society. By insisting upon a sharp distinction between voluntary associations and the state, the theory of the free society is largely influenced by the factors just considered; and the caution against entrusting diverse functions indiscriminately to the state is based upon a realistic understanding of the ambiguous and amorphous qualities of the authority of the state.

While the source from which the authority of the state derives is shrouded in ambiguity, the power actually exercised by the state is anything but ambiguous. The theory of the free society recognizes this fact, too. More than that, it insists upon universal recognition of the fact that the state is, potentially or actually, the repository of all the power which a society can command. To put this exceedingly complicated matter more extensively: the theory of the free society recognizes that sheer brute power exists in any society; that whatever persons manage to put together a preponderance of the brute force of the society are in a position to command the obedience of the rest; that peace may be preserved if this power is properly controlled; and that if the people are up to it, they have thus at hand a mechanism which can establish the peaceful conditions necessary to the free society.

But no government can operate effectively on the basis of powers limited in the manner appropriate to the voluntary association. To be a law, every law must be universally applicable to all who come within it. There is nothing wrong in having the rules of a voluntary association limited to the acquiescent membership of the association. But, as we have already seen, the state's laws are futile if they are applicable only to those who favor them or only to those who have elected the legislators who have passed the laws. Those who disapprove of a law are at least as likely to violate it as those who ostensibly favor it. Hence the state must have the power to enforce its laws against every person, even though the laws meet with the approval of only a bare majority of the people.

It is true, of course, that there are some laws which a state simply cannot enforce or which it finds entirely impractical to enforce. Usually, however, this only means that majority rule has worked even more unsatisfactorily than normally—has produced a law so ill-advised, so contrary to the wishes of so many people, that not even the greatest authorized power of the community is able to enforce it. The proper significance of this kind of a situation lies in the emphasis it gives to the generalization that law and law-enforcement, like other precious commodities and services, ought to be economized; that they ought not to be squandered. The fact that some laws are unenforceable does not mean that all laws are subject to that deficiency, or that the power of universal enforcement is not necessary to the state.

There is no known way of absolutely confining the state to the enactment and enforcement of only "good" laws, or even of laws which are simply not "bad" laws. Those who understand the theory of the free society would not presume to predict for all time just which laws should be passed in order to preserve the free society. While confident that the basic operating principles, private property and freedom of contract, must be preserved intact if a society is to be free, they are aware that the particular kinds of laws necessary to preserve those principles may vary from time to time. Such being the case, the state must be free to adjust its legislation in accordance with circumstances. And if a state is to be free to make and enforce new laws, it must necessarily be free to make and enforce "bad" laws. The founding fathers went about as far as possible in giving the federal government the power to provide for the "general welfare." The theory of the free society would identify laws maintaining the dynamic equilibrium of property rights with the "general welfare" and would therefore commend to the people and their legislators that they resist pressure for laws involving the negation of private-property rights.

Representative government—government by consent of the governed—is itself a principle of the free society; for no society can be really free, if indeed it can survive at all, which does not in one way or another, directly or indirectly, reflect the large consensus of its members. Representative governments may and often do enact and enforce measures which conflict with the theory of the free society. And yet representative government is essential to the free society because it is the best available method of changing governments without the disturbances and potential lawlessness that are inconsistent with the free society. Mises has put this matter definitively:

> Liberalism realizes that the rulers, who are always a minority, cannot lastingly remain in office if not supported by the consent of the majority of those ruled. Whatever the system of government may be, the foundation upon which it is built and rests is always the opinion of those ruled that to obey and to be loyal to this government better serves their own interests than insurrection and the establishment of another regime. The majority has the power to do away with an unpopular government and uses this power whenever it becomes convinced that its own welfare requires it. In the long run there is no such thing as an unpopular government. Civil war and revolution are the means by which the discontented majorities overthrow rulers and methods of government which do not suit them. For the sake of domestic peace liberalism aims at democratic government. Democracy is therefore not a revolutionary institution. On the contrary, it is the very means of preventing revolutions and civil wars. It provides a method for the peaceful adjustment of government to the will of the majority. When the men in office and their policies no longer please the majority of the nation, they will—in the next election—be eliminated and replaced by other men espousing different policies.[13]

There are those who may regret some of the consequences of representative government, but there is really not very much that can be done about it. Mises' remarks are relevant here, too:

> There is, of course, no guarantee that the voters will entrust office to the most competent candidate. But no other system could offer such a guarantee. If the majority of the nation is committed to unsound principles and prefers unworthy office-seekers, there is no remedy other than to try to change their mind by expounding more reasonable principles and recommending better men. A minority will never win lasting success by other means.[14]

The power of majorities to do "bad things" is thus as ineluctable as the power of the sun to destroy as well as to create. The theory of the free society is built around the awesome paradox that a free society must be free, also, to destroy itself. The hope held by those who understand the theory is that good sense will ultimately prevail among the people; that they will use the power of the state essentially to protect property rights, not to destroy them.[15]

Consequences of the Confusion of Roles

A device or method designed to perform a certain kind of service may be able to perform other kinds of services, too. But no man, no tool, no system, no agency, no institution has ever been known to have the potentiality, either as a theoretical or as a practical matter, to perform all kinds of functions in a superior way at once, or even at different times. On the contrary, among the half-dozen basically important discoveries of mankind one must rank very near the top the discovery of the utility of the principle of division of labor, specialization, and exchange. Adam Smith must be honored if only because he was the first to spell out that principle definitively.[16]

Everyone now has some understanding of specialization and exchange, and of how application of that principle has transformed the condition of men. Yet, perhaps the most portentous and most prevalent error in the world today grows out of the common failure to realize that the insights to be derived from it apply also to governments. There is nothing supernatural about the state. The state is only a human agency, created by human beings and manned by human beings. Whatever the totalitarian mystics may try to make it, the state is really, as Somerset Maugham might say, only a human institution like another. In the free society it differs from other associations only in that it is based essentially on the principle of majority rule and has the exclusive legal right to use compulsion, force, and violence.

These special characteristics equip the state particularly well to preserve the peace of society; indeed, as already noted, they are specifically designed to that end. But the trouble is that they also leave in the hands of the men in charge of the machinery of the state the power to try to do anything else they may wish to do—*and the only limiting factor of any real significance lies in a proper popular understanding of the principle of division of labor, specialization, and exchange.*

This principle declares that it is best to leave to a person or institution only the function or functions which that person or institution performs better than any other person or institution. It teaches, moreover, that if one person does several things supremely well, everyone is still better off if he concentrates on one and lets the next best men do the others. So, if Mr. X is an excellent plumber and machinist, but an unexcelled physician, he and everyone else will be much better off if he concentrates on being a physician and leaves the plumbing and machinist work to others specializing therein. If Mr. X insists upon doing them all, he may well end up doing nothing very effectively; in any case he and the plumber and the machinist will not profit as much as they would if they all took advantage of the principle of specialization and exchange.[17]

States characteristically take a hand today in a great number of activities unrelated to keeping the peace. Here in the United States, federal, state, and local governments engage in just about all the kinds of activities known to man. They run schools and hospitals; they operate golf courses, amusement parks, and other forms of recreation; they build and maintain roads and sewage systems; run production establishments of various kinds; generate and sell electric and other kinds of power; help farmers, small businessmen, and some tenants; subsidize such industries as aviation and shipping directly and others indirectly by way of tariffs. They do a virtual infinity of other little things related to the foregoing functions, but unrelated to the function of keeping the peace.

Of almost everything that governments in the United States do, one thing may be said: the means of accomplishment are derived from taxing the citizenry; that is, the governments' activities proceed by way of compulsion. This is as true with respect to the functions associated with keeping the peace as it is with the interventionist measures of the kind just sketched. But there is one great difference. In preserving domestic tranquility, the state serves the whole society as such; every member of society owes everything he has or hopes to have to civilization, and therefore has no ground for objecting to equal taxes levied in order to preserve civilized society. But interventionist measures do not characteristically serve the whole society as such; instead, as a general rule, they serve one or another minority group *at the expense of* the society as a whole.

This is not, or need not be, necessarily true of every one of the interventionist measures mentioned here. For example, in undertaking to build and maintain streets and sewers, the government of a small town is not expropriating one group for the benefit of another where it adopts a rational method of taxing those who are benefited by the streets and sewers. But suppose the same local government should decide for one reason or another that it would be desirable to build and maintain a golf course. If the golf course is operated with funds derived from general taxation of both golfers and nongolfers, the latter are being expropriated or exploited for the benefit of the former. It is no answer to say that the golf course is available for the use of all. That contention fails to modify the fact that some persons have been *forced*—by means of taxes which they cannot refuse to pay—to subsidize the recreation of others.

When one properly understands the operation of the political process, even in a tolerably advanced representative government such as that of the United States, he is forced to concede that a tradition of government action for the benefit of anything less than the whole body of taxpayers invites chaos. It tends to lead to the pitting of group against group, or at least to the process of "group accommodation," to use a current idiom. We may find ourselves once again fitting Maine's definition of the primitive society: "It has for its units, not individuals, but groups of men."

Interventionist legislation is always proposed by some group asking for a special privilege at the expense of the general taxpaying population. But if golfers get their golf course, how can one deny a similar benefit to bowlers, or chess-players, or aviation enthusiasts? If dairy farmers are subsidized, how can one resist a request for similar aid by peanut farmers or cotton planters? There is no rational basis for rejecting a subsidy request by people who would like to grow bananas under glass in New England, or orchids, or coffee; that is to say, no rational basis other than that dictated to legislators by the vagaries of politics and political alignments.

This is interventionist government by pressure groups. There are those who defend this kind of thing by saying that, in the long run, such government tends to dispense more or less equal benefits to all groups. Thus, while the general public is exploited by special subsidies, devices such as rent and price controls and "social" security measures "tend to even things out." But the fact is, of course, that in neither the long run nor the short run can such a blunt and relatively savage instrument as group political pressure produce any kind of equal distribution of benefits. Someone is always going to be hurt more than he is helped. Moreover, the fact that two wrongs have never made a right does not mean that multiple wrongs can make a right. For every special subsidy amounts to a wrong against the undifferentiated persons who make up the general tax-paying public (that is, against those who pay the taxes but do not receive the benefits for which their taxes pay); and the wrong is aggravated, not remedied, by each additional subsidy. Generally reduced productivity is the unavoidable mediate result; and the completely regimented society, engulfed in the totalitarian state, the ultimate product.[18]

Again, the never-ending potentialities of special governmental subsidies tend to divert government from its primary and essential social function. Two somewhat independent factors are at work here. First, the task of contending with all the pressure groups who come begging for special privileges becomes a labyrinthine and all-absorbing one. The newspapers daily carry stories of this or that pressure group asking the government to "step in." Congress, the Chief Executive, and his subordinates have about all they can do to placate persons and groups who want to make sure that they will not be passed up. There is little time left for careful consideration and enforcement of the laws necessary to protect the property rights which alone can secure the general welfare of the society.[19]

In the second place, contrary to some opinion, not even governments are omniscient and omnipotent; not even they can do the impossible; and there is a limit even to taxes. Interventionist government by pressure groups may be able reasonably to satisfy the demands of the most insistent seekers after special privilege; but when that has been done, there is little talent and less money left to perform the basic functions of the state.

Everywhere in this country today there prevails a tendency on the part of governments to neglect their basic function of administering justice. Court dockets everywhere, according to the findings of the Institute of Judicial Administration of the New York University Law Center, are in a shocking condition.[20] In one way or another the practice of interventionist government is responsible, either because of preoccupation with satisfying the demands of special interests, or because the state has so far exhausted tax revenues by the subsidy process that there is simply nothing left with which to run a government properly. Of the thirty billion dollars which the federal government spends annually on things having nothing to do with the common defense, about *thirty million* go to the federal judiciary. The person who understands interventionism is not at a loss to explain this insane and antisocial situation.[21]

The person who understands the theory of the free society will not take the position that a local government necessarily errs in establishing and operating schools, sewers, garbage collection, roads, and other such services. He will point out only that if government is effectively to perform functions having to do with the *general* welfare, it must refrain from giving special subsidies to anyone, no matter how persuasive ideologically or politically he may be. He will point out that the chronic discontent with the performance of the government schools and hospitals, for example, is only a natural and predictable consequence of the attempt to defy the principle of division of labor, specialization, and exchange. Residents of the City and State of New York are always complaining about the deplorable condition of their public schools and insane asylums. But if they expect their government not only to maintain civil order, schools, hospitals, roads, and so on, but also to subsidize both the users and the workers of the municipal transit system and a multitude of other pressure groups clamoring for special subsidies, what can they expect? Even the taxing power is limited.

On a still broader analysis, the problem may be said to arise as a result of confusing the role of the state with the role of private associations. The state seems to get into its worst troubles when it takes over the job of providing for the economic welfare of individuals and groups. In the free society, that is the job of individuals themselves, who are free to form voluntary associations when independent action seems inferior to association as a means of reaching desired ends. Few men are in a position to have a golf course of their own; but the free society recognizes a right in golfers to combine their resources in order to maintain a golf course. Not every person is able to make a suitable living through farming; but in the free society those who cannot make a living by farming alone are always free to join together into more efficient agricultural production units, or to try some othei occupation, the product of which is in more demand than farm commodities.

*   *   *

Men are not tied to the soil in the free society. Nor does the free society compel men who wish to remain on farms to move to other areas or occupations. But at the same time, it will not permit a minority of farmers to force nonfarmers to subsidize them; for it must never be forgotten that no one has ever proved that anything like a majority of farmers insist upon the subsidies that a few demagogues are talking about so much. One hears often today that the proponents of the free society are telling farmers to starve, or commanding them to leave their beloved farms. Not much is to be gained by spending any time on this cheap insult to human dignity and unwarranted affront to the moral stature and good sense of the nation's farmers.

Ultimately, if government by pressure group follows its inherent logic, there is no doubt that the ability of individuals to provide for themselves through their own action or through voluntary associations must be drastically impaired. All the talk we hear about "drawing the line" somewhere is merely wishful. There is just no line to draw. If the agency of force and compulsion assumes the functions allocated in the free society to persons and their voluntary associations, it must take from individual persons the wherewithal to do so. No great insight is necessary in order to realize that the individuals will then no longer have the wherewithal to provide for themselves and to forge ahead with creative plans for realizing their own potentialities.

Everyone has to pay for the projects which governments undertake for the few (or even for the many). Everyone, directly or indirectly, pays the taxes which governments exact. Simple good sense and the instinct of self-preservation then command those who pay but do not benefit to go themselves to the government, if they wish to survive in the dog-eat-dog system of interventionism. By and large that is what is going on in the United States today. Many who insist upon agricultural subsidies argue that the farmers have been discriminated against by a government which has been "doing things for" other pressure groups. There is really no satisfactory rebuttal of that contention. The argument can be met only with what the lawyers call a confession and avoidance.

The best and only way out of the vicious circle is to say to the farmers: let all men of good will and sound intelligence join together in order to put an end to a system which promises everything but which can and must deliver only the destruction of the free society. Leaders of thought among the trade unions, the farmers' associations, the businessmen, and the professions can remake this society in the image of the free society any time they wish. They need only begin directing their efforts largely to improving their own performance and guarding against interventionist legislation, instead of running to Washington with all their problems and trying to make "deals" with other pressure groups to mulct the public, as some trade unions are doing today in their *rapprochement* to some farm groups.

It is to the credit of the National Association of Manufacturers and the United States Chamber of Commerce that they have devoted so much of their energies to resisting interventionist legislation. For this indomitable resistance they have earned the contempt of many, in this day when "accentuating the positive" is the fashion. But it is inaccurate to say that one who resists interventionist legislation is a "negativist." It is such legislation which is properly to be called negativist, and in the most awful sense: for it negates personal freedom.

In resisting destructive legislation, the National Association of Manufacturers and the Chamber of Commerce have in the most critical and positive way been serving the cause of freedom and civilization. Their contribution ought to be recognized.

Instead, they are constantly pilloried as "reactionaries." Seventy-five per cent of the intellectuals would rather be dead than be caught voicing an opinion conforming to one expressed by the National Association of Manufacturers or the Chamber of Commerce. They may have their wish. For the free society is the only society in which the critical intellectual *as such* can survive. And there is nothing in the world which can more hasten the destruction of a society than the failure by its intellectuals to distinguish its friends from its enemies.

Chapter 7

TRADE UNIONS IN THE FREE SOCIETY

Marvellous are the conclusions men reach when once they desert the simple principle that each man should be allowed to pursue the objects of life, restrained only by the limits which the similar pursuits of their objects by other men impose. A generation ago we heard loud assertions of "the right to labor," that is, the right to have labor provided; and there are still not a few who think the community bound to find work for each person. Compare this with the doctrine current in France at the time when the monarchical power culminated; namely, that "the right of working is a royal right which the prince can sell and the subjects must buy." This contrast is startling enough; but a contrast still more startling is being provided for us. We now see a resuscitation of the despotic doctrine, differing only by the substitution of trade-unions for kings. For now that trade-unions are becoming universal, and each artisan has to pay prescribed monies to one or another of them, with the alternative of being a non-unionist to whom work is denied by force, it has come to this: that the right to labor is a trade-union right, which the trade-union can sell and the individual worker must buy!

—Herbert Spencer

Trade unions in a free society embody the right of working men, shared with every other member of the society, to join together in the pursuit of common interests. As a private association of men, the trade union enjoys a status no different from that occupied by any other private association. The free society has no less, and no more, interest in the existence or activity of a trade union than it has in the existence or activity of a religious group, a commercial association, a voters' league, a business corporation, or a combination whose mission it is to prove white superiority or inferiority. In some cases the job may be more difficult than in others; but in each instance society demands of the private association only that it refrain from advancing the

97

interests of its members by antisocial means. Violent, coercive, or fraudulent acts, in the theory of the free society, are as vicious and antisocial when performed by trade unions as they are when committed by the Ku Klux Klan.

The free society can no more survive if private associations take on the compulsory characteristics of the state than it can if the state emulates private associations. Trade unions misconceive their role if they assume either that they must or that they may legitimately utilize compulsion. Only the state must and may use compulsion or coercion; and the state itself should compel and coerce only in order to establish and maintain the conditions necessary to the freedom of its members. Trade unions achieve their own corruption if they coerce and compel; they tend to expend their energies in activities they do not perform very well, neglecting those more appropriate to their character as voluntary private associations; and they add substantially to the forces constantly at work in the continuous struggle against the free society by the totalitarian spirit.

Free trade unions have no hope of survival in anything but a free society. Everywhere in the world, trade unions have become little more than extensions of the political authority when the principles of the free society have been abandoned in favor of interventionism and socialism. There is nothing accidental or unpredictable in the course of events leading from interventionism to the destruction of free trade unionism and other free institutions.[1] The developments brought on by interventionism can be predicted with perfect confidence: "fair shares for all"; then decreased productivity and smaller shares for all; then more rigid controls and more autarchy; and still more poverty; and then still more controls, until socialism brings on the completely controlled society, in which there is no place for any voluntary, private association. When, somewhere or other in this sequence, members of trade unions show discontent with the situation in which they find themselves after having been taught that interventionism is the way to "social justice," their leaders receive instructions from the political authorities: "be good citizens, exercise self-control, do not be greedy." That is what the recent history of Australia, France, Germany, Great Britain, Italy, Norway, and Sweden teaches us.[2] It was what the more astute trade-union leaders learned when Mr. Truman called certain union officers "traitors" and "Communists" because they chose not to abide by the dictates of interventionist political authorities.[3] Trade-union members do not really want "social justice" or "equal shares" which always mean small shares and smaller hopes. They want all they can get, with hope for more. And these they can have only in the free society. Mr. George Meany, the solid citizen who heads the greatest aggregate of trade unions in the world, understands these things; and so do his British colleagues, who are now among the more reluctant Britons on the issue of "nationalization."

The British have extricated themselves from bad situations before; they have a talent for avoiding the ultimate evil. But things may be different in the United States. We can and do accomplish more; we are a far more complex, integrated, and productive economy than the world has ever seen before. But these attributes may make it very difficult for us to check or reverse undesirable developments. It is still true that the bigger they are the harder they fall.   *8 1160*

Notwithstanding the insights of a few great union leaders in this country, unions daily continue to take action tending toward the disintegration of the basic principles of the free society. And some union leaders reinforce their antisocial conduct with a doctrinaire propaganda which may have an even greater influence. The combination of words and deeds may make it impossible in the future for trade unions and their leaders to concur in the measures necessary to preserve the free society. The momentum of forces now in motion could become such that we or our children might one day have to watch the free society slide over the precipice toward which it always has a tendency to wander.

What the Theory Suggests

The theory of the free society only prohibits to men in trade unions the invasion of the property rights of other members of society. Beyond that there are no limitations; labor organizations are free to try to do for their members all the good or bad things that the members or their leaders can agree upon. If men wish to form or join a union, they are free to do so. If, having combined in order to promote their own economic and other interests, they decide to withhold their labor in concert, they are free to do that, too, so long as they do not invade the property rights of others by their concerted action. They are free, in short, to regulate thir own conduct in any way they see fit. The free society declares to trade unions only that they may not regulate the conduct or impair the rights of others.

Everyone must now be aware that the well-being of every member of society depends ultimately upon its productivity. However, the nature of the relationship between trade-union action and social productivity does not seem to be widely understood. Some think that trade unions necessarily reduce productivity; some that they necessarily increase productivity; some that the "nonmaterial" goals of workers are more important than the material goals and that the latter must, if necessary, be sacrificed to achieve the former.

Proper understanding of the operation of a free society teaches, however, that there are deficiencies in all these views. It teaches, in the first place, that any distinction between the material and nonmaterial goals of men is unsound, and that action based upon such a distinction leads to undesirable social consequences. It teaches, furthermore, that whether or not trade unions contribute to the achievement of the material and nonmaterial goals of men depends entirely upon whether or not they act, or are made to act, consistently with the rules and principles of the free society. If reflection upon the nature of man and society teaches anything, it teaches that freedom, well-being, and security are reciprocal phases of a single concept; and that the operating principles of the free society, private property and freedom of contract, are the indispensable means to the achievement of the spiritual and material desiderata which make up the goal of men in society.

As a matter of fact, union protagonists are basically more concerned with the "material" than with the "nonmaterial" role of unions. We may agree with the contention that unions have great potentialities for the achievement of "nonmaterial" goals; but unionists themselves put most emphasis on their material accomplishments. One commonly hears today that if it were not for the aggressive action of trade unions, the real wages of all workers in the United States would be considerably less than they are. As it happens, average wages *are* much higher than they were fifty, thirty, fifteen, or even five years ago. Hours of work, too, are much shorter on the whole. Tasks in industry are much less burdensome than they used to be. All these improvements, it is argued, are the product of unionization.

But this view does not accord very well with the facts. According to the latest researches, real wages have climbed steadily in the United States, and at about the same rate, for as long as statistics are available. Furthermore, the best estimates for periods for which satisfactory statistics are not available suggest that the climb in real wages dates back to our earliest days as a nation. Statistics demonstrate, moreover, that the share of national income going to wages and salaries has been constant at about sixty per cent of total national income for the whole of our history.[4]

Yet, extensive unionization is a phenomenon of only the last fifteen or twenty years. As recently as 1930 there were no more than four million union members in our total working force.[5] Arthur M. Ross, an economist in sympathy with the general objectives of trade unionism, has pointed out that "the spread of collective bargaining in recent years has not created any tendency for labor's share of the national income to increase."[6] If the widespread unionization of these last years has not materially affected either the rate of increase in real wages or the share of national income going into wages, it goes pretty much without saying that some other factor must have been at work in creating the steady improvement in living standards.

Other evidence suggests the same conclusion. The trade unions of the United States are by no means the strongest trade unions in the world. In fact, a greater proportion of workers belongs to trade unions in Great Britain, France, Italy, Sweden, and Germany, to mention only a few. Notwithstanding this fact, average real wages in the United States are higher—in most cases a great deal higher—than in any other country in the world.

One who contends that trade unionism is essentially responsible for the relatively high wages of American workers can certainly draw no support from these facts. If trade unionism basically accounts for high wages, then the wages of American workers should be *lower*—not higher—than the wages of workers in countries where a greater proportion of workers is organized. The fact that workers in the United States enjoy the highest real wages in the world again suggests that some factor other than trade unionism must be at work.

In the search for this other factor, certain things stand out very prominently. One of the most striking features of the economy of the United States, as compared with other economies, is the amount of capital invested per worker. The figures vary from one firm or industry to another; some have more capital invested per worker than others. But, for the economy as a whole, estimates of $10,000 of capital investment per worker are considered conservative. And this conservative estimate of the ratio of capital to workers in the United States, it need hardly be added, is very much greater than the most optimistic estimate of the ratio prevailing in any other country. No economist today questions the inference that the amount of capital invested per worker in this country is one of the important factors in the higher wage structure of American workers. All agree with Ludwig von Mises in saying that:

> The fact that the standard of living of the average American worker is incomparably more satisfactory than that of the average Chinese worker, that in the United States hours of work are shorter and that the children are sent to school and not to the factories, is . . . the outcome of the fact that the capital invested per head of the employees is much greater than in China and that consequently the marginal productivity of labor is much higher.[7]

Another prominent difference between the United States and all other nations of the world lies in our Constitution, not merely as a document, of course, but in the economic and legal *structure* it created. For most of our history thus far, the Constitution has been regarded as protecting beyond qualification the fundamental principles of the free society, private property and freedom of contract. These principles have recently been modified somewhat in the manner already described; but there is another property and contract feature of the Constitution which prevails today about as much as it ever has. This feature is the continental free trade which the Constitution commands. The Constitution declares that none of the states may erect barriers against the movement of commodities, capital, or labor from sister-states.

Largely effective in our history, this Constitutional proscription, together with the more general principles of private property and freedom of contract, has established in the United States the conditions which, according to all liberal thinkers since Adam Smith, must lead to the best possible realization of the desires of men.[8]

Other nations of the world are larger and more populous than the United States. Other nations and other areas are as richly endowed with natural resources as the United States, and some are quite possibly more richly endowed. But no nation of the world, and no area of the world, has ever enjoyed a free-trade area the equal of ours; and none has enjoyed uninterruptedly for so long a time the unqualified operation of the principles of private property and freedom of contract.

In seeking an explanation of the extraordinary well-being of the workers of the United States, these facts cannot be overlooked. Trade unions, it is clear, have had very little, if anything, to do with improving the American standard of living; and even our great capital investment is no more than the immediate cause. The underlying explanation, I suggest, lies in the fact that we have enjoyed as unassailable constitutional principles, for so long, free trade, private property, and freedom of contract.

There can be little doubt that the express constitutional sanctioning of domestic free trade has had a great deal to do with creating the elaborate, complex division of labor which characterizes the United States. And there can be even less doubt that the extraordinary capital formation and productivity of the economy of the United States owe much to the continental free trade we have enjoyed. Had there been no interstate free trade here, we should probably have been in about the same position as the nation-states of Europe from which most Americans have come. Some of our states (the ones which respected most diligently the principles of private property and freedom of contract) would have been better off than others. But if goods, capital, and labor could not travel freely to the areas where they were most in demand, we should all certainly be much worse off. Some states would have surpluses, others would have deficits, of capital, labor, and commodities; in all probability, autarchy would have produced here about the same results observable in Europe today.

There would be no such things as the nation-wide markets we know in all the commodities, the production of which may be standardized. Without national markets the economies associated with large-scale production would never have been discovered. Capital aggregates there would certainly be. But they would have been much smaller and much less efficient than they have been under the reign of continental free trade.

Our nation-wide free market, based on private property and freedom of contract, is the institution which most clearly distinguishes the United States from other societies. Trade unions in this country are both relatively newer and relatively smaller than in other nations. For a *factual* explanation of the steadily improving and relatively better economic position of the American worker, therefore, the evidence clearly tends to suggest that free trade, leading to extensive and efficient capital formation—not unionization—has been the critical causative factor.

The same conclusion is indicated by theoretical analysis. Some trade unionists advance the theory that "purchasing power" is the key to economic progress and improvement of the material position of workers. Now there is a realistic sense, as we shall see, in which it is proper to speak of purchasing power as the key to economic progress. The trouble is, however, that trade unionists do not think of purchasing power in that sense.

By purchasing power they mean the money income or wages of workers; economic problems are solved simply by giving workers greater and greater money incomes. If the wages of workers are raised, the trade unionists say, they can buy more of the products of industry. Industry is then induced to produce more and more all the time. And in the end the society has more and more goods, and everyone is better off.

The trade-union version of the purchasing-power theory is unsound in every sense. One may note in the first place that if the trade unionists are correct, we ought to raise by law the minimum-wage standard from the present $1.00 per hour to some substantially higher level—say $20.00 per hour at least. Indeed, one is at a loss to understand why unionists have been contending recently that the minimum wage should be raised to only $1.25 per hour, if they take their own version of the purchasing-power theory seriously. Under their own theory, workers now receiving $1.00 per hour would be twenty times better off if their wages were raised to $20.00 per hour.

The fact is, of course, that trade unionists are too intelligent to take their own theory seriously. They know that such a rise in the minimum wage would immediately bankrupt a great many enterprises and create almost universal unemployment. Over the economy as a whole, the wages of workingmen make up about two-thirds of the costs of production. Raising wages by 2000 per cent would involve raising costs by something like 1400 per cent. The price rise necessary to reflect this increase in costs would be something like 1000 per cent. But the demand for any product whose price rises at such a rate must virtually disappear— imagine what would happen to the sales of refrigerators if the price were to rise from $300 to $3000!

If the money income of every single person in the society could be increased by exactly 2000 per cent, the result might be different. To speak more accurately, as a theoretical matter there would be no result worth noting at all within the economy. However, the effect upon our international trade would of course be fatal; we should not be able to sell anything to foreign customers. And that would indirectly affect all of the citizens of the United States to some degree.

One should not take seriously the project just described. It is simply impossible to raise the money income of every person equally by *any* percentage. Merely finding all the persons whose incomes should be increased would be an endless job. Then there are people who at any given time have no income at all, and raising their income by 2000 per cent—involving the multiplication of zero by 2000—results in an income of zero for them. There are also the great numbers who do not have fixed incomes —the professional people, the businessmen, the intermittent workers, the investors, the old persons who are supported by their children. And why should we bother to raise all money incomes by 2000 per cent, or by any other amount, anyway? Goods and services are important, not mere money incomes.

The whole idea of money wage-increases as the key to well-being is, it would appear, absurd. The way to improvement of living standards is through increasing productivity. And the way for any particular person to improve his personal living standard is to increase his own productivity. In a free society at a relatively primitive stage, each person lives better the more competent he becomes and the harder he works. At a more advanced stage, such as the stage in which we find ourselves, material productivity is a function of the quantity, the quality, and the arrangement of the factors of production—machines, land, and men.

The purchasing-power theory makes sense if it is anchored in the reality of production and productivity. Income is, properly speaking, production. The man who produces more has more income; his production is his purchasing power. If he increases his production, he increases his purchasing power. When he increases his purchasing power in this realistic sense, he is in fact "better off," in that he can command the disposition and consumption of more goods and services, either his own or those produced by others who wish to exchange their production for his. But merely giving men more money is meaningless if there are no more goods or services to satisfy the desires of the members of society. In such circumstances the increase in money can only create price increases. It cannot create more goods. In all probability, on the contrary, it will result in the production of less goods and services, because it will bankrupt some enterprises and therefore create unemployment of some men, capital, and natural resources.

The answer supplied by economic theory to the quest for the best method of improving living standards is thus tolerably clear: more, and ever more capital equipment, until the point is reached when the addition of capital equipment costs more than it produces. Economists refer to this as the marginal-productivity theory.[9] It applies to both workers and machines. A tendency prevails at all times in the free market for employers to pay workers every cent, or almost every cent, which workers add to the value of the product. Every businessman in his right mind will be anxious to hire every worker he can, as long as the labor of each additional worker costs him less than it brings in. The same tendency prevails as regards the nonhuman factors of production. New plants and new machines will be added, or old ones will be improved, until the point is reached at which the purchase or improvement costs more than it produces.

As a matter of both theoretical analysis and empirical observation, then, free trade, leading to greater productivity and capital investment, appears to be the explanation of the economic process which creates the high standard of living prevailing in the United States. Analysis and observation coincide in suggesting that trade unions have nothing whatsoever to do with this process. And when trade-union leaders boast of how much they do as regards raising living standards for society as a whole, they are simply taking credit which does not belong to them.

This is not a harsh judgment of union leaders. It is, in fact, too charitable in respect of a good many. For a good many union leaders not only misleadingly take credit for improving general living standards; they are also responsible in many instances for substantial reductions in productivity. With this matter we shall be concerned in the following section of the present chapter. At this point we must take notice of the creative role which unions may play in the operation of a free economy if they concentrate on the social services they are in a good position to provide.

Although there is very little that unions as such may do directly in increasing productivity, there is much of utility that they can do in other ways, and which many unions already do. Experienced, well-trained union personnel of good judgment are in a position to get to know workers intimately. If they are competent and understanding, and if their energies are not absorbed in other ways, they can interpret the free society to the workers. They can convince workers that productivity is the key to the general welfare; that workers and their employers have more common than conflicting interests. Union leaders will not be suspected of bad faith if, going about it in the right way, they explain that hurting one's employer is not a very intelligent way to improve one's own position. Many union leaders may be surprised to learn that they will not be voted out of office if they tell workers that loafing on the job and exploiting employers in other ways are not good policy; they may be surprised to learn that the average worker, given a decent chance, will demonstrate as much common sense as any other man.

Union officers need not fear taking such steps, especially if they are constantly vigilant in promoting the legitimate interests of workers and if they develop a proper respect for human dignity. The stupid, ignorant, unfair foreman is one of the real problems of the free society, and of the free-enterprise system. He does not serve the employer; he hurts him. The employer, if he is sane, and most employers are sane, desires few things more than a happy working force, with every worker convinced that he is being treated fairly. He is, if anything, much more interested in achieving these objectives than any single worker. For he knows full well that his business may be destroyed if his workers get sufficiently bitter. Unions are in an excellent position to co-operate with employers in achieving working conditions which seem fair to workers, and then in enforcing fair working rules. They are in an unsurpassed position to check arbitrary and unfair conduct by supervisors. A great many employers recognize this fact and welcome unions. And a good many unions realize that in this area of employer-employee relations lies their greatest opportunity, and their greatest challenge. Unionists are always talking about the dignity and the spiritual goals of workers. More performance and less talk would be welcomed.

There are any number of other ways in which unions can serve both their members and society as a whole. They could provide employees with a great many useful services. They could be of great help to their members in planning savings and investment programs. If they were run well, they could be trusted with pension and welfare plans. They can and do run training and retraining schools for workers who are anxious to improve their productivity. They could serve as a clearing-house as regards employment opportunities. They could, in short, do many things that they are not doing at all now, or doing only rudimentarily and half-heartedly.

The measure of the failure of American trade unions is indeed provided by the fact that they are free in this society to do a great many useful things for workers that they are not now doing. Most of the things mentioned here are being done for workers, but they are not being done for them on any substantial scale by their unions. Too many union leaders in this country have been satisfied, instead, to take credit for services performed by governments or by employers (that is, by taxpayers and consumers). They have little to be proud of when they realize how often workers, asked to evaluate their union, respond that it is "just another racket."

What Is

The main reason for the poor performance of many American trade unions is that they alone, among the "voluntary" associations of this society, have tended to use violent and coercive methods at every stage of their operations. No other species of private association has displayed as much corruption and arrogance as some trade unions have. No other private association has so habitually terrorized and exploited both members and non-members, or so institutionalized the practice of compelling persons to become members. The combination of poor performance and coercive practices is no mere coincidence. The poor performance of trade unions and their coercive practices are interacting causes and consequences.[10]

These harsh charges are not addressed to every union and union officer, for many do not habitually practice coercion; many do an extraordinarily fine job under the most severe handicaps. Moreover, not a line of this book is designed as an attack upon the institution of trade unionism as such. On the contrary, the critique and the proposals to be found here are intended to establish a permanent and creative role for free trade unionism and to ease the lot of those union leaders who are willing to operate within the principles and ideals of the free society. For, as matters now stand, the creative, sincere, able union leader has an inordinately hard time of it. The corrupt, demagogic, antisocial union leader is privileged under the current system to make things very difficult for the union leader who would prefer to work within the principles and the traditions of the free society. In a word, this book proposes the elimination of coercive conduct from labor relations, so that the competition among unions and union leaders may become a competition in performance and excellence, not a competition in coercion.

Coercive conduct has been characteristic of trade unions in this country throughout our history at all levels of union action. At the first level, the organizing level, unions have often depended more upon picketing, secondary boycotts, sit-down strikes, compulsory-unionism contracts, and other kinds of physical and

economic coercion than they have upon peaceful persuasion and
other civilized methods of inducing employees to join. We shall
deal at much greater length with this matter in Part II. Here it
is necessary to emphasize that, unlike most other private associations in this country, many trade unions have not really been
voluntary associations at all. When employees have been reluctant to join a union, it has usually not left them alone, has not
resorted to peaceful sales talks, but has instead used one form or
another of aggressive economic pressure in order to compel them
to join. And when economic pressure has not been sufficient,
unions have commonly resorted to outright intimidation and violence.[11]

That is no way for a private association to operate in a civilized society. The consequences are undesirable for everyone
concerned, the unions themselves as well as society as a whole.
Many of our trade-union leaders are exceptional men. They
have, even in circumstances where the temptations to corruption
are very great, been decent citizens, faithful to the trust implicit
in their office. But, as is well known, other union officers have
been guilty of the worst kinds of conduct, ranging from petty
thievery to extortion and violence on a grand scale. There has
been a curious failure on the part of students of labor relations in
this country even to look for the causes of union mismanagement, let alone associate such conduct with its most obvious
cause. Literally no one has thought to correlate union organizational methods with the corruption so evident in some unions.

Consider one of the most egregious examples of union corruption in America today, the situation which has prevailed for so
long on the docks at the Port of New York. Details need not be
given here; everyone knows or ought to know of that affair. I
wish only to point out that if unions are given the power to control the hiring process, as has been the case on the New York
waterfront, a great deal of corruption must often be expected.
For a union, unlike an employer, does not have a functional
check upon its hiring powers. The employer who knows his own
interests and has the intelligence to follow them properly must be
concerned at all times to get the best workers he can. The employer as such is not interested in a man's racial background, his
personal convictions, or even his union membership. The em-

ployer is responsible for the efficient, profitable operation of his business. When he has the hiring power, he also has a correlative responsibility to exercise his power in the social interest; for the social interest, too, lies in the efficient, profitable operation of businesses. The employer does not need to be bribed; all he wants is work in return for the wages he pays.

But the union has no such built-in *social* responsibility.[12] Union officers in control of the hiring process are autocrats, having power without responsibility. This is especially true when the union has built up its power in the first place, not on the basis of voluntary membership, but on the basis of economic or physical coercion, forcing union membership upon unwilling employees. For then even the weak internal checks imposed by the union membership, at times, will not exist. In such circumstances some union leaders may remain men of honor, whose inner forces make them responsible despite the absence of social or functional checks such as those which work upon employers. But there was no reason ever for assuming such virtue in all union leaders; and history has, of course, proved that such an assumption is erroneous. Many union officers, finding themselves with power over hiring, have succumbed. They have bought and sold jobs, exacting terms in many cases so repellent as to put all trade unions in an exceedingly bad light.

It should have been as obvious here in America as it always has been in other countries that compulsory unionism is socially undesirable. As a British scholar, Professor J. Henry Richardson has recently put it, winning the closed shop "is a victory for the union but an undemocratic one, the additional membership being secured by force and not persuasion, and it gives to the union a potentially dangerous power over its members." Professor Richardson moves on, then, to the more important point: "The union leaders may be less considerate of their members' interests if workers no longer have the safeguard of leaving the union and still be able to find work."[13] Still more of Professor Richardson's insights are relevant:

Operation of the closed-shop principle denies the right of workpeople to withdraw from a union in the future if they have become dissatisfied with its policy or leadership. It also stands in the way of the formation of rival unions. Yet the right to set up a rival union is included in freedom of association, and to take away this right could weaken the vitality of the trade union movement. Groups of workpeople may hold quite different views upon trade union policy and methods, and if they cannot reach agreement they are likely to form separate unions. . . . Again, where only one union has hitherto operated some of the members may consider that its policy and leadership have become too extreme and aggressive or too complacent and spineless, and if they are unable to bring about a change from within, they may cease to be members or may decide to form a rival union. Differences may arise not only on the industrial policy of a union but also on the question of the union identifying itself with a particular political party.[14]

One of the great ethical products of liberal philosophy is the conclusion that means must be independently evaluated, that means tend to determine ends. The conduct of trade unions in the United States furnishes an excellent case study in support of the conclusion. Fashioned to a great degree by coercive methods, trade unions in this country tend to use coercion habitually. In an all-too-typical pattern, a trade union will begin by forcing every worker in a particular trade to join the union. If strikes, picketing, and boycotts are not sufficient to induce membership, violence and intimidation will be used.[15] Then, having built itself coercively, the union will, once it has gained sufficient strength and has the power to control hiring in an industry, bar union membership in some more or less arbitrary way.[16] Formal initiation fees, as set forth in union constitutions, may be moderate; but not everyone offering to pay the formal fee will be admitted to membership. A man may have to buy his way into the union, if indeed he is admitted at all. Or he may have to be a son of an existing member, or a close relative, or exert some other kind of "influence." The actual fee required for admission to membership in certain trade unions in Chicago ranged from $500 to $2000 at one time. Some unions in the New York metropolitan area will not admit anyone to membership, no matter what fee is offered.

The effect is a general structure of unionization in this country which bears no necessary relationship whatsoever to the desires of individual workingmen. A free market in commercial affairs tends to produce the structure of business enterprise which reflects the wishes of consumers and the most efficient technological methods of serving those wishes. Never having had a free market in labor organization, we have no way of telling whether trade unions are at present organized in the best possible way. What we do know is that organizations built upon coercive devices usually reflect the wishes only of those using the coercion.

Recent researches show that participation by workers in the daily affairs of their unions is at a minimum. Attendance at meetings is normally very low, in large unions much lower than in smaller unions.[17] In the nature of the case it is very difficult, if not impossible, to make a correlation between the degree of member participation and the organizing methods of unions. One is pretty safe in assuming, however, that a union which frequently coerces membership is not likely to have interested and active participation by its coerced members. Strong-arm methods at every stage are to be expected of such unions, and they do not often disappoint expectations. Unions built upon organizational picketing and compulsory unionism are the unions which most frequently engage in racketeering and other corrupt practices. It seems almost axiomatic that a union which has not forced its members to join will be a better-run union in every way.

The right to strike for higher wages and better working conditions is a fundamental right of working men in a free society, and it must be preserved largely intact if the society is to remain free. Yet, one of the certain indications of a badly run union is that it frequently calls prolonged strikes, only to settle them thereafter largely on the terms offered by the employer in the first place. Satisfactory statistics on this matter are unavailable, but one gets the impression that a large number of strikes are settled pretty much on the terms originally offered by the employer. This fact, too, to the extent that it prevails, is a necessary consequence of a unionism out of touch with its members and with economic realities. It is a sign of stupid, arrogant mismanagement by union officers. It indicates that these men, who insist that they are dedicated to the welfare of workingmen, really care very little about the men over whose lives they have chosen to exert so much authority. And that is to be expected of a unionism built upon coercion.

Of all groups in the United States today, only trade unions frequently use violent methods. Usually they do so, it seems, in order to divert attention from the mistakes made by union officers in calling strikes which should never have been called in the first place. Calling a strike is a sound move when an employer arbitrarily refuses to meet the economically justified demands of his employees. Two circumstances must exist: first, the employer must be insisting upon substandard wages and other working conditions; second, the employees themselves must be deeply dissatisfied with their wages and working conditions. When these circumstances obtain, a simple work-stoppage—unaccompanied by picketing, violence, or threats of violence—will in every case bring the employer to heel.[18] When these two conditions do not exist, a strike is unjustified; and, more important, it will not be successful unless the union uses violence or some other antisocial, monopolistic method in order to carry off its coup.

For if the employer is not insisting upon substandard conditions, some of his employees will not be in sympathy with the strike; and other workers, previously employed at less attractive terms, or unemployed, will seek the jobs vacated by the strikers. When the latter occurs, the strikers themselves will reconsider their decision to participate in the strike and will, unless forcibly prevented, seek to get back the jobs they have left. If the union leaders are not willing to admit they have been mistaken in calling the strike, they will establish mass picket lines and all the other paraphernalia of fear and violence so familiar in labor relations. It is fashionable among "experts" in labor relations to minimize the extent to which violence prevails in the strategy of union leaders. But no person who takes the trouble to keep himself informed as to what actually goes on will be misled by this refusal to face the facts. The truth is that year after year fear and intimidation, amounting often to civil insurrection, continue to be standard tools of incompetent union officers who are out of touch with the real sentiments of their own members, conditions on the labor market, and economic reality in general.[19]

Each and every time that a union establishes a picket line during a wage dispute in an attempt to obstruct access to employment premises, or uses other coercive, intimidatory, and violent devices, the observer may be sure that the leaders of that union have made one or another kind of an error in judgment. They have misjudged conditions on the labor market or the temper of their own members or both. The businessman who thinks that the price of his product is too low attempts to correct the situation by the peaceful, civilized method of simply raising the price. If the product does not move at the new price, he may seek to increase demand by advertising or by improving quality. Using violence against his purchasers or competitors is simply unthinkable to him. The union leader, however, is not satisfied to proceed in this manner.

The strike itself is a far more drastic and effective method than anything normally available to businessmen. When justified by economic conditions, the strike alone will cause an employer to come to terms. Still, for reasons which should be apparent by now, union leaders have become accustomed to hiding their bad judgment by resorting to methods which are destructive of the basic principles of the free society. There can really be no doubt that the compulsion and coercion built into the structure of unionization are basically responsible for the way in which union leaders operate. Natural selection in such an environment brings to positions of authority in unions men who have neither the innate nor acquired characteristics necessary to intelligent union leadership. The strong-arm man finds an environment cut to his order; the able man of peace often finds the environment unsuited to his qualities.

Earlier in this book it was said that one of the best ways to the improvement of the material well-being of workers lies in the improvement of the market position of their employers. Efficient, profitable businesses are in a much better position to compensate their employees well than those which are losing ground. Many unions have grasped this point; but, instead of lending their efforts to improving the performance of employers, some unions have created monopolistic situations in which particular employers, and their employees, have profited at the expense of society as a whole. The closed shop is usually the key device in such cases. A union having a monopoly of all work assignments in a particular industry will exercise its power in a way which eliminates all business competition. Protected by such action, the employers will then make higher profits than they otherwise would, and the "take" will be split among them, the union, and the union members, in the form of relatively high wages, elaborate fringe benefits, and "gifts" to union officers. One must not conclude from this that unions thus raise the living standards of all workers. Quite the contrary: some workers (the employees of the employers excluded by the union's monopolistic practices) are impoverished for the benefit of others.

Thus, if the union controlling all installation of electrical products in the city of New York refuses to permit the installation of electrical products manufactured outside the city, it has in effect raised a barrier against such products which neither the city nor the state government, under our Constitution, could raise. The effect of this barrier is to deny to consumers in the city of New York the benefits of competition in the production of electrical equipment. It is also to impoverish the employees of the employers who have been barred from the New York city market. This kind of monopolistic restraint of trade is not uncommon in the United States, as reference to official court records will demonstrate.[20]

In the preceding section it was shown that unionization seems to have had no effect in terms of raising the average wages of all workers. We are now in a position to understand the precise nature of the effects of unionization upon general wages. When unions destroy free markets, through either violent or monopolistic conduct, they actually do raise the real wages of those of their members who still have jobs, despite the fact that the new and higher wage levels require higher prices and less production.[21] But wages and prices raised above the free-market level create unemployment in the industry affected by the monopolistic practices. The workers squeezed out of employment must then go somewhere else, bidding down wages in the free-market areas to which they gravitate. At the same time, consumers as a whole are exploited; they must pay higher prices for the products of the industries in which unions follow monopolistic practices. Many are concerned today over the plight of the nation's teachers, whose incomes have not kept pace while the prices of the things they buy have been soaring. Many other members of society—pensioners and those not in a position to exert monopolistic pressures—suffer in exactly the same way. They ought to know the real cause of their disagreeable position. Unions and their members can and do raise their own wages over free-market levels; but in each and every instance that they do, they exploit their fellow-workers and consumers.

Compulsion and coercion as normal union methods, therefore, do not exhaust their vicious effects in the corruption and mismanagement of unions alone. They have untoward consequences for all workers and for society as a whole. Such situations as the one just sketched could not exist if unions were unable to monopolize job opportunities. Without the closed shop and other violent, monopolistic methods, no union would be in a position to block off markets; no union could frustrate the continental free trade which the Constitution commands and which has meant so much in the development of this nation.

Compulsion and coercion as standard union practices have also produced a structure of unionization in this country which tends to be industry-wide in character.[22] The chances are very great that if unionism had proceeded on an entirely voluntary basis, a different structure would have resulted. Quite possibly, union structures would have tended to reflect our single-firm structures, with one or possibly several unions for each firm—a large union for, say, General Motors and United States Steel; and smaller unions for the employees of smaller firms. Had our unionization been so structured in fact, we should be much better off in many ways.[23] As matters now stand, industry-wide strikes, always possible and very often imminent, have potential consequences so grave that it is questionable whether society can tolerate them. This is an unimaginably complicated and integrated society. The effects of an industry-wide strike are so widespread and unpredictable that there seems to be no end to the harm they may do.

Yet, the structure of unionization being what it is, union leaders are virtually compelled to take broad-scale action, even though they might prefer not to do so. For one thing, the leader of one big industry-wide union can scarcely agree without a struggle to different wage and other standards for the employees of different companies, even though the economic circumstances may vary considerably from one company to another. Political and other pressures within the union will compel him, against his better judgment in many cases, to insist that all members of the union receive more or less the same wages for similar types of work. But such a wage structure is as unnatural as a rule decreeing equal sizes of families or equal production rates would be. The consequence in many cases must inevitably be the disadvantaging of some firms and employees relative to others. Unemployment, too, must frequently result. Still, while realizing the probability of such undesirable results, union leaders are driven inexorably by the inherent nature of industry-wide unionism to strive for equal wages and working conditions for all their members.

Such unionism puts the union leader in an impossible position also in the sense that it tends to set one big union against all the other equally prominent unions. The railroad unions cannot afford to lag behind the other transport unions. The steelworkers must keep up with the mineworkers. The automobile workers must show that they, too, are up with the others, or ahead of them. Whereas we put pressure upon business leaders to offer high quality at the lowest possible prices, the structure of unionization as we know it creates an irresistible pressure upon union leaders to exact the highest possible wages for the least amount of work.

The instinct of self-preservation applies to societies as well as to persons. Although industry-wide unionism has been allowed to develop in this country, aided in many ways by governmental intervention or by failure of government to restrain lawless conduct,[24] there can be little doubt that a line will be drawn somewhere, some time. As the dangers to a complex society posed by monopolistic unionism emerge more clearly, the freedom of unions will certainly be narrowed more or less drastically, and with this restriction will probably come the restriction or even the abandonment of other phases of economic freedom intimately related to the freedom of action of labor organizations.[25]

Many thoughtful persons have in recent years predicted that industry-wide unionism must sooner or later lead to the destruction of the free market as the basic system of economic organization.[26] Such predictions are based upon the assumption that current trends toward monopoly unionization either will or should continue unchecked. On such an assumption, the prediction is doubtless well founded. There can really be no doubt that society will take the steps necessary to protect itself from the exploitative action of monopoly unions. Unions are minority groups, and will always remain such in the United States, as they are in most other industrial nations. That being the case, they can have no long-run delusions about what will happen to them when they achieve the goals toward which they now seem to be striving. "Public opinion" is always the same in the great strikes we experience: the strikes must be called off. More than that, "public opinion" is resentful of union leaders who fail to comply with the requests of politicians for "moderation." Only a relatively few people were upset when Mr. Harry Truman, as President of the United States, threatened to take drastic action against the railroad unions during one of their nation-wide strikes.

Everywhere in the United States that unions have achieved monopoly status, the consequence has been a narrowing of their freedom to act. Speaking realistically, even the right to strike in a peaceful way for higher wages and better working conditions is already disappearing in certain areas of the economy. The form of the right remains, but the reality is almost gone—in the railroads and other transport industries, in the coal mines, in steel, and in other basic nation-wide industries.[27] A society such as the United States simply cannot afford a universal strike in such basic industries for any extended period; and as this becomes more fully appreciated, the form of the right must vanish with the reality.

If wages and working conditions are not established by the interaction between employers, employees, and labor organizations, they must be established by some other process. One or another version of compulsory arbitration is the most likely alternative. But this will involve the substitution of compulsion for agreement in the wage-setting process. Government agents will tell employers what wages they must pay and employees what wages they must accept. If wages are to be fixed in this manner, there can be no doubt that prices, too, will have to be fixed. Once wages and prices are both fixed by governmental decree, it will be idle to think in terms of a free society.

*   *   *

It is not a thesis of this book that the possibilities just sketched are "inevitable." We can have pretty much the kind of society we wish to have. But if we wish to have a free society, we cannot condone or encourage conduct inconsistent with the basic principles of such a society. If unions are permitted to compel and to coerce, we are already tolerating conduct inconsistent with the free society, and we should not be surprised to find that the end results are inconsistent with those to be expected of the free society. An attempt has been made in this section to demonstrate that violent, coercive, compulsory unionism is the cause of both internal corruption in unions and an external structure of unionism which could, if allowed to continue unchecked, produce gravely antisocial results. It is even possible that the structure of unionism which we know could contribute to the total abandonment of the free society. For it must never be forgotten that there are many other tendencies in the same direction: discriminatory taxation, inflationary governmental policies, special subsidies to almost all powerful pressure groups, tariffs, and the many other similar interventionist measures which have been referred to in the preceding pages. There is no way of telling in advance just when the free society is lost; as David Hume said long ago, "it is seldom that liberty of any kind is lost all at once." The only sensible thing to do is to guard against those developments which reason defines as inimical to the free society. When one can say that a society is no longer free, it is too late to do very much about it.

What Can Be

On the level of generalization, the problem of establishing a decent labor policy for the United States is not a very difficult one. Evils existing in American trade-union practice today are serious, even critical, for the free society; but they are also few, prominent, and easy to recognize: compulsion and coercion at the organizing level, violence and monopolistic pressures at the collective-bargaining level. A viable, effective labor policy would need only eliminate from unionism its violent, coercive, monopolistic practices. To put the matter another way, an enduring labor policy need only be oriented in terms of the basic operating principles of the free society—private property and freedom of contract. If this were done, it would not be necessary to engage in extensive, interventionist regulation of the internal affairs of trade unions, any more than it has been necessary extensively to regulate business partnerships and corporations, or any of the multitudinous other voluntary associations of the free society. Again, the collective-bargaining process could be left pretty much alone, with the peaceful interaction of unions, employers, and employees determining wage rates and other conditions of employment, much as the pricing process generally is permitted to proceed in an unhampered way in the free society.

Unions which grow to be large and powerful because of the services they render, rather than because they excel in coercion, need not be disturbed, any more than large business firms need be disturbed. For public opinion in regard to such unions will be as favorable as it is beginning to be in regard to large business aggregates, especially when the public is not induced by demagogic propaganda to fear large aggregates merely because they are large. In short, on the level of principle, with coercion and violence eliminated, unionization may be allowed the natural and free course of development which the intelligently operated free society allows to all private, voluntary associations.

Settling things on the level of principle, however, is not enough. We are interested in establishing an enduring labor policy, not in the abstract, but for the United States *as we know it today*. Success in such a project depends, among other things, upon familiarity with the particular problems of history, tradition, and law of the United States. The principles of bridge-building must everywhere be the same, but bridges are erected in particular places; and the engineer who hopes to construct a good bridge must know all he can about the site upon which the bridge is to stand. *What can be* in the labor policy of the United States depends to a great extent upon the way in which our policy has thus far developed. If we should find, for example, that there is absolutely no relationship between the policies suggested by the theory of the free society and the policies which actually have emerged in the United States, we should probably have to conclude that the analysis in the foregoing pages has been a mere intellectual diversion. But if we find that there is an intimate relationship between the theory and the actual evolution, we may be greatly encouraged to hope that the labor policy suggested by the theory of the free society may easily be translated into the labor policy of the United States. And we shall, in such a case, be in a position to make a more practical judgment as to the feasibility of measures suggested by the theory of the free society.

No policy, no code of laws, can be effective unless it enjoys the support not only of the citizenry as a whole but also of the persons to whom it is immediately applicable. Laws are effective only when most people obey them, and this is true no less of labor laws than of other laws. On the other hand, laws are not needed in order to discourage conduct which no one engages in, anyway. Thus, no objection can be made to labor-law proposals merely because they forbid conduct now common among trade unions. Yet, unless at least some trade unions and their leaders are disposed to obey the laws applicable to their activities, the problem of enforcement can become difficult.

These considerations, too, indicate the merit of the policies and laws suggested by the theory of the free society; and they point up the desirability of an examination of the labor policies and laws which have evolved naturally in the history of the United States. For the policies and laws of the free society are few in number and generally applicable in character; as a consequence, even though a majority of trade-union leaders should be reluctant to submit to them, the fact that other members of society on the whole submit to them gives promise that they can be made to work in labor relations, even though the job may be difficult. Experience with the actual evolution of labor policy in the United States must give valuable aid in settling upon the particular rules and methods most likely to achieve success in the future. We turn now to a survey of the experience of the United States in the field of labor policy and law.

Part II

EVOLUTION OF LABOR LAW AND POLICY IN THE UNITED STATES

Employees shall have the right to self-organization, to form, join, or assist labor organizations, to bargain collectively through representatives of their own choosing, and to engage in other concerted activities for the purpose of collective bargaining or other mutual aid or protection, and shall also have the right to refrain from any or all of such activities...

—The National Labor Relations Act, as Amended

Chapter 8

EVOLUTION OF LABOR POLICY: THE PRINCIPLE OF FREE EMPLOYEE CHOICE

Standing as close as we do to numerous disputes in the field of labor relations, we tend to see sharply and vividly some features, while others are blurred, out of focus, sometimes completely out of sight. This is unfortunate. The subject is broad and complicated. It has a history which cannot be neglected if we seek to understand. Institutions, activities, rules of law in labor relations which seem unimportant, which lack vividness in a narrow view of the subject, take on new importance when the perspective is broadened and deepened. Others, of colossal dimensions in a short view, assume more moderate proportions when the focus is lengthened. One can block out the sun with one's thumb.

This chapter is designed to cover the field panoramically, and in historical depth. The aim is to establish the proper relative proportions of the various features of the labor relations field: to show what looms large in proper context.

Organization of Employees and Collective Bargaining

Sometimes facts are so large as to be virtually invisible. Beyond much doubt the rules governing labor disputes have over the years been the topic of the liveliest public debate, have provoked more sustained public interest than any other internal problem, and have excited the most notable political activity. For all that, not more than seventeen million of the nation's sixty-odd million workers belong to trade unions; and the rate of union growth has shown no material increase for a number of years now.[1] Whatever the explanation, we are far from being a nation of unionized workers. And this fragmentary unionization is one of those huge facts which, even though not obvious to all at all times, is of crucial importance in the real world.

Some attribute our fractional unionization and the sticky rate of union growth to the so-called anti-union character of the current labor relations legislation (the Taft-Hartley law). Others contend that there is an inherent limit to the organizing potentialities of labor unions and support their position by citing the fact that the proportion of unionization in the United States today is approaching that in other industrialized countries. Still others argue that unionism in general, and in the United States in particular, has really not very much to offer the workingman; that economic conditions in the United States are sufficiently favorable to make the average workingman at least vaguely aware of this; and that, therefore, if unions are prevented by law from coercing employees to join, as the current law purports to do, the natural result will be a decrease in the relative size and power of labor unions.

We shall make no attempt to weigh the merits of these hypotheses. For present purposes it is sufficient to note the basic fact that unionization of the American working force is far from complete, the further fact that the unionization which now exists is by no means stable, and the consequence that organization of the working force remains today a notably important subject for everyone concerned. Many unions are intent upon expanding their membership, either by enlisting employees who presently belong to no union or by raiding the ranks of other unions. "Organization" of nonunion workers is, in short, one of the important features of the field of labor relations. In the light of these factors it will come as no surprise that one of the major phases of labor relations *law* involves rules governing the organization of employees.

While unions number among their members considerably less than one-third of the working force, their social and economic influence may be far greater than that proportion suggests. And this possibility accounts for the second of the two major phases of the law of labor relations—that is, the rules governing the collective-bargaining process itself. For several reasons this process is considered more important than the bare membership figures of the unions would suggest; two of the reasons should be noted here.

In the first place, under current legal principles, a union representing only a bare majority of the employees within a given employment unit is nevertheless the exclusive bargaining representative for all employees in that unit, nonunion as well as enrolled members. In a unit of 10,000 workers, a union bargains exclusively for all even though it has only 5,001 members in that unit. Thus, bargaining by unions may directly affect many more employees than the bare union membership figures suggest.

In the second place, unionization is virtually complete in the basic industries which directly affect the whole country and the living costs of every consumer: mining, steel, manufacturing, transportation, and construction. With collective bargaining thus affecting production costs and prices to a substantial degree throughout the economy, it is entirely natural that the law assumes an interest in the process.

Another capitally important feature of our subject matter is that these two major areas of labor relations law—union organizational activities and the collective-bargaining process—have a single, common point of departure in the current legal structure: the principle of *free employee choice*. This principle, as conceived and largely as applied today, declares that individual employees have a protected legal right to join or not to join unions, or to participate or to refuse to participate in the concerted activities of labor organizations, according to their own choice, and free of coercion by either employers or unions.

Development of Free Employee Choice

The evolution of labor relations law in the United States may be described largely in terms of the history of the principle of free employee choice. Contrary to a rather common interpretation of American industrial history, this principle has always existed in the United States, at least in rudimentary form; it has never been unlawful for workers to form and join unions.[2] On the other hand, it is entirely accurate to say that the principle has only recently come to occupy the central, dominant position which it holds now in the structure of labor relations law. For a time, the bare legal principle was subordinated in the real world to the right of employers and unions to use economically coercive techniques. Then for another period, labor relations law consciously and directly subordinated the principle of free employee choice to the national policy which gave central importance to the promotion of the growth of unions.

Until recently, despite the fact that an employee broke no law in joining or in refusing to join a union, both employers and labor unions were largely free, in the legal sense, to exert economic pressure in order to discourage or to compel, as the case might be, membership in labor unions. Employers had a right, according to common-law concepts, to refuse to hire or to discharge workers who showed an interest in unionization.[3] Economic necessity or voluntary acceptance of trade unionism induced some employers to forego the use of their legal right to resist unionization. But this did not alter the legal principle; it only qualified the employer's exercise of his undoubted legal right. Thus, in a period of labor shortage an employer might accept unionization, only to resist it when market factors were more favorable to him. On the other hand, for a longer time, extending indeed to the present, unions also were and have been largely free under the law to use certain forms of coercion as a means of compelling employees to accept union membership.

Toward the end of the nineteenth century there emerged in emphatic form the opinion that the power of employers to discourage unionization was much greater and more effectual than it should be. Put in more realistic terms, this point of view probably reflected the judgment that the power of employers to discourage unionization was much greater than the power of unions to compel unionization. For the aim of those who voiced such sentiments was not to free employees of coercion by both unions and employers. The aim, instead, was to eliminate only coercion by employers. At the same time that it was proposed to eliminate all possibilities of coercion by employers, the proponents of the point of view in question strove equally vigorously to erase such checks upon union coercion as the then-current law provided.[4]

This point of view achieved its widest acceptance among intellectuals, the people, and the politicians in the years between the two world wars. And the period of maximum acceptance coincided with the flourishing of interventionist economic thought. By interventionism we mean, of course, the theory that the state must intervene to correct the so-called imbalances and inequities which are presumed to be inherent in a free economic system. Naturally this interventionism was operative in much more than the labor sector of the economy: in the United States during the 1930's it influenced farm, fiscal, and trade policies. But in the labor sector it started with the assumptions that the purchasing power of the so-called "masses" is the key to economic prosperity, that free market factors are always unfavorable to the "masses," and that universal unionization is the most desirable method of correcting the unfavorable market situation and securing for the "masses" a high degree of purchasing power.[5] These assumptions were translated into action consistent with general interventionist theory by throwing the force of government behind the union movement.

The product of the convergence of these two lines of thought was the period—roughly 1930 to 1947—during which tight legal restraints were imposed upon employers and virtually all legal restraints were removed from unions. The essential character of the period is reflected in two basic federal laws, the Norris-LaGuardia Act of 1932[6] and the Wagner Act of 1935.[7] The Norris Act prohibited the federal courts from enjoining economically coercive activities by labor unions. The Wagner Act systematically outlawed *every* conceivable type of coercive activity by employers. Of these two laws, the Wagner Act was the more typical representative of the then-current interventionist theory. It not only prohibited all forms of employer coercion, but also created an elaborate governmental apparatus whose function it was to enforce the strictures of the law against employers and to direct the development of the expanded unionization which, under the circumstances, seemed inevitable.

Employees during these years had a clear, legally protected and enforced right to join unions. Their right to refrain from joining unions was not so clear.

This was the period when the labor unions flourished. Union membership grew from three million in 1934 to sixteen million in 1947. The American Federation of Labor, the parent organization of the craft unions, expanded its membership to more than six million. The new Congress of Industrial Organizations (CIO), originally a part of the AFL, brought unionism to workers in the mass-production industries: autos, steel, oil, and electrical equipment. Unions representing workers in the railroad and mining industries, already large and powerful, practically completed the unionization of employees in those industries. Unionization of the maritime and motor transport industries was likewise extended greatly. Stranger-picketing, sit-down strikes, mass picket lines, and secondary boycotts—either expressly condoned or ineffectually prosecuted—were commonly and frequently used organizational techniques during this period.[8]

The national government's aid to unions during this period was not limited to the legislative branch and to favorable legislation; all branches of the government came to their aid. The Supreme Court of the United States, in a series of decisions which are called famous by some and infamous by others, erased the restraints upon union action which had formerly been applied under the Sherman Anti-Trust Act.[9] Moreover, in an interpretation of the Constitution which it has now largely abandoned, it held that picketing, one of the most common of the coercive organizing devices of unions, was a form of freedom of speech which no court, federal or state, could constitutionally enjoin.[10] Finally, it adopted a jurisprudential principle according to which the National Labor Relations Board, a quasi-judicial agency in the executive branch of government, was largely freed of judicial control in applying the already pro-union Wagner law in disputes between unions and employers.[11] At the same time, in the opinion of many, the purely executive branch of government was likewise favorably disposed toward the large labor unions. By acts of the President himself, the Department of Labor, and the National Labor Relations Board, the weight and prestige of the executive department were thrown usually on the side of the unions in labor disputes, although the usual formalities of nonpartisanship were observed and even perfected.

This, then, was the period in which the principle of free employee choice, subordinated to the policies encouraging collective bargaining and the growth of labor unions, became in effect the principle favoring only the employee right to join unions. And it is interesting to note that the statement of "employee rights" in

Section 7 of the Wagner Act made no mention of any right to refuse to join unions. That statement read as follows:

> Employees shall have the right to self-organization, to form, join, or assist labor organizations, to bargain collectively through representatives of their own choosing, and to engage in concerted activities, for the purposes of collective bargaining or other mutual aid or protection.

If the Wagner Act's statement of employee rights reflects the subordination of the principle of employee free choice to the policy favoring collective bargaining and concerted union action, the analogous statement of employee rights in the Taft-Hartley Act symbolizes the emergent dominance of the principle of free employee choice. As amended by the Taft-Hartley law, the statement of employee rights declares that:

> Employees shall have the right to self-organization, to form, join, or assist labor organizations, to bargain collectively through representatives of their own choosing, and to engage in other concerted activities for the purpose of collective bargaining or other mutual aid or protection, and shall also have the right to refrain from any or all of such activities. . . .

The Taft-Hartley law does not limit itself to a simple declaration of the bare legal right of employees to refuse to join unions. It goes as far in declaring unlawful the coercion of free employee choice by unions as the Wagner Act went in declaring unlawful such coercion by employers. Thus, on the level of principle, it is entirely accurate to say that free employee choice is the dominant concept in the Taft-Hartley law. The fact is, however, that according to interpretations of the law prevailing today, there are certain forms of coercion by unions which are permissible. As we shall see, there is also a strong opposing current of opinion, among students as well as judges, to the effect that the Taft-Hartley law was designed to prohibit every form of union coercion similar in principle to the forms of employer coercion prohibited by the Wagner Act.[12] Here, however, we need only note that the promotion of collective bargaining is no longer the dominant feature of the national labor relations law. By specifically declaring an employee right to refrain from collective bargaining and by specifically prohibiting all union coercion of free employee choice, it becomes evident that collective bargaining, while still encouraged by national law and policy, has yielded the center position, and that the concept of free employee choice has taken its place. Both employers and unions are, under the Taft-Hartley law, prevented from coercively interfering with that choice.

The Appeal of the Principle

To understand the process whereby the principle of free employee choice has become dominant is to understand some of the most important features of economic, social, and legal thought in the United States. Understanding of this process is important also to a fruitful grasp of the character of the current labor policies and laws. It seems worthwhile, therefore, to sketch the factors which have been at work in the elevation of this new central principle, and then to note the extent to which the principle prevails in practice.

There has been an entirely natural and forseeable reaction during the last ten years to the excesses resulting from the relatively swift growth of labor unions and the substantial economic power which this growth has placed in the hands of union leaders. To put the matter simply, the American people, who have always been suspicious and resentful of great economic power, now suspect and resent the power of union leaders and are well disposed to arguments suggesting both diminution of that power and safeguards against abuses of the remaining powers of labor union leaders. Before unions achieved great power, many seemed to think that union leaders, unlike other men, could somehow be trusted absolutely. With experience of arrogant, antisocial conduct on the part of union leaders, the weight of opinion has shifted to the conclusion that labor union leaders are, after all, only men; and that, as such, they must be carefully watched and checked. This attitude has an importance in the current structure of labor policy in the United States which cannot be exaggerated.

At the same time, many in the United States remain sympathetically disposed to the "workingman," and most people are convinced that much good is to be expected from collective bargaining. The problem, therefore, has been one of preserving collective bargaining while at the same time checking the arbitrary powers of union leaders.

With such a problem to solve, it has been natural for American thought to turn to the economic, social, and political philosophy of classical liberalism—the philosophy which over the years has exerted so strong an influence in our public and private lives. In this almost unconscious process of deliberation, the concept of free employee choice has again and again emerged as the most satisfactory practical expedient for reconciling antagonism toward arbitrary power with sympathy for the individual worker and faith in the institution of collective bargaining.

Classic liberalism has always regarded the individual, the freely choosing individual, as the only rational starting point in social, economic, and political analysis. Representative government has been the consequence in political life. The free market has been the consequence in economic life. And great emphasis on individual freedom of choice has been the general social consequence. Against this background, it becomes evident that the concept of free employee choice in the elaboration of labor policy must have an extremely strong appeal. It is literally unthinkable to many that everyone should be forced, if he wishes to work and live, into union membership.

Principle and Practice

Besides its strong influence on the law applicable at the organizing level, the traditional emphasis on the uncoerced individual permeates the law relating to collective bargaining as well. It is true that a valid collective agreement binds even those employees in a bargaining unit who have voted against the union; and to that extent individual bargaining has given way to the collective, majority-rule concept. But it must be remembered that under the law freely choosing individuals—a majority of them in any bargaining unit—decide in the first instance whether there should be any collective bargaining at all. Furthermore, a feature of labor relations legislation in the United States is a provision safeguarding the right of individual employees to present their grievances directly to their employer, without operating through the union. Naturally, a grievance so presented is in a somewhat disadvantageous position. The union itself is likely to discourage the employer from giving nonunion employees favorable treatment. But the fact remains that even in the area where the greatest inroads have been made, the principle of individual autonomy has prevailed to the greatest practical extent.[13]

Furthermore individual freedom is a definitely vital factor in the stages leading up to the conclusion of a collective agreement and determining its content. The individual has a legally protected right to refuse to participate in the strikes and other activities in which unions engage during the collective-bargaining process. As a matter of legal principle, a union may not either physically or economically coerce an employee who has refused to participate in a strike. One of the central problems in labor relations law, however, is that of translating this legal principle into practical operation. For as matters stand today, the law and law-enforcement agencies do not effectively protect the individual employee against various types of union coercion. Picketing, with its frequent concomitant of violence, is still permitted; and union control of many job opportunities constitutes another legally permissible method, in many states, of coercing employee acquiescence in union action.[14] The fact that compulsory unionism and picketing are two of the most frequently discussed of all topics in the field of labor relations is largely explained by the continued emphasis on individual free choice.

Liberal orientation in terms of the individual and the free market account likewise for the rule that, during a strike, new workers may apply for the position vacated by the strikers.[15] The existence of this rule establishes, in fact, that free-market principles still theoretically control the determination of wage rates, notwithstanding the elaborate apparatus of collective bargaining; for the rule merely embodies the classical liberal principle that conditions on the market shall be the determining factors in the establishment of wage rates. As long as unions may not prevent employers from advertising for workers, and workers from seeking employment during a strike at wages satisfactory to themselves if not to the strikers, the strike itself is no more than an evolved form of the traditional technique indispensable to the operation of any free market—namely, the refusal to deal on unsatisfactory terms.

Again, however, it must be noted that inadequate laws and law-enforcement permit unions to engage in activities, such as picketing, which carry a menace directly or indirectly of physical violence. While sit-down strikes, outright violence, and other physical interferences with the peaceful operation of the labor market are prohibited, it is not at all rare to witness depredation and violence during strikes, especially in areas where union leaders are both politically powerful and unscrupulous, and where the police are either unable or unwilling to establish order.[16] Nevertheless, there is no doubt of the theoretical illegality of such union conduct and, consequently, of the theoretical legal dominance of the position of the individual worker.

The continued vitality of free-market principles is responsible also for the existing rules which limit the degree to which independent union organizations may combine their forces and thus impose monopolistic pressures in the collective-bargaining process. It is unlawful, for example, for a union to call a strike against one employer, or to refuse to work on that employer's products, simply because another union has a dispute with another employer (the so-called secondary boycott tactic). Here too, however, the logic of the law is not entirely clear in some respects, and the law itself is by no means effectively enforced.[17] Secondary boycotts and the degree to which they should be prohibited likewise represent an area of current public debate.

Of all the subjects of present-day debate, however, the outstanding one is that concerning so-called industry-wide bargaining. The term itself, like others in labor relations, creates considerable difficulty. In some instances it refers to the situation in which a union bargains collectively with all the firms, throughout the nation, engaged in a particular form of production, such as coal mining, petroleum production, or steel fabrication. In other instances it may be used to describe collective bargaining with all the firms in one industry in a smaller area, such as a part of a city, an entire city, or some larger region. Another source of difficulty lies in the uneven extent to which such bargaining prevails even within given geographical areas. In other words, it is rarely true that a union bargains simultaneously with all the steel companies, coal companies, etc., in *any* given area. A final difficulty is created by the fact that the agreements actually reached in this ambiguous process of industry-wide bargaining do not apply exactly the same terms and conditions of employment even to all the companies which have participated. For all these reasons it is extremely difficult to discuss the so-called subject of industry-wide bargaining in coherent and precise terms. Or, to put the matter another way, it may well be that there is no single intelligible subject of discussion presented by the term "industry-wide bargaining."[18]

The fact remains, however, that a strike simultaneously of a large number of railroads, steel mills, or coal mines has distinct effects upon the general public. It can be disastrous for many people if prolonged.[19] And the pressures for a solution of the so-called problem of industry-wide strikes are therefore great. (Incidentally, the same kind of pressures exist, and pose generally the same kinds of problems, in cases of strikes against local, monopolized transit and utility systems.) Under current federal law, "industry-wide" strikes are subject formally to basically the same rules as all other strikes; and collective bargaining, aided by the mediation efforts of governmental agents, is relied upon as the ultimate technique of settlement.[20] The only important formal difference in the legal treatment of these strikes today lies in the provision for a temporary injunction against them when they are found to imperil the public health or safety, whereas other purely economic strikes are on the whole lawful and unenjoinable as such.

The basis of the current legal approach to these "emergency" strikes is the traditional reliance upon voluntary methods of settling economic disputes, the traditional liberal reluctance to impose upon private parties a governmental determination of economic issues. The hope is that the dispute will ultimately be settled through collective bargaining during the eighty-day period of the temporary injunction, without substantial governmental intervention and coercion.

Many state and municipal governments in the United States have chosen to impose compulsory governmental arbitration in cases of local transit and utility strikes.[21] And on the national scene, considerable dissatisfaction with the present law is shown, especially by labor union leaders and by scholars and politicians sympathetic with the point of view of those labor leaders. These critics contend that the current device of the temporary injunction is unfair to the unions, that it penalizes them and favors the employers. They assert that the industries should be seized by the government and profits confiscated. They do not take the further logical step of proposing that wages be confiscated, or that individual workers be compelled to remain at their jobs during the dispute. Nor do they insist upon compulsory arbitration or the fixing of wages and working conditions by government fiat. Their aim is instead to weaken employer resistance to union wage demands by expropriating profits for as long as the employers refuse to grant increases in the amount asked by the union. The objective seems to be, not to destroy or supplant the market determination of wages, but merely to rig the market heavily in favor of the unions.[22]

This objective, as we shall see repeatedly, rather than socialism or communism, seems to have been historically the dominant one of the union movement in the United States.[23] Constantly in opposition, traditional liberalism attempts to preserve the free and peaceful market determination of wages and working conditions. While accepting and promoting the principle of free association, subject to the principle of free employee choice, traditional liberals hope to preserve the right of individuals or groups of individuals to work or not to work in accordance with their own, uncoerced desires.

Chapter 9

FREE EMPLOYEE CHOICE AND EMPLOYER COERCION

The labor relations legislation of the 1920's and the 1930's did not create the legal right of employees to form and join trade unions; that right was recognized by the common law, prior to the enactment of the labor relations legislation.[1] Accurately stated, the effect of the labor relations legislation was to extinguish another right recognized by the common law: the right of employers to resist and discourage employee organization by means of the peaceful exercise of their own property and contract rights.[2]

The Common-Law Background

The common law, while recognizing the right of employees to form and join labor unions, also recognized the right of employers to hire or fire workers at will, at least to the extent that the employers themselves had not voluntarily relinquished such a right by means of an express contract of employment. In the absence of a limiting contract, employers were free at common law to refuse to hire or to fire employees who insisted upon joining unions.[3] Of course, if an employer chose to hire or to maintain in employment workers who belonged to unions, he was free under the law to do so. Thus, in periods of labor shortage when economic conditions were exceptionally favorable to workers, employers would find it more difficult to resist unionization, assuming that they would want to do so. More or less continually favorable economic conditions probably account for the substantial employee organization which existed at different times, even during the common-law period when employers were legally free to resist unionization through lawful, nonviolent means.[4]

Besides being in a legal position to hire and fire at will, employers could prohibit organizational activities on company premises, criticize unionization freely, threaten to fire or to deny promotion to employees who joined unions, hire only on condition that employees refuse to participate in union activities, and could, in general, utilize all peaceable means to discourage unionization. About the only peaceable economic means of resisting unionization which the common law denied to employers derived from the common-law principle against combinations in restraint of trade. Some courts held that separate employers could not agree among themselves to refuse to hire workers who were known to favor unionization (the so-called blacklisting technique).[5]

Under the common law, therefore, the question of whether or not there should be unionization of employees was considered a question of no special or unique significance. It was viewed in very much the same way as the question of the particular wage level. The common law established no upper or lower limits on the wage level; wages to be paid or received were left to the free play of economic forces. Employees were legally free to ask whatever wage they wished; employers were legally free to offer to pay whatever wage they wished. The actual wage paid was fixed, not by law, but by the interrelationships of the wishes, desires, and capacities of employers and employees.

The common law recognized the right of employees to refuse to seek work at wages unsatisfactory to themselves. And, despite uninformed opinion to the contrary, it likewise recognized the right of groups of employees to cease work in concert, to strike, where the wage level was unsatisfactory to them.[6]

The same situation prevailed in regard to the preliminary stage of self-organization. On the whole, in both cases, the common law prohibited only violent or monopolistic action. As we shall see later, in dealing with common-law restraints upon union action, there was considerable difference of opinion among common-law judges in the United States as to the exact types of union action which fell within the prohibitions of violent or monopolistic conduct.[7] And it is in a certain sense regrettable that positive labor relations legislation intervened before the evolutionary processes of the common law could operate to smooth out these differences, or at least to pose the central issues in a succinct and manageable manner. It is entirely possible that certain problems which vex labor relations law today, even under the comprehensive statutes, might have been solved sooner and more satisfactorily had the common law had more time to clarify the issues, if not to advance definitive solutions.

The fact is, however, that only five years or so after the production of the common law's most definitive statement of its attitude toward unionization and collective action by employees, political forces became so strong as to produce the so-called pro-labor legislation. It was in 1921 that Chief Justice Taft, speaking for the United States Supreme Court, eloquently stated the common-law attitude toward, and acceptance of, the right of employees to organize labor unions.[8] Five years later, in 1926, came the first of the more significant interventionist types of labor relations legislation, the Railway Labor Act;[9] in 1932 came the Norris-LaGuardia Act which, by drastically limiting the jurisdiction of the federal courts in labor disputes, virtually denied them any role in shaping the common law;[10] and then, in 1935, the enactment of the National Labor Relations Act (the Wagner Act) gave to an administrative agency, the National Labor Relations Board, the major, if not exclusive, function of developing labor relations law and policy.[11]

These two statutes, the Norris-LaGuardia and Wagner Acts, changed the course of development in labor relations law. While physically and economically coercive union action had been the major concern of the common law, the federal Norris Act and its counterparts in state legislation went a long way toward erasing this concern by denying courts jurisdiction except over the most flagrantly violent union conduct. Meanwhile, although the common law had scarcely concerned itself with the use by employers of their economic position to resist and discourage unionization, the Wagner Act intervened to eliminate employer resistance to unionization much more efficaciously than the common law had ever been able to control union organizational activities.

The National Labor Relations Act

The original Wagner Act was designed to eliminate every type of effective employer resistance to unionization. With certain relatively unimportant modifications, the same is true of the current version of the Wagner Act; that is, the Taft-Hartley Act. (The official title of the Wagner Act was the National Labor Relations Act. The Taft-Hartley Act is merely the informal title of the amendments made in 1947 to the NLRA. Thus the current statute is officially known as the National Labor Relations Act, as Amended. When speaking of the current law, we shall use the abbreviation "NLRA." In instances where the current statute differs from its predecessor we shall use the terms "Taft-Hartley" and "Wagner.")

The NLRA went about eliminating the employer as an obstacle to employee organization by means of two interrelated legal provisions: first a broad declaration of the right of employees to form and join labor unions and to participate in concerted activities;[12] and then a positive definition of five so-called employer "unfair labor practices."[13] Viewed as a whole, these five unfair practices cover every conceivable type of employer activity which might have the effect of coercively impeding unionization. Moreover, the Act does not rely upon traditional judicial methods and private legal actions brought by employees or labor unions as means of enforcing its policies. Instead, the expense and the burden of prosecuting the policies of the Act are borne by the government; i.e., by the taxpayers. The National Labor Relations Board was specially created both to prosecute and to judge cases brought under the Wagner Act.

The Taft-Hartley Act changed the procedure slightly by putting the function of prosecution largely in one agency and the function of adjudication in another; it also expanded somewhat the role of the constitutional courts in reviewing the activities of the National Labor Relations Board.[14] Both the Wagner and Taft-Hartley Acts include among employer unfair practices any form of employer coercion designed to discourage employees from cooperating with the government in the prosecution of the policies of the NLRA.[15] It seems accurate to say, in summary, that under the NLRA the employer's use of economic power as a means of discouraging or frustrating employee organization is totally prohibited.

Employer Unfair Labor Practices

A brief sketch of the five unfair practices defined in the Act will more concretely demonstrate the extent to which employer interference in the organizational process is prohibited. The first unfair practice is a generic prohibition which covers all the others. It states that it is an unfair practice for an employer to interfere with, restrain, or coerce employees in the exercise of the rights to form and join labor unions and to participate in concerted activities.[16] The second unfair practice forbids the employer to dominate or interfere with the formation or administration of any labor organization or contribute financial or other support to it (that is, an employer may not do anything which would tend to weaken a union's total allegiance to the employees).[17] The third unfair practice, specifically addressed to the employer's control of employment terms and conditions, declares that he may not deny employment or adjust the conditions thereof on the basis of an employee's sentiments in regard to unionization.[18] The fourth unfair practice repeats the prohibition of the third, but is applicable only in instances of employee participation in the prosecution of suits under the Act.[19] The fifth unfair practice declares that it is unlawful for an employer to refuse to bargain collectively with the union designated as their representative by a majority of employees in an appropriate bargaining unit.[20]

Property Rights and Unfair Practices

The central problem in the vast majority of employer-unfair-practice cases concerns the degree to which these prohibitions qualify rights and privileges accruing to employers under pre-existing traditions, customs, and laws. Freedom of speech, private property, and free contract are concepts of a certain vitality and force even today in the United States. They are, in fact, rather widely considered as more than mere abstractions or empty generalizations which time and the so-called complexities of modern life have robbed of real significance and social utility.

The most critical of these concepts today, the concept of private property and the practical incidents thereto, is often considered to be not a mere shibboleth designed to shelter privilege but the best practical method of serving the social aim of utilizing human and material resources in the manner most advantageous to society as a whole; that is, the most sensible basis of production.

The operation of the NLRA can be best demonstrated and appreciated in terms of the accommodation which has been effected between its provisions and the traditional common-law view of the scope of private-property rights.

A fundamental aspect of the traditional right of private property accords to every proprietor the control of the use of his land, buildings, factories, or other subject of the property right. As a proprietor, an employer has the right to place such limits as he wishes upon the activities of workers on his property. The workers are usually admitted to that property in order to perform the work for which they have been engaged. Activities unrelated to that work may, under the traditional view, be permitted or prohibited, as the employer wishes. Viewed purely in the light of the common law, the employer might prohibit the use of his property for any purpose related to organization of a labor union, while permitting other types of employee activity unrelated to production—as, for example, athletic events or social gatherings.

The NLRA declares, however, that an employer may not interfere with, restrain, or coerce employees in the exercise of their right of self-organization. And thus the question arises whether the pre-existing right of private property has been modified, for if the employer forbids the use of his property for organizational purposes, it may be contended that he is interfering with or restraining employees in the exercise of their right of self-organization. The same argument may be advanced if the employer refuses to permit union organizers to enter upon his property. On the other hand, it is highly doubtful that the Congress of the United States, in passing the NLRA, intended to compel employers to help employees in their organizational efforts. The provision prohibiting employers to contribute support to labor organizations is relevant here. It can scarcely be contended that by prohibiting employer interference or restraint the law intended to force employers to make a positive contribution to organizational efforts, when a provision of the law clearly prohibits such contributions.

The practical application of the law has resulted in a series of adjustments of the property rights of employers and the rights of employees as declared in the NLRA. No employer has ever been compelled to permit organizational activities on his premises during working hours; but, unless employees have abused the privilege, they are held to have the right to engage in organizational activities during nonworking time (lunch periods, or periods before work begins or after it ends).[21] In those situations where employees live as well as work on the employer's premises, as on merchant ships or lumber camps, the employers are required to permit access at reasonable times to union organizers.[22] This rule has been extended to the point where, in a company owned town, the employer has been required to permit union organizers to rent a meeting hall if that meeting hall is made available to other organizations in which the employees are interested.[23] Along similar lines, unions are sometimes held to have the right to distribute their propaganda on property owned by the employer, although the highest legal authority is now to the contrary.[24]

The theoretical goal of the courts has been to provide some practical scope for the right of self-organization without impinging upon the social values which underly the employer's property rights. Thus it has been common for the courts to say that "working time is for work."[25] And, where use of company premises even during free time might reasonably be expected to result in serious impairment of the essential commercial function (as in the selling area of a department store) the courts have upheld the right of the employer to prohibit all organizational activity during free time as well as during working time.[26]

Similar considerations have led to largely similar conclusions in reconciling other features of the NLRA with the property or contract rights of employers. Thus the traditional right of the employer to hire or fire at will, or to control promotions, demotions, wage increases or reductions still prevails.[27] But the courts have interpreted the NLRA as prohibiting the exercise of this right in a manner designed either to *discourage* membership in a union which the employer disapproves or to *encourage* membership in a union which the employer favors.[28] The NLRA itself contains a modification of this general rule. Employers may enter into "union-shop contracts" with unions which represent a majority of employees in an appropriate bargaining unit. Such contracts provide in general that after a nonunion employee has been hired he must join the union, or at least offer to join and to pay union dues, as a condition of continued employment. If he refuses, he may, under such a contract, be discharged; and the law itself provides that a discharge pursuant to such a contract is not unlawful, even though the effect may be to encourage union membership.[29] (It should perhaps be mentioned here that, as a general rule, the employer may consistently with the NLRA concede entirely or share with a union, pursuant to a collective agreement, all or any part of the control of employment terms and conditions derived from his common-law private-property rights.)

Freedom of Speech and Free Employee Choice

One of the profound problems raised by the NLRA's prohibition of employer interference in the organizational process concerns the right of employers to criticize and condemn labor unions. By and large, this has been considered a constitutional problem. It has been thought that a prohibition of employer criticism of unions must necessarily be analyzed in the light of the constitutional right of free speech. Here, however, as in many areas of so-called "constitutional law," the emphasis upon the constitutional analysis may have done more harm than good. It may have tended to conceal the true dimensions and character of the problem.

In the first place, analysis must be addressed to the legislation itself. One must ask whether the NLRA intended to silence the employer entirely during the organizational process. It is academic at this time to relate this question to the original NLRA (the Wagner Act), since the Taft-Hartley amendments in part addressed themselves specifically to the problem. A provision added by the Taft-Hartley Act expressly declares that a statement of opinion by an employer may not be regarded as an unfair practice in itself, or evidence of an unfair practice, unless the statement contains a threat of force or reprisal or a promise of benefit.[30]

The mere fact of the deliberate insertion of this provision suggests the acceptance by Congress of the social utility of permitting employers to speak freely on the subject of unionization. It also strengthens the inference that labor policy in America is today oriented primarily in terms of free employee choice, rather than in terms of the single-minded promotion of labor unions and collective bargaining. For the new "free speech" provision, by condemning only those statements which contain threats or promises, recognizes the continued existence of a right in employers to speak out liberally on the merits of unionization.

Of course the law does not limit employers to scholarly, objective dissertations on the general subject of unionization. The employer is permitted to address himself specifically to the union which seeks to organize his employees, to point out defects in that union or its administration, even to state in a general way that employees will gain nothing by designating that union as their bargaining representative.[31] But he may go no further. He breaks the law if he offers any concrete benefit in return for a vote against the union, or if he threatens to withdraw benefits from the employees should they vote for the union.[32]

In summary, the extent to which the law permits employers to speak on the subject of unionization does not impair the principle of free employee choice. On the contrary, by maintaining the prohibition against economic coercion on the part of employers but at the same time making available to employees such arguments as employers can adduce against unions, the probability is that the area of effective choice by employees has been widened and deepened. The opportunity now available to both unions and employers to point out each other's defects tends to give employees a broader basis of judgment. It also emphasizes to unions and employers that the employees themselves are the central subjects of the national labor policy. Unions and employers are made strikingly aware of the power of the employees, and in the process it can hardly be doubted that substantial advantages accrue to the employees. The Taft-Hartley Act's emphasis on employer free speech is therefore to be regarded in principle not as a favor to employers but as an integral element of the concept of free employee choice.

Free Employee Choice and Majority Rule

The current emphasis upon employee free choice may be perceived in another aspect of the modification made by modern legislation on pre-existing employer rights. Previously an employer was legally free to recognize as exclusive employee representative even a union which had enrolled none or only a small minority of his employees.[33] As a matter of history, many unions had through the use of economic pressure gained bargaining status while lacking representative status. By means of picketing and secondary strikes and boycotts, strong unions had been able to compel employers (and employees) to accept them as exclusive bargaining representatives, even though none of the employees involved were members of those unions.[34] In some cases unions even found it possible to compel employers to discharge nonunion employees and to replace them with union members.[35]

These possibilities were condemned in principle even by the Wagner Act and have been more explicitly condemned in certain changes made by the Taft-Hartley Act. The implicit condemnation of the Wagner Act was to be seen in three of its provisions: the provision prohibiting employer interference with the exercise by *employees* of the right to form unions of their own choosing; that declaring unlawful any employer assistance to a labor organization; and that requiring employers to bargain *only* with unions representing a majority of employees in any bargaining unit.

The clear implication of these provisions was, of course, that an employer should not recognize and bargain with a union which represented less than a majority of his employees. However, since the law did not provide any direct method of preventing minority unions from exerting economic pressures for recognition, employers were often compelled to deal with such unions if they wished to continue in business. No help could be expected from the National Labor Relations Board under the Wagner Act, since that agency felt that its primary function was to promote collective bargaining, entirely without regard to the question whether such bargaining was desired by the employees concerned. And so, while the Wagner Act condemned and prohibited employer interference with the free choice of employees, it condoned such interference where union coercion compelled the employer to interfere.

In the light of these factors it is entirely accurate to state that the Wagner Act was not basically preoccupied with any meaningful concept of free employee choice. It was concerned with that choice only when employees happened to be interested in unions. In short, the Wagner Act presented and protected one choice alone: the choice of belonging to a union.[36]

One of the central purposes of the Taft-Hartley Act was to make equally effective the choice of not belonging to a union And to this end several of its new provisions were directed. But proper appreciation of this phase of the current legal structure requires systematic analysis of the provisions dealing with union action in connection with employee organization—the subject of the following chapters.

Chapter 10

UNION ORGANIZATIONAL METHODS
AND THE FREE CHOICE OF EMPLOYEES

It has become evident in the last few years that one of the great problems in American economic life concerns the methods used by unions in organizing employees. Attempts to hide, to disguise, or to ignore the existence of this problem have failed. Events have demonstrated that the common law's preoccupation was not, as has so often been charged, mere proof of the class-conscious prejudices of common-law judges against the legitimate economic aspirations of the working population. Instead, it now seems that the common-law judges were concerned with maintaining only the dynamic equilibrium of human rights, and especially the right to be free of coercion and intimidation. For recent legal developments, reflecting profound and widely shared sentiments among all the people, have taken up again the analysis and even the precise approaches of the common law, after an interregnum during which the nation as a whole seemed to have accepted the contentions that the common-law attitude had been misdirected, that in fact unions could do no wrong, and that only the subservience of judges to the arbitrary and unfair principles of "capitalism" stood between employees and universal unionization.

Actual experience with a unionism allowed to utilize all conceivable organizational techniques has produced unforeseen results. For one thing, under the most favorable circumstances unions have not succeeded in organizing the entire working force. Even more important, the organizing methods themselves have become the subject of widespread criticism and, consequently, of a legislative control which seems to have taken up where the common law left off.[1]

Peaceful Solicitation versus Coercion

Union organizational techniques in the United States have varied remarkably little over the years. Methods practiced around 1800 prevail today.[2] There have been some refinements and extensions, a greater efficacy in some instances because of the greater and more widespread power of modern unions, but nothing new in principle. Today, as 150 years ago, union organizational devices fall into two great categories—coercive and noncoercive.

The simpler of these categories is that of the noncoercive techniques. Among these may be mentioned the peaceable solicitation of union membership at the place of employment, at the worker's home, or at a meeting place which may be rented by the union for the occasion. The characteristic element in peaceable solicitation is an appeal to the nonunion employee's conception of his own interest. In effect, the union organizer tells the nonunion employee that he will be better off if he joins the union. The argument is addressed to the employee and the decision rests with him. In peaceable and noncoercive solicitation, the employee is subjected to no threat of economic or physical reprisal emanating from the union if he rejects membership. He may be told that the employer or the "market" will treat him badly if he does not join the union (just as the employer in the analogous situation may tell him that he will be worse off if he joins the union). But a union oversteps the bounds of noncoercive solicitation if it also asserts, expressly or implicitly, that it will harm the employee physically or economically should he decline to join.

Coercive Techniques: Picketing

The coercive organizational techniques all carry an express or implicit threat of reprisal, in the form of either physical or economic harm; but, unfortunately for analysis, they are very often "mixed categories." They often combine both physical and economic coercion, and in some instances contain also elements of noncoercive solicitation—a fact which has led to confusion in the law.

The coercive organizational techniques are imbedded in the

classic union activities: picketing, secondary strikes and boycotts, and compulsory unionism. Some of these activities may be carried on in a noncoercive manner; but in practice they are usually coercive—physically, economically, or both physically and economically. For example, picketing, a union activity which has created considerable ambiguity in the law, may be analytically subsumed under all the known categories: entirely noncoercive, physically coercive, economically coercive, or any combination of the three. A single person walking up and down before a factory, carrying a sign exhorting the employees to join his union, certainly coerces no one if his conduct actually signifies nothing more than an attempt to secure the attention of the nonunion employees. Such picketing is the simple equivalent of noncoercive solicitation of union membership. But it becomes entirely another thing if it is designed as, or understood to be, a signal which places an embargo around the factory and thus threatens its economic life.

In the United States, picketing, even by a single person, has commonly, if not usually, such embargo effects and purposes.[3] It is commonly understood, and even made a part of union "laws," that no member of a union will enter picketed premises.[4] A member of the truck drivers' union will usually not deliver items to a picketed factory. Members of the building trades unions will not enter a picketed construction project. Little imagination is needed to realize that under such circumstances picketing which appears innocuous may, in the complicated American economy, carry with it a threat of economic suffocation of the business involved, and with it the livelihood of its workers. It is, in short, an effective weapon. In many instances it is a deadly form of economic coercion. Employees otherwise inclined to refrain from joining the union will be coerced economically by the embargo into joining. In fact, one may usually infer from the mere existence of picketing that the employees have in the exercise of their own free choice already refused to join the picketing union. Had they not refused, the picketing would not have been necessary.

For there is no need of picketing when employees voluntarily join a union. When they do so, the law requires their employer to recognize and bargain with that union.[5] It is not necessary for the union to picket in order to secure bargaining status. So the simple existence of a picket line, however peaceful it may seem on the surface, carries in itself a strong implication that the union is intent upon economic coercion. The implication is stronger than ever today, since unions and employees have a protected right to engage in all forms of peaceable, noncoercive organizational activity. Today the very presence of picketing is a sign, usually, that noncoercive methods of solicitation of union membership have failed to persuade employees to join the union responsible for the picketing.

Secondary Action

Very closely related to picketing among the coercive organizing techniques are those union activities known as secondary strikes and boycotts. Secondary strikes and boycotts are usually, though not always, used as organizational techniques. In a secondary strike a union creates a work stoppage in one employment unit as a means of putting pressure on some other employer and his employees. As a general rule, the mere existence of a secondary organizational strike, like the mere existence of organizational picketing, definitively indicates that employees have refused to join a union. The secondary strike is a form of economic coercion applied when peaceable and noncoercive organizing techniques have failed to persuade employees to join the union.[6]

A study of hundreds of secondary strikes and boycotts in American history, past and recent, makes it possible to present a characteristic example. Employees of one employer refuse to join a certain union. That union represents the employees of a second employer, whose services or patronage are essential to the continued existence of the first employer. By calling a strike against the second employer, the union thus squeezes tightly the first employer, endangering both his business and, accordingly, the livelihood of his employees. This is economic coercion of a most stringent kind. It might be called economic blackmail or, better, predatory monopolistic pressure.

Employers and employees who find themselves in such a predicament can usually resist only for a very limited time. If the law does not afford them immediate relief, either the employees will give in and join the union, or the employer may feel that he must, in order to preserve his business, add his own economic pressure to that of the union and compel his employees to join, threatening to discharge them if they refuse. Consider the pressures which the truck drivers' union may exert when attempting to organize the employees of any employer whose business depends entirely on the delivery or consignment of raw materials or finished products by means of trucks. Such pressures become very great where the products involved are perishable or where time exigencies are otherwise imperative. Always a powerful weapon of economic coercion, the secondary strike in the latter circumstances is irresistible.[7]

The secondary strike need not involve a complete stoppage of the work done by the employees of the secondary employer. The union may command those employees to refuse to perform services related only to the business of the primary employer under attack, leaving them free to continue to perform those parts of their duties which relate to the affairs of other employers.[8] If those other employers happen to be competitors of the employer primarily under attack, the coercive character of the secondary strike, even though it be only a partial secondary strike, becomes greater.

The secondary boycott is a broader and less well-defined method of imposing the pressures evident in the secondary strike. In fact, the secondary strike may be regarded as a species of secondary boycott. In all secondary action the union seeks to apply coercive pressures indirectly on the primary employer. This is necessary in the nature of things because, owing to its failure to organize the employees directly by peaceable, noncoercive means, the union must work in other ways. In the broad category of the secondary boycott, the union will bring to bear on the primary employer the economic pressures of his suppliers or customers.

There is no general agreement on the use of this terminology in the United States, but for present purposes we may distinguish the secondary boycott from the secondary strike on the basis of the means utilized to impose the pressure.[9] The secondary strike imposes the pressure through the indirect means of a secondary work stoppage. We shall call a secondary boycott the imposition of the pressure by demands addressed directly to the suppliers or customers of the primary employer. Thus, where a union appeals to the public to cease purchasing the products of a certain employer, the activity may be called an attempt to induce a secondary boycott. If the general public does in fact refuse to purchase, the refusal itself may be called a secondary boycott. Some may question whether such a secondary boycott is properly categorized as coercive. There is merit in such doubts, but they are largely irrelevant. Of all the kinds of secondary boycotts, that involving a simple appeal to the general public is the most rarely used and the least successful. It is rarely used for the simple reason that a union has no entirely effective means, as yet, of coercing the general public; it is unsuccessful for the same reason. The public is generally more interested in the quality and the price of an employer's product than in whether or not his employees have chosen to be represented by a union.

Accordingly, union appeals to the general public are rare. Such appeals are usually directed, instead, to persons or groups against whom the union is in a position to exert one form or another of economic coercion. One of the more common types of secondary boycott is known as "blacklisting" in union publications which are read by both union members and employers interested in the union.[10] When a business is "blacklisted," union members are under an obligation, more or less strictly enforced, to refuse to purchase the products of that business. If they are found purchasing such products, different penalties may be imposed, ranging from social ostracism, to reprimands, to fines, or even expulsion from the union. If an employer persists in dealing with a "blacklisted" employer" he takes the risk of being added to the blacklist himself or of having a strike called against him.[11] There can thus be no doubt of the accuracy of defining the "blacklisting" types of secondary boycotts as fundamentally coercive: they are not disinterested appeals; they contain threats of economic reprisal.

An essentially similar, but even more efficient, type of secondary boycott is the one imposed by what are colloquially called "hot-cargo" contracts. "Hot-cargo" clauses are often to be found in collective agreements between unions and employers.[12] By the terms of such clauses, the employer undertakes to refuse to do business with any employer who is involved in a labor dispute.

It makes no difference that the labor dispute arises from the refusal of employees to join a union and from the efforts of that union to coerce them into joining. The secondary employer undertakes in either case to refuse to deal with the primary employer. As regards the primary employer and his employees, the secondary boycott imposed by means of a "hot-cargo" contract is as economically coercive as picketing or the secondary strike. We need not inquire at present, therefore, into the means whereby unions induce employers to participate in "hot-cargo" contracts. We are concerned here only with the methods used by unions to compel employees to join, after peaceful, noncoercive attempts at persuasion that are privileged and protected by law have failed. In the context of such an investigation, the "hot-cargo" type of secondary boycott must definitely be characterized as economically coercive, especially as regards the employees of the primary employer. It is an instrument of reprisal.

Compulsory Unionism

There is one other form of economic coercion which must be mentioned here because of its widespread use and historical importance in the United States. That is the institution of "compulsory unionism."[13] Compulsory unionism means that an employee *must* be a union member and keep up his union membership if he wishes to be given a job or to be maintained in employment. It is the logical counterpart of the condition in which employees are compelled by an employer to *refuse* to join unions if they wish to secure or to maintain employment. If it is economically coercive for an employer to refuse employment to men who insist on joining unions, good sense and logic require that union insistence upon union membership as a condition of employment be likewise characterized as economically coercive. There is no basis of distinction, in fact or in theory. Indeed, insistence upon *non*unionism as a condition of employment is much easier to justify than compulsory unionism. For the employer who insists upon nonunionism is providing a job in return. But a union which makes union membership a condition of employment is usually offering no job in return; it agrees only to refrain from interfering with the relations between employers and employees.[14]

In the United States, compulsory unionism takes four different forms: the "closed shop," which means that a man may not secure employment unless he already belongs to a union; the "union shop," which permits an employer to hire a man before he belongs to a union but which compels the employee thereafter to join the union if he wishes to remain employed; "maintenance of membership," according to which no employee is compelled to join a union, but if he chooses to join is required to remain a member for the duration of the collective agreement; and finally, "preferential hiring," an arrangement whereby the employer agrees to give first preference in employment to union men. Under each of these conditions economic pressure of a more or less critical nature is exerted, compelling the employee to belong to a union if he wishes to work. Some economic coercion of employee choice exists in even the mildest form of compulsory unionism, maintenance of membership. In the most stringent forms, the closed shop and the union shop, the economic coercion is irresistible. If he wishes to work at the job in question, the employee must belong to the union.

Physical Coercion

Nothing has been said thus far of the second major category of coercive interference by unions in the exercise of free employee choice; that is, physical coercion. It will not do to neglect this category, however. For, while it is true that such coercion is always theoretically unlawful, many forms of physical coercion go unnoticed as such; and in regard to all forms, even the most evident, the law's methods of prevention and control have often been and still are to a large degree ineffective.

There is another extremely important reason for emphasizing the physically coercive aspects of union activities at this point. As a matter of history in the United States, the economically coercive activities have usually occurred in a context, immediate or more remote, of either outright violence or threats of such violence.[15] Unless this fact is emphasized and fully appreciated it is impossible properly to understand some of the most important trends in the development of the common law prior to the enactment of the modern labor relations legislation.

The overtones of violence in almost all union activities in earlier days induced some judges to view as unlawful many forms of union activity which, if viewed abstractly and in isolation, could be considered, and would be considered today, only economically coercive, not physically so. The point may perhaps be made most swiftly by noting that aspects of violence were present in three of the most famous and influential cases in American labor law history, cases which span the whole common-law period: the Cordwainers case, decided in 1806;[16] *Vegelahn* v. *Guntner*, decided in 1896;[17] and *American Steel Foundries* v. *Tri-City Central Trades Council*, decided by the Supreme Court of the United States in 1921.[18] An examination of the facts in these important decisions will demonstrate the role which violence has played in both labor activities and the development of the common law.[19] There is some reason to believe that, had there been no violence mixed with the union activities involved in those cases and in practically all the others heard by judges during the common-law period, the common law relating to economically coercive union activities would have developed in a manner largely similar to the common law concerning economically coercive activities by employers in regard to organization of their employees.

Proper appreciation of the common-law developments regarding union organizational activities requires familiarity with certain other factors. During the common-law period, employers were under no obligation to refrain from economically coercive interference in the organizational activities of their employees. Employers could recognize and deal with unions as they wished, or they could refuse to do so. On the other hand, there was no governmental mechanism by means of which a union representing a majority of employees in an appropriate bargaining unit could compel the employer to recognize it as exclusive bargaining representative of these employees. The principles of free employee choice and majority rule, it will be remembered, were not dominant in the common-law scheme of things.

In consequence, an employer was legally free to refuse to deal with a union representing a majority of his employees, and he was equally free to deal with a union representing none, or only a small minority, of his employees. There was, in short, only one way for a union to secure bargaining status from an employer unwilling to grant such status voluntarily: the union had to apply coercive pressures, physical or economic. It is probable that where a union actually represented a majority of employees, the simple straightforward strike for union recognition was most often utilized. Where the union did not represent enough employees to make such a strike effective, it could secure recognition only by means of the use of the physically and economically coercive methods which have been described here.

There are very few instances of courts ruling that simple, straightforward strikes for recognition by majority unions were unlawful during the common-law period. All common-law courts seem to have been agreed that employees could leave their work in concert where their objective was to secure better wages and working conditions, or recognition of their union as bargaining representative.[20]

*   *   *

The common-law situation was vastly different, however, as regards other methods utilized by unions to gain recognition. But it is necessary at this point to make some general observations about the common law. As known in the United States, the term "common law" means the system of judge-made rules (as contrasted to laws passed by the legislatures) in each of the forty-eight states. Owing to a certain reluctance on the part of the Supreme Court of the United States, our "common-law" system is really *uncommon*, since it lacks a common head, a supreme court, which would make the courts of the various states conform to a single set of common-law principles. Therefore it is somewhat misleading to refer to *a* "common law" relating to union organizational activities, or to anything else for that matter, in the United States. To be accurate, one must refer to the common law of a particular state.

In labor relations law it has been customary to use the developments in the federal courts and in the courts of the industrialized states, such as New York, Massachusetts, Pennsylvania, Ohio, New Jersey, Michigan, and Illinois, as a means of illustrating the so-called common law. It will be convenient for present purposes, although not completely accurate, to represent developments in New York and Massachusetts as the conflicting prototypes of the so-called common law concerning organizational activities by unions.

In speaking of current labor relations law, we shall be referring most frequently to the statutory norms established by the National Labor Relations Act, as amended by the Taft-Hartley Act, and the interpretations by the courts of those norms. However, it will be necessary upon occasion to refer also to decisions by state judges which have carried the development of the "common law" forward during the period of the comprehensive labor relations statutes.

Chapter 11

THE LAW GOVERNING UNION ORGANIZATIONAL METHODS

Common-law rules applied by state courts constitute an interesting and important part of the current law in the United States concerning union organizational methods; but that field of law is at present dominated by federal legislation. According to recent decisions of the United States Supreme Court, the states and their courts and legislatures may, generally speaking, regulate only those labor disputes which are strictly local in character; in other words, those which have no effect on interstate commerce.

In the integrated economy of the United States, practically all labor disputes have interstate effects; consequently, in the immediate present, the federal law is usually applicable, to the exclusion of state law.[1] Still, despite the current dominance of federal law, there are several reasons why it would be unwise to neglect state common law. Historically, the common law has been the most important source of rules governing union organizational activities. Moreover common-law attitudes and approaches have intimately affected federal legislative rules in the past, and continue to do so. Finally, considerable current dissatisfaction with the Supreme Court's views toward the powers of the states suggests that before long Congress may deliberately restore to the states the power to govern labor disputes which they have had so long. For all these reasons, it is desirable to include here a summary of the attitudes of state courts toward the principal organizational activities of labor unions.

Picketing

Picketing has always had an ambiguous legal status in the United States, and the situation is no different under current legislation. Owing to the inherent character of the principles which formed the basis of its operation, the common law could never declare that picketing, as such and in the abstract, was unlawful. It could only find that the specific example of picketing involved in the specific case under consideration was lawful or unlawful on the basis of consistency or conflict with general common-law principles. The Massachusetts view went as far as the common law could in outlawing picketing in the abstract; the New York view went as far as it could in legitimatizing picketing in the abstract. Current federal legislation makes no specific mention of picketing as such, leaving the control of that activity to depend upon its effects and purposes.

According to the Massachusetts view, picketing was unlawful and enjoinable because it possessed an inherently intimidatory quality.[2] Union men had a right to quit work in concert. Nonunion men had a right to continue work or to seek work vacated by union men. Employers had an inherent right to seek workers. These several rights could be given the effectiveness which the law required, according to the Massachusetts view, only if all aspects of intimidation and coercion were eliminated. In *Vegelahn* v. *Guntner*,[3] the Massachusetts court, over a dissenting opinion by Mr. Justice Holmes, found that in the context of a labor dispute, picketing has the effect of coercively interfering with the employer's right to seek workers and with the right of nonunion men to seek work. This famous decision was handed down, however, in a case in which there was evidence that the pickets had used some physical violence. The same is true of the United States Supreme Court's most notable decision on the subject of picketing, in which the Court ruled (strangely enough with the acquiescence of Mr. Justice Holmes, who had meanwhile moved from the Massachusetts to the United States Supreme Court) that all picketing had to be enjoined in the case then before the court because of its inherently coercive character.[4]

The Massachusetts view did not condemn picketing as a form of economic coercion. It held that picketing was physically or at least "morally" intimidatory. Thus the Massachusetts court and the other state courts which adopted its point of view were never called upon to take the additional logical step of condemning those acts of employers which might have been considered economically coercive. But it is certain that they would have held unlawful any employer activity which was physically intimidatory. In fact, the Massachusetts court went so far as to declare that employers could not in concert refuse to make employment available to workers who were interested in unionism.[5] In terms of principle, this decision represents an extremely important development and must be considered in evaluating the "objectivity" of the Massachusetts view toward picketing.

New York courts, seemingly entirely oblivious of the physically coercive aspects of picketing, took the position that this activity occupied the same legal status as a simple strike under the common law.[6] The New York courts recognized that picketing imposed substantial economic harm on the employer and nonunion employees; but they insisted that, in the absence of outright violence, this harm was no more unlawful than the type of harm which ordinary economic competition between businessmen created for the less successful competitors.[7] So, if a union picketed in order to compel the employer to recognize it as bargaining agent[8] or even to compel the employer to replace existing workers with union men, the New York courts held the picketing privileged.[9] When it was pointed out that picketing in the latter case destroyed the livelihood of nonunion men, the New York courts merely observed that such is often the consequence of economic competition. Aside from its insensitivity to the physically coercive aspects of picketing, the New York view may be considered as a reasonably logical application of laissez faire attitudes. The law did not at the time forbid economic coercion by employers; picketing was a form of economic coercion; hence, if the law was to be fairly applied, the courts could not forbid peaceful picketing.[10]

The important role which this logic played in the decisions of the New York courts is demonstrated by the facts involved in its abandonment. When positive legislation intervened to prohibit the use by employers of economic coercion in combating unionization, and imposed a duty upon employers to recognize and bargain with majority unions, the New York courts changed their attitude toward at least some types of "peaceful" picketing. At present, the New York courts are in the process of modifying the rules which they had formulated prior to the modern labor relations statutes.

The process is not yet complete. But as of this time, the New York courts are holding that a union may not even "peaceably" picket for recognition when another union has been certified by the government as the representative of a majority of employees in the bargaining unit involved. They have also held that a union may not picket for recognition at a time when there is a dispute as to whether that union represents a majority of the employees.[11] Only a relatively small logical step is necessary for the New York courts to hold that a union may never picket for a recognition at all, unless it is able to prove that it represents a majority of the employees. This culmination, if and when it occurs, will demonstrate an exceedingly interesting adaptation of common-law principles to paramount public policy as declared in legislation.[12]

As to the currently dominant legislative rules, the situation is extremely complicated. Federal law forbids a union to restrain or coerce employees in the exercise of their right to refrain from joining a union or participating in its concerted activities.[13] As already shown, a similar prohibition of employer coercion has been construed as making it unlawful for an employer to grant or deny any economic benefit, to discharge, or even to threaten to discharge, a man for joining a union. In short, the prohibition of coercion by employers has been construed as outlawing *all* forms of economic coercion.[14] The statute uses the same words to outlaw union coercion. Still the National Labor Relations Board has thus far refused to hold that those words mean the same in regard to unions as they do in regard to employers. It has held that peaceful picketing for organizational purposes, though undoubtedly a form of economic coercion, is not prohibited by the NLRA.[15] One important federal court has disagreed with this interpretation of the NLRA,[16] and other federal courts, including the Supreme Court,[17] have indirectly indicated that they are confused by the Board's refusal to apply the legislation consistently to both employers and unions.

Basically, this situation presents a political problem, not a legal one. Until very recently, the Board was composed of men appointed by a President who was out of sympathy with the law

governing union activity. It is really not surprising that such
men should have hesitated to condemn so commonly used an
organizing technique as picketing, even though a straightforward
application of the law would require such a result. Whether or
not the new members of the Board will reverse the decisions of
their predecessors in regard to picketing cannot be predicted with
any certainty, for it is still a political question, not a legal one.
So far as the law is concerned, there is no substantial doubt that
picketing violates the prohibition of coercion. Picketing threatens the livelihood of the workers of the picketed company, and
as such coerces them economically. As matters now stand under
the NLRA's prohibition of union coercion, a union agent may
not say to a nonunion man that he will lose his job unless he joins
the union,[18] yet the same union agent may establish a picket line
whose primary objective is to blockade the place of business and
thus cut off the worker's means of livelihood. It would seem that
the NLRB has been careful to preserve to unions the right to
continue using their most effective and most drastic form of
economic coercion.

The Board has not been very vigorous, either, in preventing
physical coercion. Of course, this agency does hold that physical coercion violates the law. But it insists that it has no power
to make unions pay for bodily harm inflicted upon employees
who are reluctant to join unions.[19] The fact that the law
expressly gives the NLRB complete power to order any remedy
which effectuates the national policy against union coercion of
employee free choice has been disregarded by this agency[20]—the
same agency, it may be noted, which has not hesitated to impose
every conceivable kind of order upon employers who have been
guilty of interfering with the free choice of employees.

In summary, it may be stated generally that most state courts
are inclined to go further than national authorities in holding
peaceful picketing for organizational or recognition purposes
unlawful. This is by no means to say that injunctions against
such picketing are readily and freely granted, even in the state
courts. It is only to say that in terms of principle, the logical
basis for such injunctions has been established in the common-
law jurisprudence of the states, and that one finds the state courts

ever more frequently following that logic to its natural conclusion.[21]

In the federal system, on the other hand, notwithstanding the explicit prohibition of union coercion, and notwithstanding the fact that picketing for organizational and recognition purposes is undoubtedly economically coercive, the stronger tendency is to hold such picketing privileged. As to the physical violence which sometimes accompanies picketing, the common remedy in the state system is an immediate injunction, which is often, when promptly issued, an effective remedy. The immediate injunction is rarely available in the federal system, however, and for that reason the reluctance of the NLRB to make unions pay for the physical harm they do is a factor of considerable importance.

The truth is that control of union coercion has been more effective in the state courts than it has been in the federal system. And it is this fact, not elegant arguments about federalism or philosophical disquisitions about the dominance of the federal government, that accounts for the current movement to oust the state courts of their historical jurisdiction in labor disputes.

Unfortunately for the national policy against union coercion, the Supreme Court has recently gone a long way toward eliminating the jurisdiction of the state courts over cases involving union coercion. It has held that state courts may control physical coercion by unions, but not economic coercion. There is neither a statutory nor a constitutional basis for this distinction; there is no legal or logical basis for it.[22]

Secondary Strikes and Boycotts

Historical and current trends in the law concerning secondary union action have many points in common with those concerning picketing for organizational and recognition purposes. As a matter of history, there was the same split of opinion among common-law judges concerning the legality of secondary union action;[23] and in terms of current law, there has been the same tendency among state courts toward prohibiting all secondary organizational action and the same tendency in the federal law toward condemning such action in principle but holding the most effective forms of secondary action to be privileged in actual practice.

The "Massachusetts view" imposed rigorous controls upon secondary union action. The basis for this control was, however, not the violence which figured in the picketing cases, but the common-law principles against monopolistic action in restraint of trade, against deliberate interference with advantageous commercial relations among third parties, and against the deliberate imposition of economic harm without justification.[24] The judges did not always make entirely clear which of these principles they were relying upon in holding secondary strikes and boycotts unlawful. But attention to the decisions will reveal that one or the other figured largely in the conclusions. The judges frequently called secondary strikes and blacklisting "combinations in restraint of trade," and for forty years such union activities were held in the federal system to be violations of the Sherman Anti-trust Act.[25] At other times, judges found "secondary boycotts" to be unlawful as "willful" or "malicious" inflictions of harm upon third parties who, according to legal theory, had a right to be protected against such damage.[26] The most general legal theory was the so-called prima-facie tort theory, according to which any deliberate infliction of economic harm upon a third party was unlawful unless justified.[27] This theory left with individual judges the responsibility and the power to determine when a legal justification existed. In the absence of legislative standards, the economic and social predilections of the judges controlled. Judges unsympathetic with unions naturally found justification relatively rarely; those sympathetic with unions found justification relatively frequently. The standard was subjective, and variable.

Massachusetts and other "conservative" judges found justification under this theory more rarely than New York and other "progressive" judges.[28] It has been fashionable in recent times to condemn the Massachusetts judges and to praise the New York judges.[29] But it would have been much more helpful had scholarship worked out a coherent rationale for the prima-facie tort theory, or had legislatures supplied an intelligible concept of justification for the guidance of the courts, as they later did in giving prominence to the principle of free employee choice. The law of labor relations suffers today mainly because of the reluctance of some authorities to accept the principle of employee free choice as the central principle of labor relations policy.[30]

After the Supreme Court held in 1940 that the federal Norris-LaGuardia Act cancelled the Sherman Act's prohibitions of secondary union action,[31] the only legal control against such action in the United States, until the enactment of the Taft-Hartley law in 1947 was that which existed in some state courts. And even in those courts, controls were notably minimized as a result of pro-union legislation in many states and certain "constitutional" doctrines of the United States Supreme Court.[32] In a very general way it is accurate to state that in the years between 1940 and 1947 legal restraints upon aggressive, economically coercive secondary union action were at a minimum in most states as well as in the federal system.[33] Consequent abuses, the war and its exigencies, conspicuous wastes of manpower as a result of union power and political favoritism—all these factors coincided during the immediate postwar period to produce a change in public sentiment toward unions. These factors, and others, also produced another thing: a preponderantly "conservative" Congress. At the same time, however, the Chief Executive of the nation was representative of the political and social sentiments which had prevailed during the preceding period. He was in a certain sense an anachronism.

The confusing consequence of the political situation was a statute unequivocally prohibiting every kind of secondary union action, but an administration of that statute which permitted the kinds of secondary organizational action which unions had historically found most effective.[34] Stated very generally, the statute declared unlawful every kind of inducement which unions might use, during a dispute with one employer or his employees, to make employees of some other employer refuse to perform services connected with the first employer. It is not necessary to trace here in detail the history of the methods used by the NLRB to modify the broad reach of this prohibition.[35] It will be sufficient to note that whereas the literal terms of the statute would prohibit every kind of union action except a strike called by a majority union against the employer with which it was primarily disputing, the NLRB tended to hold that only clear secondary strikes, or inducements to such strikes, were made unlawful. As a result, unions retained the privilege to continue to use the inducements to secondary action which had been most effective historically. Primary picketing was allowed, and blacklisting and "hot-cargo" contracts as well, although some modifications have been made recently in regard to the latter.

The character and distribution of American unionization being what it is, to permit these methods constituted in a practical sense encouragement of the use of the most efficacious forms of economic coercion of employee free choice. Few businesses in the United States can get along entirely without the services of trucking companies. The employees of the trucking companies belong for the most part to the Teamsters' Union. That union usually insists upon "hot-cargo" contracts, according to which its members may not be required to make deliveries to businesses which are involved in "labor disputes," even when a so-called labor dispute arises from the refusal of the employees to join a union. Having privileged both organizational picketing and "hot-cargo" contracts, the NLRB established the framework within which the truck drivers' union could lawfully exert enormous economic coercion against any group of employees who refused to join a union. It was necessary only to establish a picket at the place of business of those employees. The truck drivers' union, with its "hot-cargo" contracts would be privileged to isolate that business and ultimately to ruin it if the employees and their employer did not give in.[36] And all this drastic economic pressure was held privileged in spite of a statute whose central principle is the free, uncoerced choice of employees concerning unionization, and in spite of that statute's broad, unqualified prohibition of secondary labor pressures.

The Supreme Court of the United States has, on the whole, affirmed the NLRB's modification of the Taft-Hartley Act.[37] But the Court's more original and creative activity in guiding the national labor policy away from that declared by Congress has been of another kind, as already mentioned here. At the same time that the NLRB was refusing to apply the Congressionally declared policy against economic coercion and secondary action by unions, the state courts were doing their best to enforce that policy and to provide the immediate relief against union coercion that the NLRB withheld.[38] The unique contribution of the Supreme Court has been its holding in effect that the state courts may no longer take jurisdiction in labor cases involving interstate commerce.[39] The consequences of this recent ruling have not as yet been entirely clear. And the fact that a new political administration has changed the composition of the NLRB tends to create certain additional problems. But one consequence of the elimination of the jurisdiction of state courts is certain: the indispensable, immediate relief against union coercion which only the state courts have been able to afford in recent times is no longer forthcoming.[40]

Compulsory Unionism

Unlike the situation prevailing in regard to other coercive organizational activity, current federal law expressly provides that compulsory unionism is subject to state law.[41] This is not to say, however, that federal law is unconcerned with compulsory unionism. On the contrary, the closed shop, the most rigorous form of compulsory unionism, is prohibited by the Taft-Hartley Act, as is the preferential hiring of union members. Only union-shop contracts and those providing for maintenance of union membership for a limited period are permitted by the federal law. Furthermore, the type of union-shop contract permitted is substantially different from that which unions have traditionally sought.[42]

Historically, unions have sought a type of union-shop contract which would oblige the employer immediately to discharge any person who lost or was denied union membership for any reason whatsoever. Unions want employers to be obliged to discharge employees who are denied membership because they have refused to participate in strikes, because they are political opponents of the union leaders, because they are personal enemies of influential union officers, because they work too hard, because they are "communists," because they have been members of a rival union, and so on.[43] Current law has changed all this. It permits an employer to discharge, or a union to request the discharge of a person, pursuant to a union-shop contract *only* if that person has refused to pay uniform and nondiscriminatory membership fees and dues.[44] So, regardless of the personal relationships between employees and union leaders, they may be secure in their jobs as long as they continue to pay dues to the union. And if a union attempts to force an employer to discharge an employee who has continued to pay or to offer to pay his dues, the union violates the law.[45]

The plain intent of the law was to implement the national policy against economic coercion of employees by unions. This fact becomes clear when one realizes that, as a practical matter, the law does not really permit any compulsion of union membership, even under a union-shop contract. The law permits only the compulsion of the payment of union dues. For as long as the employee continues to pay dues, he may be secure in his job, even if he refuses to obey the orders of union leaders or is vocally and expressly against the policies of the union.[46] There are those who see in this legal structure an antipathy to unionization. But it is at least equally rational to characterize this phase of the law as being fundamentally concerned with implementing the principle of free employee choice which underlies so much of the current structure of labor relations law.

The important role of state law in this field is to be seen in the fact that by the express terms of national law the states are permitted to outlaw even those forms of compulsory unionism (that is, the union shop and maintenance of membership agreements) which continue to be permitted by the federal law.[47] Seventeen states have laws at present which unequivocally prohibit all kinds of compulsory unionism.[48] By and large, however, the industrially developed states continue to permit all forms of compulsory unionism, subject to certain complicated conditions. Such important states as California, New York, and New Jersey have shown a tendency to permit the closed shop only to unions which have liberal membership policies—unions, that is, which do not arbitrarily limit membership to white men, to sons of existing members, and so on.[49] But this tendency has neither gone very far nor produced any results worth noting.

Even though state law may permit the closed shop, it must be remembered that the federal condemnation of that form of compulsory unionism is controlling in businesses in interstate commerce. Certain paradoxical situations result. For example, in a state such as New York a single union may represent the employees of both interstate and local businesses. In regard to the interstate business, the union may not, under the applicable federal law, even ask an employer for the closed shop. But since the law of New York permits that institution, the union may seek to compel the local employer to agree to the closed shop. When one appreciates the fact that it is not always possible to tell in advance of litigation whether a business is subject to federal law, and that unions (like many other persons and groups) are often insensitive to such legal niceties, one understands why it is that the federal prohibition of the closed shop has not proved to be an extraordinarily effective one, except in states where all forms of compulsory unionism are prohibited.[50]

Thus, in regard to compulsory unionism as in the other forms of economic coercion which unions have traditionally used in their efforts to compel unwilling employees to become union members, there is a definite gap between policy and practice, between principle and action. Viewed abstractly, the national legal structure is coherently oriented in terms of free employee choice and the prohibition of all forms of physical and economic coercion by both unions and employers. The ban against economic coercion by employers is both coherently conceived and effectively prosecuted. But the same is not true of the prohibition of economic coercion by unions. As a matter of fact, the most effective union instruments of economic coercion have been left virtually unimpaired by the administration of the law. Unions are largely free under national law to use the coercive weapons of picketing and secondary boycotts as means of compelling employees to become union members. While national law prohibits the closed shop, the fact that this rigorous instrument of economic coercion is available to unions by law in the large industrial states, has had the effect of minimizing the effectiveness of the national law, at least in those states. On the other hand, the Supreme Court's refusal to permit the state courts to enforce the abstract national policy against coercive picketing and boycotting has created immunity for those activities, owing to the lack of vigorous practical enforcement of that policy on the national level.

Chapter 12

COLLECTIVE BARGAINING, THE LAW, AND THE FREE MARKET

Law in the United States today is not concerned as a general rule with establishing the exact wages and conditions of employment of the working population. In regard to the large number of workers whose wages and working conditions are established by means of direct negotiations between them and their employers, without the intervention of labor unions, the law is relevant, indeed, in only the same general and minimal rule-making way that it applies to all private contracts.

The role of the law is notably different, notably greater, however, in connection with collective bargaining, the process by means of which the wages and working conditions of more than fifteen million workers are directly established and those of an indeterminately larger number indirectly affected. Collective bargaining is a process governed at almost every stage, procedurally and substantively, by a code of laws which stops short only of establishing quantitatively exact wages and conditions of employment.

Law governs the manner in which employee representatives are selected, establishes procedures which unions and employers must follow in the actual process of negotiation, indicates permissible and prohibited subjects of collective bargaining. Perhaps most important of all, it regulates and defines the economic techniques available to and used by unions and employers as means of enforcing their respective bargaining positions. In a somewhat less detailed way, the law also defines the juridical status of the collective agreement and is even concerned, although on a very general level, with the manner in which collective agreements are administered by unions and employers.

Any legal structure can be effectively applied, intelligibly described, or fruitfully understood only in terms of the principles and social goals which determine its content. The more complicated legal structures are the most difficult to apply, to describe, or to understand; and largely for this reason it is both more difficult and more necessary to deal carefully with the principles and goals of a complicated legal structure.

Conceptual Confusion and the Shifting Framework

These observations have an especial significance in relation to the law governing the collective-bargaining process. For the truth seems to be, in some instances at least, that this single legal structure simultaneously houses principles and goals which are contradictory and conflicting. In its current form, the law governing collective bargaining reflects different political pressures and competing political, social, and economic concepts. To make things even more difficult the situation is fluid; rules change from year to year, if not from week to week. It is difficult at times to gauge the true import of a shift in the application of a rule; it may indicate merely a technical correction, but it may also be the surface manifestation of a profound and massive realignment of basic principle.

Examples come readily to mind. In amending the Wagner Act, the Taft-Hartley Act took supervisors out of the category of "employees" and may thereby have indicated a change in collective-bargaining policy, the complete significance of which has never yet been adequately evaluated. A recent decision of the Supreme Court of the United States concerning the degree to which an employer may resist union demands for participation in the disciplining or rewarding of employees surprised a number of scholars and induced others to begin to think in a substantially different way concerning the basic orientation of national policy toward collective bargaining.[1] With some frequency, at the present time, the National Labor Relations Board is handing down decisions which indicate views materially different from those of the preceding personnel.[2] The situation is fluid on all levels, legislative, judicial, and administrative; and the difficulty of evaluating basic principle and policy is accordingly heightened.

But the volatility of the present situation does not eliminate the necessity or desirability of examining basic principle. Its effect is, instead, to emphasize the need for examination of historical trends concurrently with the analysis of the competing principles and goals. If it is true, as someone has said, that current views affect our reading of the past, it can scarcely be less true that past events determine to a considerable extent both the present and the future.

The Market as the Ultimate Determinant

One very large idea must be re-emphasized at the outset, both because of the perspective it affords generally, and because of the aid it gives in evaluating specific, complex aspects of existing rules and policies governing the collective-bargaining process. With very limited and relatively unimportant exceptions, wages and working conditions are established, even under collective bargaining, on a market basis. Neither law nor executive fiat fixes the actual details of the labor contract; those details are established by the interplay of the individual goals and wishes of workers, unions, consumers, and enterprisers, representing the consumption, labor, and capital factors which make up a market. But although it is true that the law has not supplanted the market, it is equally true that the law has had a great deal to say about the way the market operates. The market controls, but who controls the market is another thing.

Few in the United States, responsible labor leaders least of all, wish to abandon the market determination of wages and working conditions. The fate of labor unions in Soviet Russia has created a strong tendency to believe that there is an enduring and independent role for labor unions only in a market economy; hence there is no strong desire among labor union leaders to substitute socialism for the private-enterprise system of organizing production. Furthermore, union leaders on the whole are opposed to compulsory arbitration, the other nonmarket method for determining worker income.

The realistic context of discussion, therefore, is the market determination of wages and other working conditions, and the relationship of law to collective bargaining in that context. A structure of law and governmental policy that is unintelligible upon any other basis yields to rational analysis and evaluation when examined in the light of market theory. For market theory, viewed in terms of both jurisprudential and economic principles, provides intelligible standards of measurement. And these standards render possible a logical, rational evaluation of law and policy.

The Free Market and the Hampered Market

There are two main conceptions of market theory prevailing in the United States, and in the world, today. One is the conception of the free market; the other is the conception of the state-controlled and administered market.[3] The free-market conception envisions interpersonal economic relationships proceeding largely on a basis of voluntary, individual negotiations between buyers and sellers of all commodities and services. It is erroneous to say, as so many have, that free-market thinking opposes and rejects all state action. On the contrary, the market itself is nothing if it is not a manner of acting within a sharply defined legal environment.

The right of private property is a legal right; and without this right, insuring to its possessor the faculty of controlling the material subjects of the right, a free market could not operate. The right to contract, to make binding exchanges of the things which one owns and controls in virtue of the legal right of private property, is in turn another legal right without which a free market is impossible. The right to live and act, to follow the normal pursuits of men, to seek work, to set a price on one's labor, to work, indeed to refuse to work under unsatisfactory conditions— these are all rights absolutely indispensable to the operation of a market. Needless to say, they are all juridical rights—rights which are only illusory or at best hypothetical except to the extent that the instruments of organized society embodied in the law and law-enforcement agencies protect them and punish their invaders. No market system can function properly without the aid of an agency intent upon extirpating, preventing, and punishing the use of brute force.

Far from opposing law and government, therefore, it is distinctly probable that free-market concepts created the idea and the actuality of the rule-making and law-enforcing nontotalitarian state. As Part I of this book was intended to demonstrate, the free-market concept is really only a technical term for the idea of liberal civilization. It is a restrained way of evoking the rights of man and personal freedom. It means that men shall be free to engage in normal, peaceable pursuits without fear of physical restraint from either their fellowmen or agents of the state.

The concept of the interventionist state differs precisely at this point. It would use the force embodied in the state and its agents to prevent some and redirect other peaceable human activities which the concept of the free market would insulate and immunize. The free-market concept is one which would permit all men to price their labor or their goods or services at whatever level pleases them. The interventionist concept would put some men in jail for asking prices above an arbitrarily determined level; would put other men in jail, or impose other types of penalities, for asking or giving prices below a certain level. It is the interventionist state which imposes maximum prices, rents, and interest rates, and which prescribes minimum rates for certain types of labor, agricultural products, and rail, motor, and steamship transport.

The free-market concept considers the act of pricing like other human acts and would, therefore, make it subject to similar legal rules. When a man states a price, he is voicing an opinion concerning the value of the commodity or the labor or the service which he is offering; and free-market thinking, aware of this important fact, would have the law treat price-opinions in the same way as other opinions. It would permit individuals or groups of individuals to have the same freedom in pricing their labor, their goods, or their services and in thinking or voicing political opinions. It says to any individual or any group: you are free to voice whatever opinion you wish or to set whatever price you wish, but you are not free to prevent any other individual or group from voicing other opinions or setting other prices. The free-market

concept produces both the right of free speech and the Sherman
Act.

It is necessary to note very carefully that this consequence is
neither accidental nor arbitrary, but the ineluctable result of a
logical application of the free-market concept. The concept itself
forbids one individual or group, whether private or governmental, to restrain the peaceful activity of others. The moment such
restraint is permitted, the free-market concept no longer prevails;
and the interventionist concept has taken its place.

The Free Market: More Sinned Against Than Sinning

Many have asserted that the market concept represents an impractical ideal, unsuited to modern life and to the necessary role
of government therein; and that interventionism is absolutely
necessary. It is said that the very goal of the free-market concept
—a free, secure, productive society—cannot be obtained within
the structure of law and government required by the concept;
and that, in consequence, interventionism is necessary if only to
achieve the admittedly attractive result. In an unhampered market, it is alleged, people are free to lie and to cheat and to sell
"harmful" things; wealth is progressively more unequally distributed; the rich get richer and the poor get poorer; the total
wealth of nations tends to decrease; and, worst of all, free-market
nations are subject to periodic economic crises with all the misery,
tragedy, and terrible human sorrow which they involve. The
state must intervene to eliminate the objective evils and to
minimize the inequities of the unhampered market economy.
The free-market concept is unrealistic, outmoded, irrelevant, irresponsible.

If our task here is to understand the free-market analysis, it is
necessary to examine these charges, for they contain some rather
strong statements. We have already dealt with some of these
allegations (in Chapter 5), but some others must be considered
at this point. Thus, it should be noted, in the first place, that
free-market ideas have never in the known history of man had
an opportunity to control completely the affairs in even one nation. This single fact must indicate that one cannot convincingly

attribute to the free-market economic and legal system all the evils which have occurred in the past.

Critics of the free market may have committed other equally significant errors. Their acquaintance with history has at times been superficial. Furthermore, they have very often not really understood the economic and legal theory which they have condemned. During the period of the maximum flourishing of the free-market concept and its attendant legal institutions, the wealth and the productivity of the largely free-market world has increased astonishingly; and social and economic distinctions among men, previously enormous and categorical, have begun to diminish. Absolute social distinctions have tended to disappear. The comforts of life, vastly improved, have tended to become more widespread. And wealth and honor have tended to go to the men who were most astute in the production and distribution of these comforts—not to men most astute in war and politics. Perhaps we should read the last fifty years of interventionism as partly the history of the politician and war-maker striking back at the man of commerce for his impudent assault on their medieval rank and privilege.

Free-market ideas do not privilege lying and cheating; they certainly do not reward them. Classical common law, not interventionism, created the legal prohibitions against fraud and misrepresentation. Market theory protects the right to voice opinions concerning either ideas or prices, not because it approves all ideas or prices, but because there is no way of testing their validity other than by exposing them to the free choice of the people. The market place of ideas is no more nor less indispensable than the market place of prices. It is only a less effective, less smoothly working market; people know much sooner in a free society whether a price-opinion is "right"; it takes longer for a "wrong" political opinion to be rejected and eliminated. Thus, market theory would approve the outlawing of both wrong prices and wrong political opinions if there were some objective, reliable, authoritative method of proving them wrong in the beginning and by legal methods, just as it outlawed fraud and misrepresentation. But there is no such thing as a true or a false price. Prices are opinions; they are either acceptable or unacceptable to the people. And there is no way of telling whether they are acceptable without a try. Political ideas and proposals are the same. They are neither true nor false; they are acceptable or unacceptable. Only experiment determines whether they are acceptable.

Market theory resists and exposes all fraud and falsehood. It differs with interventionism on this point in insisting that *all* frauds be prosecuted by the most effective available means. It declares that if fraudulent advertising by businessmen is to be prosecuted, so too, then, should the frauds of labor union leaders be prosecuted. Significantly enough, recent interventionism has created an elaborate mechanism for prosecuting merely deceptive advertising, while at the same time erecting a special privilege for picketing, an inherently fraudulent activity engaged in constantly by labor unions.

Free-market theory proceeds along the same lines in regard to harmful merchandise. If it can be proved that merchandise is harmful, its sale should be prohibited. The only doubts of free-market theory lie in the accuracy of the definition of harmful and in the practical possibilities of legal control. Prohibition of the manufacture and sale of alcoholic beverages is the classic case in point. Market theory says only that we should not make a fool of the law. Where there is doubt as to the harmful quality of merchandise, and where at the same time people strongly desire that merchandise, the law makes a mistake in forbidding it. There is nothing more important in civilization than respect for law and legal institutions. Persons who bend the law to silly, futile ends do a great deal of harm.

It is inaccurate to say that free-market theory passively stands by to permit the propagation of harmful things. For centuries men have been trying to reconcile the ideal and the practical, have been trying to solve the problem of freedom and control. Free-market thinking effects the reconciliation, provides the answer to this old problem. It teaches us to distinguish between what we as individuals subjectively consider harmful and what is inherently and objectively harmful; in either case it proposes the use of appropriate controls. It knows that the law is not the instrument to use in propagating and enforcing convictions which are only personal and subjective and not shared commonly by most members of a society. This is simple good sense, not the passive acquiescence in evil which it has sometimes been said to be. Only the naïve rush headlong into the enactment of laws and the creation of elaborate political controls on the basis of subjective notions of "right" and "wrong," "good" and "bad," "equity" and "inequity," "fair" and "unfair," "just" and "unjust."

More and more sensitive and intelligent persons are beginning to realize that the free-market concept has been maligned during the past fifty years. They are beginning to realize that it is inaccurate to say that free-market thinking favors the do-nothing state, inequality, social injustice, the rich, sharp business practice, exploitation of the consumer and the worker, and so on. A great many thinking persons would probably agree today in saying, with that great and eloquent leader of free-market thinking, Ludwig von Mises, that

Those fighting for free enterprise and free competition do not defend the interests of those rich today. They want a free hand left to unknown men who will be the entrepreneurs of tomorrow and whose ingenuity will make the life of coming generations more agreeable. They want the way left open to further economic improvements. They are the spokesmen of progress.[4]

But at the same time it is common to hear that the free market must be modified, if not abandoned, because of the recurrent, tragic, business depressions it inevitably produces. The answer of free-market analysis is that, not the free market, but the very methods used to thwart and to limit it are responsible for the recurrent depressions noted in societies which are largely free and industrialized. They show a significant correlation between depressions and state intervention in the market, between unemployment and state tampering with the wage structure. Free-market analysts make the logical point that you cannot blame a free market for a given consequence when important interventionist institutions are present and can be shown to bear a logical relationship with that consequence at the crucial time. They point to state policies tampering with interest rates, fiat money, tariffs, state-established or protected monopolies and cartels, subsidies, encouragement of interference by labor unions with the free working of the market—and ask whether it is sensible to blame the free market for consequences which ensue when the market has not been allowed to work in an unhampered way.

Their case is made in a convincing way by pointing out that, although the United States has experienced many so-called depressions, none was so tragic or so long as the one which government attempted to "cure" by a virtually complete abandonment of free-market principles. Before 1930, depressions in the United States were of relatively brief duration. Without significant governmental intervention, economic activity rebounded to reach new heights of production, consumer satisfaction, and, naturally, employment. But during the course of the depression of the 1930's, government used all the age-old interventionist measures and even created some new ones; yet the depression went on and on; the economy remained stagnant in 1939. The conclusion of free-market analysis is that interventionism, not the free market, creates depressions; and that interventionist measures only aggravate depressions, do not "cure" them.[5]

Labor relations and collective bargaining present a special case (an especially illuminating one) of the differences and the issues between the free market and the hampered one. In surveying the developments in the law concerning collective bargaining, we shall use the market principles developed by the common law as the point of departure. We shall thus operate within a context which will render the existing situation more intelligible; and it is to be hoped that the use of this method will even enable us to fix more precisely than would otherwise be possible the exact nature and character of the existing legal structure. By noting the body of rules which prevailed earlier, moreover, we may be able to grasp more realistically the character and scope of those which came later.

Chapter 13

COLLECTIVE BARGAINING IN THE GENERAL JURIDICAL STRUCTURE

The common law, tracing to a large extent to free-market thinking, is a system of general rules for governing relationships, economic and otherwise, involving individual natural persons and such artificial "persons" as corporations which have been given a legal identity by positive legislation. An unincorporated labor union had no legal identity and therefore could not be a party to a common-law action. It could not sue or be sued as an entity, in its formal name. Contracts between an employer and a labor union as such could have no legal reality; they could not be enforced in favor of or against the union.

It is accurate to say, in general, that labor unions had no existence as juridical entities in the pure common law.[1] This situation might easily have been changed if labor unions had chosen to incorporate, for nothing in the law prevented such incorporation. The probability is that union leaders refused to incorporate because they wished to avoid legal responsibility; there is no other satisfactory explanation for the refusal.[2] Existing state and federal legislation which establishes legal status for unincorporated labor unions is properly viewed as a positive effort to bring unions within the legal control which they have always avoided.[3]

The Common Law and Collective Bargaining

There were two factors at work in the common-law rule which accorded employers legal freedom to deal or not to deal with unions. In the first place a "contract" with a union under the common law would be a nullity—an arrangement lacking qualified legal parties as well as legal methods of enforcement. In the second place, the idea of compelling even two legal persons to enter into a contractual relationship had no place in the common-law scheme of things, a scheme which viewed such relationships as strictly voluntary. The common law never compelled one legal entity to bargain with another. For a common-law judge, therefore, it would have seemed idiotic to compel a legal person, the employer, to bargain with a legal nonentity.

It is something of a mistake, then, to speak of a common law concerning collective bargaining. The common law, because of its inherent character, could deal with the situations arising among employers, employees, and unions only in terms of its concepts concerning individual, voluntary action. The common law did not, however, prohibit or even discourage collective bargaining. It permitted employers to deal with employee representatives on a collective basis. It permitted employees to cease work in groups as a means of putting pressure on employers to deal on that basis. Still, since the accord reached between union and employer had no legal standing, it could confer no legal benefits and could create no legal duties as regards the individual employees, the union, or the employer. The employer could specify one rate of pay in the "collective agreement" and actually pay another; as far as the law was concerned, he could equally disregard any or all other features of the "agreement." So too, of course, could the union and the employees.

That far the common law went, and, as a practical matter, that is about as far as it could go so long as unions refused to acquire legal identity and so long as the legislative and administrative branches of government did nothing to facilitate the process of collective bargaining. Viewed in proper legal context and with an understanding of the nature of constitutional government in the United States, it becomes evident that the judiciary and the common law could not be held responsible for the situation in which the institution of collective bargaining found itself in the common-law period. Unions themselves, in refusing to incorporate, were primarily responsible for the vague and chaotic legal status of the collective agreement. One may certainly understand why unions refused to incorporate; it is in many ways more convenient to operate beyond the reach of the law. But then one who understands this point is scarcely likely to praise the law-evader or to support his criticisms of the law.

Collective Bargaining Under Interventionism: Planned Chaos

Unions were engaged, however, in a more subtle strategy. They wanted the advantages of legal status without its disadvantages. They wanted legal rights without legal duties. They wanted government's force used in labor relations and collective bargaining, but always on their side, and never in control of their activities. Interestingly enough, they were largely successful, for a time. During the triumph of interventionism in the 1930's, when the national government changed from a largely free-market state to a substantially interventionist state, the labor unions got almost exactly what they wanted: legal rights without any legal duties; power without responsibility.[4]

This result was reached through a complex series of ambiguous legal maneuvers. The interventionist legislation did not take the straightforward step of giving full legal status to labor unions, or of declaring collective agreements legally enforceable contracts. It declared, instead, that any union representing a majority of employees in an appropriate bargaining unit was the exclusive collective-bargaining representative of all employees in that unit for purposes related to wages, hours, and terms and conditions of employment.[5] All the language of democracy and majority rule were to be found in the Wagner Act. There was to be free choice by employees, and secret-ballot elections, and the right of individual employees to present their own grievances.[6] But the fact is, as we have already seen, that neither the law nor its administrators was greatly interested in preventing unions from coercing employee free choice.[7] The administration of the law was prejudiced against independent unions and in favor of unions affiliated with the AFL and the CIO.[8] While the law spoke in terms of majority rule, the administration encouraged unions which represented *no* employees to force employers to deal with them exclusively in establishing the wages and working conditions of those employees.[9]

The law compelled employers to bargain with majority unions, and it set up elaborate administrative machinery whose function it was, through standard election methods, to ascertain which union employees wanted. But all the while there was nothing in the law to prevent any union from exerting economic pressure to secure bargaining status, even though the government had already certified another union as bargaining representative.[10] It was as if the defeated candidate in a secret ballot election were to be authorized to oust his successful opponent by the use of one or another coercive measure. And at the same time, the Norris-LaGuardia Act specifically denied judges the power to prevent unrepresentative unions from exerting such coercive pressures.[11]

One other feature of the Norris-LaGuardia Act must be noted at this point. At common law, union agents were subject to the same rules of responsibility which applied to all other persons. Stated very generally, the common law rule declared that any person was responsible for acts which his agent committed within the scope of his authority. This common-law rule did not go very far in controlling unlawful union acts, largely because of the nonentity status of the union under the common law. Thus a union could not be compelled to pay out of its own treasury for unlawful acts committed by one of its officers.[12] Still, unions had a certain, qualified legal status under the federal Sherman Act, and had in a few instances been fined for the unlawful conduct of their officers.[13] While union funds had scarcely ever been reached by judges under the common law itself, equity courts had often, on the basis of the common-law rule of responsibility, extended to members of a union as a whole restraining orders based on the unlawful activities of certain officers and members.[14]

Even these crude and inadequate measures for imposing responsibility upon unions were erased by the Norris-LaGuardia Act.[15] It and similar legislation in most of the states declared that a union could be held responsible for acts of officers or members only upon proof that the union had ratified, authorized, or participated in the specific unlawful activities.[16] The more extended and more realistic rule of responsibility created by the common law and applied to all other persons and legal entities was thus specifically made inapplicable to labor unions.[17] A better example of the essential character of interventionist measures can probably not be found. This one had everything, special privilege and deviousness especially.

The situation seems on the whole to have been one of deliberately calculated legal chaos—a special kind of planned confusion in which strong affiliated unions had all the arms and all the immunities, and in which employers, employees, and independent unions were both unarmed and defenseless. Employers could not interfere in the formation of unions. When unions acquired even a semblance of majority status, the law forced employers to bargain with them. But if unions did not have majority status the law still protected them in using coercive methods to compel collective bargaining. Once written, a collective contract was worth little more than the paper it was written on, since there was no method of enforcing it. As far as interventionist legislation was concerned, there was no such thing as an unlawful union activity; furthermore, to the extent that some union activities were unlawful under the common law, the interventionist legislation made it virtually impossible to hold unions responsible for those unlawful acts. Nothing comes out perfectly in this world, but for a while unions got from law and government almost exactly what they wanted—legal rights without any legal duties or responsibilities.

Collective Bargaining and the Taft-Hartley Act: Order, Integrity, and Responsibility

We are now in a position to evaluate the historical and legal significance of the Taft Hartley Act, the legislation about which so many complaints have been registered. The Taft-Hartley Act gives unions a juridical status: it declares that unions may sue or be sued in their formal name,[18] applies to them the same rules of responsibility which bind all other persons or legal entities,[19] and declares that union treasuries may be made to pay damages resulting from some unlawful union acts.[20] On a historical basis, these measures can be accurately characterized only as progressive accomplishments vitally necessary to extend the rule of law.[21] They place no special burdens on labor unions. In the long view, they represent society's acceptance of unions. Union criticism of these measures may thus be properly thought of as a reflection of the traditional union reluctance to take a responsible position in society.

The Taft-Hartley Act declares that a properly executed collective agreement is a legally enforceable contract, for the violation of which both unions and employers are subject to damages and other legal remedies.[22] This, too, is a measure about which unions have complained long and vociferously. Their complaints acknowledge a fact the existence of which has long been plain: unions do not always take collective agreements seriously and wish to have them remain in the same ambiguous, nonlegal environment that used to prevail in relation to the status of unions. The complaints reflect again the long-run desire of union leaders to remain outside the law. And again the Taft-Hartley Act may properly be viewed, on a historical basis, as an attempt to extend the rule of law to the labor relations field and to its central institution, the collective contract.

The accuracy of these observations concerning the essential character of the Taft-Hartley Act is established by the fact that other, related features of the Act, whether viewed separately or together, all point to the same end: the acceptance of unionization, subject to relatively clear-cut rules of law. Thus the Act continues to provide the election machinery whereby agents of the government are enabled to ascertain the free choice of employees concerning union representation for collective-bargaining purposes.[23] But Taft-Hartley differs from the Wagner Act in that it is actually concerned with the free choice of employees. It declares that employee choice is to be as carefully respected when it is registered in favor of an independent union or no union at all as when it is registered in favor of a strong affiliated union. The special legal privileges and protection which the Wagner Act gave to strong affiliated unions have been removed.[24] There is no need here to explain the reasons for the complaints of the affiliated unions in this regard. But one cannot help pointing out that these complaints tend to prove that unions wish to renounce law only when it regulates their activities, not when it accords them special privileges.

The Taft-Hartley Act's concern with rationalizing collective bargaining and providing it a stable legal context is again displayed in the provision making it unlawful for one union to take aggressive, coercive action which is aimed at breaking down a legally established bargaining relationship between an employer and another union. Taft-Hartley makes it an unfair labor practice for a union to strike, picket, or boycott for recognition when another union has been certified as the exclusive bargaining representative in the appropriate bargaining unit.[25]

Unions once based their plea for interventionist legislation partly on the charge that the prevailing common-law situation was one of "jungle law." We have already referred to the chaos which existed under the interventionist legislation, where a legal certification of one union did not prevent another from inflicting all kinds of severe harm upon an employer who was intent only upon abiding by the certification.[26] In making it possible for courts to enjoin such union aggression, the Taft-Hartley Act seems to have been seriously intent upon replacing the law of the jungle with the law of civilization. Perhaps, after all is said and done, that is what some present union leaders are really angry about. The great union leaders of the future will view the Taft-Hartley Act more favorably, just as present business leaders praise the Sherman Act as the legal charter of a free business community, in spite of the criticism of their predecessors.

Chapter 14

COLLECTIVE BARGAINING, VIOLENT
UNION ACTION, AND THE LAW

To this point we have been dealing with the more abstract juridical framework of collective bargaining. We have noted a progression whose net result has been to bring within the rule of law the union as an entity, the concept of collective bargaining through employee representation, and the collective contract itself. Perhaps the most interesting and notable feature of this progression is the manner in which legislation in the United States, after an interlude of chaos, has succeeded in putting into effect legal institutions consistent in spirit with those of the common law and of the free market, but which the unaided common law found beyond its powers.

To say that the Taft-Hartley Act represents governmental action of a more interventionist nature than the Wagner Act, however, would be an error. Interventionism means the use of the state's force to create special privilege; it does not necessarily mean the mere existence of more law. As a matter of fact, it usually means less law and more special privilege. It means, in short, the type of situation which prevailed under the Wagner Act and the Norris-LaGuardia Act. The Taft-Hartley Act gives us more law, but only in the sense that a great institution actually existing in society (that is, unionism) has been made to adhere to the same rules of law which apply to other social institutions.

The Common-Law Background: An Accurate Perspective

The same general phenomenon is to be seen in the development of the law relating to the economic tactics used by unions; namely, strikes, picketing, and boycotts. At its most fully developed stage, the common law perfectly reflected free-market theory, holding it a right of all men to offer or to withhold their services, individually or in groups, on the basis of their own opinions or desires.[1] Beyond any question it is true that British statutes and court decisions up to and through the eighteenth century went pretty far in restricting collective labor action.[2] In the period in question there was some authority to the effect that any concerted activity by workers aimed at raising wages would be considered unlawful.[3] However, business activity was at least as rigorously regulated. Statutes and court decisions minutely controlled and defined all gainful activity during the Middle Ages,[4] and continued to do so until the strong, clear current of eighteenth and nineteenth century liberalism began to set men free.

Early English law may therefore not be characterized as having been discriminatorily restrictive of labor action only. Reflecting the relatively rigid security-concepts of the age, it was generally restrictive; everybody was supposed to live by the rule. Mercantilism was the dominant economic theory; free trade had not yet arrived.[5] James M. Landis, formerly Dean of the Harvard Law School, has put the matter in appropriate perspective:

> Secondary authorities uniformly concur in [the] view that the general crime of conspiracy embraced all the common collective activities of employees. Indeed, the conception that there was no such common law crime capable of making illegal the ordinary employee combination, seems not to have been seriously argued until in a later era, men sought a legal justification for their humanitarian impulses and a defense for their avowal of the desirability of trade unionism. The philosophical difficulty involved in the conclusion that ... two or more could not combine to do what each of them acting individually could lawfully do disturbed none of the judges during this period. Instead they reacted to the inevitable impulse of trying to protect their economic society against the thrust of collective action by both employers and employees, trying either to retain the earlier concept of governmental determination of wages and hours or the later assumption that as to these and other conditions of labor only individual bargaining was to be allowed. They perceived concretely enough the dangers to their traditional economy involved by any recognition of the legality of collective action and, in seeking for an appropriate legal instrument with which to avert that danger, naturally enough seized upon the convenient and flexible device of conspiracy. By making the legality of combination depend upon the test of "illegal purposes" or "unlawful means," they were enabled to mould a legal doctrine that

would [keep] . . . their civilization true to what they conceived to be its objectives.[6]

Eighteenth and nineteenth century liberalism, although born and bred in Great Britain, thrived better in America, perhaps, than anywhere else. Medieval institutions and status relationships had never acquired the grip upon society in the United States that they had in other countries.[7] The United States became a nation at just that point in history when liberalism was most vigorously stimulating the minds of men. It made greater progress here because there was less of mercantilism and statism, with their rigidifying tendencies, to slough off. One consequence is that the personal freedom of both businessmen and workers to enter into voluntary combinations occupied a generally more favorable position. It is indeed doubtful that, aside from carry-overs of older notions concerning "restraints of trade" in some state statutes,[8] the right of workers to combine and to take peaceful action in their own interest was ever seriously questioned in the United States. Labor organization was a constant feature of the nineteenth century. It increased and declined during various periods, but it was always overt, never institutionally clandestine.[9] These facts tend to suggest general acceptance of the right to organize in the United States. Those who contend that common law in the United States prohibited unions as criminal conspiracies must be at a loss to explain these phenomena.

Scholars taking the position that the common law of the United States prohibited labor organization as such usually cite a case dating back to 1806, the Cordwainers case.[10] But that case is defective in more ways than one. In the first place, it does not stand for the proposition for which it is so often cited. A careful examination of the case shows that union men were charged with using threats and violence in an effort to keep employers from hiring nonunion workers. One completely misunderstands the common law if he fails to keep carefully in mind the distinction between voluntary, peaceful strike-action aimed at raising wages, on the one hand, and physically coercive conduct aimed at preventing workers from offering their services, on the other. The former is action indispensable to the working of a free market and, therefore, privileged by the legal counterpart of market theory, the common law; while the latter action destroys the free market and is therefore prohibited by the common law. It is not at all surprising, accordingly, that the activities involved in the Cordwainers case were held unlawful. To hold otherwise would have been, in fact, to negate, not only the law of the free market, but civilization itself.

The second defect in the Cordwainers case, as cited, relates to the authority of the judge involved. Those contending that early common law in the United States condemned unions and concerted labor activities as such, usually quote the following language from the Cordwainers case: "A combination of workmen to raise their wages may be considered in a two-fold point of view; one is to benefit themselves . . . the other is to injure those who do not join their society. The rule of law condemns both." Now, as we have seen, the bare decision itself, viewed in the light of the facts of the case, may not be criticized on any basis; and if the judge had confined himself to a statement to the effect that violent interference with the market is unlawful, no one could have said very much about it. It is therefore the language used by the judge, not the decision itself, which is pointed to as symbolic of the unfairness and prejudice of the common law toward organized workers.

But for the mere language to carry any weight, it must be demonstrated that the judge in the Cordwainers case—known in history as Recorder Levi—was an authoritative representative of the common law. This, of course, no one has ever been able to do. Levi was a judge on the lowest level of the American judiciary, a municipal trial-court judge in Philadelphia.[11] To speak of a judge on that level as representative of a broad nationwide common-law view is unsound. It is far more sensible, far more accurate, to confine oneself, in searching for an indication of the broad common-law view of the United States during the nineteenth century to the known and accepted leaders among the common-law judges of the time.

When that is done, an entirely different conception of the common-law principles applicable to labor organization emerges. The Massachusetts Supreme Court was acknowledged to be the leading common-law court of the country during the nineteenth century; and of the many notable judges who sat on that court,

Chief Justice Shaw was regarded by many as the greatest and the most authoritative. In attempting to reconstruct the common law concerning union organization and concerted action by workers, it is more appropriate to examine Judge Shaw's opinions than those of a member of the lowest and least influential rank of the judiciary.

And when Judge Shaw's opinion in the most important labor case of the first half of the nineteenth century is examined, the case of *Commonwealth* v. *Hunt* (1842),[12] we find an unqualified acceptance of the right of workers to organize and to take peaceful, nonfraudulent concerted action in pursuit of their own legitimate economic interests. Judge Shaw even went so far as to say that organized workers might lawfully agree to refuse in concert to work for any employer who hired nonunion men. Of such concerted action, he said: "If it is to be carried into effect by fair or honorable and lawful means, it is, to say the least, innocent; if by falsehood or force, it may be stamped with the character of conspiracy."

The vast mass of authoritative judicial opinion from the second half of the nineteenth century establishes beyond any doubt the common law's acceptance of the right of workers to organize and to take peaceable, nonfraudulent, and noncoercive concerted action in pursuit of higher wages. The legal rules were largely those which a logical application of free-market principles would require. Employers had a right to free access to the labor market. All workers had a right to join or to refuse to join unions, to apply for work at wages satisfactory to themselves; to refuse to apply for work, or to cease work, individually or in concert, when wages were unsatisfactory. No one had the right to use fraud or force against others in the exercise of these various rights.[13]

So, where workers were dissatisfied with their wages, they had a common-law right to cease work in concert. But they violated the law if they used force or fraud to prevent other workers from seeking the jobs they vacated. For such forcible prevention negated the right of employers to seek other workers, and the right of other workers to seek employment.[14]

Trade-Union Violence: "Government by Injunction" Reconsidered

A true and accurate understanding of what our American judges were doing during the so-called common-law days is impossible without an understanding of the frequent, fundamentally lawless character of union action during that time. Anyone who takes the trouble of reading the reported cases carefully will find either outright violence or a menace of such violence so immediate and so overpowering as to create its virtual presence. A strike would be called. It might be aimed at an understandable, even laudable, purpose: higher wages, the elimination of ugly or dangerous working conditions, even perhaps to check a supervisory employee whose conduct was as detrimental to the interests of the employer as it was damaging to the honest and praiseworthy instincts of the workers. The strike might also have less attractive ends: it might be designed to force the employer to pay higher wages when he simply could not afford to do so without cutting down employment or going out of business; or it might be designed to get for the members of one union the jobs held by members of another union or by employees who belonged to no union.

In the vast majority of the cases, the courts were not preoccupied with the strikes themselves or even with their objectives. This was certainly true if a strike was aimed at higher wages or the improvement of working conditions. Such strikes were universally held lawful and unenjoinable. This rule was so well established that petitions for relief filed by employers rarely, if ever, asked that the strike itself be enjoined, or that the court order the strikers to return to work.[15]

Once this fact is appreciated it is possible properly to evaluate the character of the outcry by unions and their apologists against the so-called government by injunction which allegedly prevailed during common-law days in the United States. These complaints were so misleadingly phrased as to induce many to believe that the courts were preventing workers from striking against low wages and bad working conditions.

But nothing could be further from the truth.[16] The judges were not concerned about the strikes; they were concerned about the violent, militant activities which unions used in connection with such strikes. "At the beginning of the present strike the pickets had large tents at important points of ingress to the company's property, and were accustomed to assemble there, especially in the night time, in large numbers. I became convinced from the evidence that such tents, or the assembling of large numbers at or near the company's property was a serious intimidation to workmen going about the yards in the necessary performance of their duties."[17] This is a statement, not by an "anti-labor" judge, but by Federal District Judge Amidon, whose opinions in labor disputes have frequently been cited favorably by labor union leaders and their apologists. The descriptions fits any number of labor cases during the nineteenth century, and it fits a large number of those which occur in the United States today.[18]

Of course any sensitive person can understand and appreciate the point of view of the organized workers. In an attempt to improve their economic position, they strike; but if production continues during the strike, if the employer is able to hire replacements, if substantial numbers of their fellow-workers stay on the job, the strike is likely to be unsuccessful; and the strikers themselves may in the end even lose the jobs they previously held. Strong emotions are likely to be aroused; they are in fact aroused.[19]

Then, too, it is necessary to understand something about the character of private mass action, especially in earlier days in the United States when police control was even more inadequate than it is today. There is, in short, something of a tradition of mob violence in the United States. We know well the phrase, "take the law in our own hands." There is the "posse," the Ku Klux Klan, the vigilantes. The story is told fully and well in the excellent novel, *The Ox-Bow Incident*. When high feeling is shared among a number of men, when police control is slight, when there is a tradition of mob law, violence is to be expected. And all this applies in labor disputes as well as anywhere else.

The Role of the Law in Labor Disputes

Now the job of the law in labor disputes is not to take sides; nor is it, in a free economy, to say that the economic merits of any particular dispute lie with the organized workers, the unorganized workers, or the employer. Its job is simply to provide the civilized framework within which all the interested parties can peaceably exercise their established legal rights. The law's job is to secure the right of the organized workers to leave their jobs if they wish, the right of other workers to continue working or to seek work if they wish, and the right of the employer to continue operations by all peaceable and lawful means.

Some will attack this statement by declaring that it presumes the answer and that it hides the real problem. They will say that the real problem concerns the degree to which the law should privilege organized concerted activity which goes beyond a simple strike. There is some merit in this suggestion; it does state the real problem which we face today. Yet the previous formulation of the role of the law contains the answer to this problem when the inner realities of labor disputes are properly understood. For the point is that, all social, psychological, and historical factors considered, the law cannot adequately insure the peaceable solution of the economic problems which cause labor disputes, consistently with the basic rights of all the parties concerned, unless it eliminates the conditions within which intimidation and violence may be expected to occur.

In order to preserve all the basic legal rights, in short, the law simply must, by precluding the occasion and the context of intimidation, confine organized workers to the basic right to strike. To permit strikers to congregate at the scene of the labor dispute is to invite violence.[20] A proper understanding of the psychological realities involved can lead to no other conclusion. And that is why so many common-law judges felt they had to enjoin all picketing, all congregation at the scene of a labor dispute. That is what Federal District Judge McPherson meant when, in reviewing the evidence of one case, he said: "At times the paths and walks are obstructed. At times the pickets are near by, making grimaces, and at times acting as if violence were intended, and at times uttering profanity and vulgarity. There is and can

BARGAINING AND VIOLENT UNION ACTION   197

be no such thing as peaceful picketing, any more than there can be chaste vulgarity, or peaceful mobbing, or lawful lynching."[21]

This was the voice and the conclusion not only of good sense and sound psychology. It was something even more important than those admirable qualities: it signified the intelligent and courageous acceptance by the law of its share of the responsibility for preserving civilization. Courts have not always been so courageous or so intelligent.

It is irrelevant to assert that sometimes employers are responsible for the violence which occurs in labor disputes. Employers or their agents may at times have committed the particular act which precipitated violence, but the fact is that had there been no congregation of union men, aimed at interfering with production, there would have been no occasion for any incident of any kind. Another perceptive judge, Judge Henshaw, said many years ago (1909):

> A picket in its very nature tends to accomplish, and is designed to accomplish these very things [riots and disturbances of the peace]. It tends and is designed by physical intimidation, to deter other men from seeking employment in the places vacated by the strikers. It tends and is designed to drive business away from the boycotted place, not by the legitimate methods of persuasion, but the illegitimate means of physical intimidation and fear. Crowds naturally collect, disturbances of the peace are always imminent and of frequent occurrence.[22]

Regardless, then, of which party may be responsible in a particular case for the act of provocation, a sensible, acute legal structure will aim at eliminating the conditions which make violence virtually inevitable. When union leaders object to injunctions forbidding all picketing, they are really insisting upon the special privilege to intimidate others. They have been extraordinarily successful.

Many common-law judges did their best to eliminate all picketing and other forms of congregation, or at least to limit severely the numbers of the participants in such activities. Other judges, especially in New York, seemed curiously insensitive to the facts of life so apparent to some—perhaps because they were more than normally sensitive to the realities of politics and the obvious political appeal of unionism. In 1953 for example, a

New York judge thought he was doing his duty in "limiting" the number of pickets in a busy Manhattan area to 200![23]

The Problem of Union Violence in Current Context

The common law and the judicial process are, more than likely, essentially inadequate by themselves to the role of policing labor disputes. Picketing and other forms of congregation at the scene of a labor dispute must be expressly prohibited by legislation; and the legislation must be so clear and unequivocal as to be readily and effectively enforced by police methods. For the job of the law, if it is to serve its purpose in society, is to prevent such inflammatory conduct, not to punish it later, which is the only thing judges can do. Unless picketing is enjoined, a labor dispute is never satisfactorily resolved. For the free market is the only satisfactory social technique for the resolution of economic disputes, and the purpose and effect of picketing are to destroy the free market.

These facts and desiderata, too, were appreciated long ago, by policy makers in some states anyway; and there has actually been state legislation directly and expressly prohibiting all picketing. But the fate of that legislation represents another triumph in the historical search of unionism for special privilege, and another episode in the recent history of the Supreme Court's cooperation with unionism in the achievement of that goal. Finding it impossible to prevent the states from prohibiting picketing in any other way, the Supreme Court declared in effect, in one case, that picketing is a form of freedom of speech and as such not constitutionally subject to previous restraint by either state judicial or state legislative action.[24]

This astounding identification of picketing and speech was not, of course, plainly and directly expressed; the Supreme Court is not always audacious.[25] Nor did the identification survive very long; the Supreme Court is not always stubborn, either.[26] But the fact is, to this day, that no state has repeated the outright prohibition of congregation at the scene of a labor dispute, which the Supreme Court once held unconstitutional. This hesitancy does not trace to a universally shared conviction in favor of picketing. On the contrary. Since the Supreme Court has given ground on the picketing–free-speech theory, state after state has outlawed one or another form of picketing. The hesitancy, at least in those states where it is politically feasible to outlaw all picketing, is probably owing to existing doubts as to just how much picketing the Court will allow the states to prohibit.

The picketing–free-speech doctrine undoubtedly also influenced the manner in which the Congress dealt, in the Taft-Hartley Act, with picketing and the violence factor generally. The term "picketing" is nowhere used in the Taft-Hartley Act, although it is evident from the general structure of the legislation, and from other things, that the Congress was greatly preoccupied with the problem of labor violence and intimidation. The Act specifically declares that workers have a right to refrain from joining in the concerted activities of unions.[27] In declaring this right, Congress was manifestly concerned with the problem of the worker who refuses to join in a strike—the worker who wishes to continue on his job or who wishes to apply for work vacated by strikers.[28] Thus, the Act goes on to provide that it is unlawful for a union or its agents to restrain or coerce workers in the exercise of their right to refrain from concerted action. Now, when it is remembered that the national labor law has always permitted employers to replace strikers with other employees, it will be seen that the Taft-Hartley Act must have been intent upon re-establishing the conditions within which a free labor market could prevail during labor disputes. Considered together, all these measures evoke the common-law and free-market structure which has just been sketched here: with organized workers having a right to strike, other workers having a right to seek work or to continue working during the strike, and with employers having a right of access to a free and peaceable labor market.

The inescapable logic of this set of rules, expressly set forth for the first time in legislation, clearly called for either an express prohibition of picketing or a limitation of that activity so narrow and so precise as to eliminate any possibility of the restraint and coercion which the Act prohibited—for example, say, a limitation of only one union observer at the scene of a legitimate economic labor dispute.[29] Of course no one can be absolutely certain of the reason for Congress's failure to pursue its own logic to that extent; but, everything considered, the probability is that Congress was discouraged by the uncertainty which prevailed concerning the degree to which the Supreme Court would apply such fragments of the picketing–free-speech doctrine as still remained in 1947. Probably as a result of that uncertainty, Congress limited itself to outlawing union restraint or coercion only in general terms.

It is entirely possible that Congress intended this general prohibition to cover all picketing. Congress might have hoped that the National Labor Relations Board and the courts would find most picketing coercive, as common-law courts had done. But, if this hope was actually held, it was to be disappointed. Far from condemning picketing generally as restraint or coercion, the members of the NLRB (appointed by a President vehemently opposed to regulation of union conduct) took the position that no matter how clearly the Act prohibited union restraint or coercion, it could not have been intended to prohibit picketing. Thus, this agency never issued an order against picketing associated with a primary strike, even when it occurred in numbers so great as to constitute an obvious menace. The furthest it went in implementing the clear Congressional ban on union restraint or coercion was to issue cease-and-desist orders against specific threats or actual acts of violence. It even refused to make unions pay, in money, for the wages which workers lost as a result of physical harm or intimidation by unions during the course of strikes and other labor disputes.[30]

This general situation continues to prevail, even though the composition of the NLRB has been changed, and it is therefore evident that the national law's prohibition of union restraint and coercion is as a practical matter meaningless. A mere cease-and-desist order, after violence has been done, does not even discourage, let alone prevent, violent interference by unions in the operation of the labor market. It goes without saying that if an employer should by similarly coercive means force union men to refrain from joining unions or participating in concerted union activity, the NLRB would make him pay for such conduct. The Act provides in exactly the same terms for remedies against unlawful conduct by both unions and employers, but the NRLB makes only employers pay.[31]

The situation, then, in regard to violent interference by unions, is this: unions continue to have today, despite the existence of clear legislative prohibition, a special privilege under national law to engage in violence. Only in those relatively few states where courts are quick to perceive the realities involved in picketing and other menacing union action does the labor market have the possibility of working in any kind of a free and peaceable environment. Everywhere the picketing–free-speech doctrine and other special privilege are operative to hamper or to preclude entirely a clear-cut and definitive elimination of union violence and coercion.

Chapter 15

COLLECTIVE BARGAINING AND NONVIOLENT UNION ACTION

The historical quest of unions for special economic advantage has not been confined to efforts to interfere by violent methods in the free operation of the market. It has been implemented also by nonviolent, monopolistic, economically coercive methods, by legal maneuvers aimed at placing employers in a position more readily vulnerable to union demands, and by devices designed to bring to the aid of unions involved in economic controversies the prestige and influence of political forces. We have already seen how difficult it has been for the law merely to bring unions within the juridical structure and effectively to control their violent interferences in the operation of the market. The law's attempts to control the more subtle economic and political efforts have been even more awkward and confusing.

Monopolistic and Economically Coercive Union Methods

While it was relatively simple for common-law judges to perceive, at least in principle, that organized society could not afford to tolerate violent union action, the problems posed by monopolistic and other economically coercive interference by unions with the free market were much more difficult and produced conflicts in principle as well as in practice. Some courts held that any action which went beyond peaceable direct strike action—for example, picketing and secondary boycotts—should be condemned as monopolistic coercion in restraint of trade.[1] But others held such action privileged.[2] And still others took intermediate positions in regard to the tactics which unions use in enforcing or strengthening their bargaining positions.[3] An indication of the confusion may be conveyed by noting that while practically all courts condemned the "secondary boycott" as unlawful, there was no universally accepted definition of this tactic. An act held unlawful in one state as a secondary boycott might be held lawful in another state on the theory that it was *not* a secondary boycott.[4]

Similar confusion existed in regard to the substantive purposes of collective labor action. All courts agreed that a strike for higher wages or a direct improvement in working conditions was completely lawful. But while one court might hold a strike for the closed shop unlawful, another court might hold such a strike and its objective lawful.[5]

There was obviously a need for a unifying factor, and, as we are told by Professor Crosskey in his recent great work on the Constitution, the national government had been designed precisely to serve that function.[6] However, doctrines created by the Supreme Court made unification and uniformity impossible.[7] The Court held itself to be without power to control common-law developments in the states,[8] and it held for a long time that Congress lacked power to legislate in the field of labor relations.[9] If it is necessary to have a "villain in the piece," the role belongs to the Supreme Court.

The role certainly does not belong, historically or theoretically, to the Constitution of the United States or to the common law. And free-market theory, the villain chosen by the historical version which has been orthodox for the last twenty or thirty years, fits the role least of all. Free-market theory calls for a uniform rule of law prevailing throughout every economic unit. For it is only in such circumstances that economic activity distributes itself effectively and rationally. In a system of conflicting laws, the distribution of economic activity may be influenced as much by the laws as it is by the more objective considerations of productivity and efficiency. In a very real sense, therefore, the confusion in the law hampered the market, and the effective distribution of productive activity, in much the way that most interventionist measures do. Hence it is a mistake to say that the confused status of the common law, even though it may have worked out in some instances to prevent labor union interference with the free market, was a situation tracing essentially to free-market thinking. It was a situation calling for a political remedy, a coherent national legal structure.

The first national statute applicable to concerted labor activities was the Sherman Anti-trust Act.[10] This law was addressed not to labor activities specifically but to all monopolistic interferences with the market, whether by businessmen or labor unions, which affected interstate commerce. During the period of its applicability to labor action—roughly 1890 to 1930—the Sherman Act was held to prohibit, by and large, only various types of secondary union action, or combinations between unions and employers designed to eliminate business competition in interstate markets.[11] In one famous case there was an implication to the effect that even a primary strike might be held unlawful where it affected an entire field of production, an entire industry, and was intended to affect the market price of the product of that industry.[12] But this implication, as significant as it is in terms of present problems of industry-wide strikes, never became a fixed part of the law of the Sherman Act and was, in fact, expressly abandoned by the Supreme Court at a later date.[13]

On the whole, then, the national law under the Sherman Act broadly resembled the common law as regards acceptance of the basic right of self-organization and the right to strike. In going further to outlaw secondary boycotts and combinations in restraint of trade, the Sherman Act was similar to one of the competing branches of the common law. This branch may be called, for lack of a better term, the antimonopolistic one, or the free-market branch, since it was concerned with eliminating monopolistic and coercive interferences in the working of the market.

During the period in which the Sherman Act was applicable to labor activities, the Supreme Court's narrow conception of the scope of the national commerce power made the law, despite the importance of the principles it reflected, relatively unimportant in terms of any real limitations upon monopolistic union action. And when the Supreme Court's conception of the scope of the national commerce power expanded during the decade 1930–1940, the Sherman Act's applicability to labor union conduct was largely erased.[14] In its place were substituted those laws and judicial doctrines—mainly the Norris-LaGuardia Act and the picketing–free-speech doctrine–whose aim and effect were to put in a specially privileged position the monopolistic and economically coercive union action which one version of the common law and which the Sherman Act had held unlawful.[15]

The decade 1930–1940 was the period in which union leaders secured almost everything they had so long been seeking: a favorable climate of opinion; a national administration anxious to please and many state administrations similarly obsequious; laws which forbade employers to interpose any effective resistance to unionization but which at the same time permitted unions to engage in all kinds of strike and boycott activity. Some resistance remained in a few state courts and legislatures, it is true.[16] But widespread labor violence, the success of sit-down strikes, and the phenomenal growth in union power and prestige, all suggest that such resistance as existed was minimal and unimportant.

Beginning in 1940 and culminating in 1947 there began, as already noted, first among the states and finally in the national government, a movement in the direction of removing the special privileges. States began applying their own antimonopoly laws in an effort to control secondary boycotts.[17] The national government, in the Taft-Hartley Act, made a more comprehensive effort to remove all the special privileges which unions had enjoyed during the preceding years.

We have already discussed the Taft-Hartley measures designed to control union coercion of free employee choice and to bring unions within the juridical structure. We deal at this point with that law's rules concerning monopolistic labor union action during economic disputes.

Those rules can be adequately understood only in terms of free-market principles; for it is fairly evident, from analysis of the Act as a whole, that its aim was to eliminate all monopolistic, economically coercive trade-union interference in the operation of the market. In the first place, the Act absolutely forbids the closed shop, that institution which serves double duty as a means not only of coercing free employee choice, but also of tightly controlling the labor market. In terms of the present discussion, the prohibition of the closed shop is properly viewed as an endeavor to free the labor market of the monopolistic control of labor unions. Of course, labor unions and their agents and apologists object strenuously to this measure. But that is to be expected; monopolists do not usually take kindly to measures which deny their privileges.

The influence of free-market thinking is seen equally clearly in what are perhaps the most important measures of the Taft-Hartley Act: those defining the types of concerted labor union activity which are privileged and those which are forbidden. The law expressly privileges a direct strike called by a union representing a majority of employees against the employer with whom the union is primarily disputing.[18] Either expressly or by clear implication it prohibits every other kind of strike, boycott, or inducement to strike or boycott.

This prohibition is expressed in general terms. The Act nowhere uses the specific terms "picketing" or "secondary boycott." The legislators undoubtedly intended to avoid the confusion and ambiguity in which history has clothed those terms. But it will be seen from a careful reading of Section 8(b)(4) of the law that no union may call a strike, or induce employees to engage in any kind of a concerted refusal to work, where an object of such action is to make any person (including an employer) cease doing business with any other employer. Such language obviously prohibits every type of secondary strike and every type of inducement to secondary-strike action, including inducement by means of picketing.[19] But it goes much further. It also forbids, in general terms, even a primary strike; for *an* object of every strike is to cause a businessman to cease dealing with other persons.[20] It is impermissible, however, to apply these terms literally against all strikes; for, as already mentioned, there is in the Act a provision expressly preserving the right to strike.[21] Such being the case, standard rules of statutory interpretation require that the specific provision be given effect. And the effect to be given to the provision specifically declaring the right to strike is indicated by still another provision of the law. Significantly, this other provision is located at the end of Section 8(b)(4)—the very section which, literally read, would outlaw all strikes. It rather clearly, though not expressly, establishes a special privilege for strikes called by a majority union against the employer with whom it is disputing.

Current interpretation of the Taft-Hartley Act does not, on the whole, agree entirely with this analysis. While holding that the Act forbids all secondary strikes and "secondary boycotts," whatever they may be, the weight of current opinion is that the law does not prohibit minority strikes and even minority picketing in certain important situations.[22] This current interpretation, it is admitted by the very persons and authorities who most strongly support it, does not apply the terms of the Act literally. Nevertheless, they insist, it is consistent with the legislative intent. When they say "legislative intent," they mean, apparently, what they think the legislature should have intended or must have intended. They obviously do not mean the legislative intent as expressed in the legislation; for they admit that their interpretation is not based on the natural meaning of the words which all the members of the legislature voted upon in registering their intent.[23]

One of the most serious consequences of the currently prevailing misinterpretation of the Taft-Hartley Act is that it disguises what would otherwise seem obviously to be the aim of the law, namely, to apply and to implement the free-market concept toward which the common law was aiming: to establish the right to strike but to prohibit all other interference in the free operation of the market. Any kind of combined concerted action going beyond the simple strike and peaceable persuasion, according to market theory, represents coercive restraint and amounts to a combination in restraint of trade, if not to clearly monopolistic interference in the market. One union has the right to withhold its labor in a dispute with an employer; but when it enlists the aid of another union or another employer against the primary employer, the latter is being made the victim of a market-manipulating operation. That is what the principles of the free-market concept suggest, and, except for the current misinterpretations to the contrary, that is the kind of conduct which the Taft-Hartley Act seems to have attempted to forbid.

Political Intervention in Collective Bargaining

The problem in labor relations which receives the most attention, and which is probably uppermost in the minds of the people of the United States today, is that which arises when a union calls a strike against all or most of the companies involved in a basic industry, such as coal, steel, railroads, or steamship lines. The effects of such a strike are rather drastic and are felt relatively soon; and one can therefore readily understand why they receive such widespread attention, even though there may be some ground for believing that other problems in labor relations are more important in many ways.[24]

There is a sense, however, in which the industry-wide strike is of the most profound importance. The existence of such strikes, with the overwhelming economic power which they demonstrate and the incredibly complicated damage they can do, compels rethinking on the most basic levels concerning labor-relations policy. While few students in the field have been induced by such strikes to go so far as to challenge the wisdom of the policy of establishing the basic right of self-organization or the basic right to strike, some have begun wondering whether it is wise to give those rights any positive legal protection. This line of thought ends in a reconsideration of the advisability of the features of the current law which prohibit employers from interposing economic resistance to the organization of their employees. It suggests that perhaps employers should be allowed to combat unionization with all the legal means which used to be at their disposal prior to such legislation as the Wagner Act.

Another approach to the problem would preserve the basic protections afforded by the Wagner Act, but would establish an arbitrary limit on the collective-bargaining process or would restrict the magnitude of strikes. It would declare, for example, that no single union could bargain *for* more than a limited number of employees or *with* more than a limited number of employers, and that bargaining strikes be limited accordingly.[25] The trouble with this approach is that it is fundamentally interventionist in nature and thus creates all the kinds of problems which are normally to be expected from interventionist measures. Whatever bargaining area might be defined, it would be fundamentally arbitrary in relation to the natural developments in union organization and collective bargaining. It would probably be impossible to set forth legislative rules clearly enough for application by the regular courts in traditional forms of litigation.

In the end, legislation would have to be vague, and a large degree of administration, rather than pure adjudication, would be necessary. The result would be the same as that usually to be expected from administration rather than adjudication: politics rather than law would dominate.

Probably for these reasons, liberals take the position that the problem should be treated indirectly and entirely in terms of clear-cut rules of law. They point out that industry-wide strikes are not nearly so grave and important as they are sometimes said to be. What they actually mean is that there is no overwhelming need of immediate, drastic, arbitrary action. The sensible approach, they insist, is to adhere to the basic elements of labor-relations policy which have naturally evolved consistently with traditional liberal principles: let employee organization develop as naturally as possible in as completely noncoercive an environment as possible, with both unions and employers subject to clear-cut and effectively enforced rules prohibiting all forms of coercion. The fundamental assumption of this point of view is that in a completely uncoerced environment the natural checks and balances of a market economy will keep collective bargaining and strikes within socially desirable limits, will preserve intact the basic liberal principles accepting the right of self-organization and the right to strike, and will permit unions to grow and mature gradually and naturally into their important role in a free-market economy.

A good deal of thought is being given by some people who are basically influenced along these lines to approaches which follow the pattern of the present legislation. The present legislation is based on no perceptible principle other than that of postponement. Fundamentally, beneath all the complicated language, the Taft-Hartley Act declares simply that any strike which, in the opinion of the President, affects the public health and safety because of its nation-wide effects, may be enjoined for a period of eighty days.[26] During this period the law obliges the parties to continue bargaining, and commands the mediation machinery of state and national governments to extend itself in the search for a solution of the dispute. A goodly number of variants of this approach have been proposed; but, aside from the time and effort involved in excogitating these variants and the labor and materials expended in publishing them, they provide little of interest. There is, of course, much to be said for the principle of postponement. In some instances, time is all that is necessary in order to reach an agreement; and if the losses caused by strikes to union, workers, employer, and the public can be avoided, so much the better. But that is about all that can be said about it.

Much more can be said about a competing plan, which would eliminate the eighty-day injunction, leaving the union free to strike at will, and at the same time authorizing the government to seize the businesses involved, confiscate profits or some part of them, and restore the businesses to their owners only after the dispute is settled and an agreement between the union and the employers reached. By and large the forces behind such proposals are the interventionists—union leaders and some academic people—who have always sought to weight the so-called process of collective bargaining in favor of unions by bringing to bear on their side the force of government, whether by means of law or administration.[27] Such a measure would probably not entirely supplant the market, just as compulsory arbitration in accordance with standards adjusted to comply with realities of the market would not completely supplant the market determination of wages. But, like compulsory arbitration, which unions and their apologists generally resist, government confiscation of profits for the duration of a labor dispute would have the effect of rigging the market in favor of unions. It would say in effect to the employers involved: either give in or you will be hurt even worse than you would be by the unions and the free play of market forces. This is, in terms made familiar by antitrust litigation, predatory monopolistic pressure; it is the kind of tactic used by some monopolistic-minded business firms to eliminate the inconvenience of vigorous competitors: raise your prices or you lose all.[28]

There must be no mistaking this last point. Immediately, ultimately, in the short run and in the long run, the effect of putting all businesses in an industry under such extra pressure to increase wages will certainly be substantially the effect of a price increase in one form or another, direct or indirect, actual or potential. Prices will be higher than they otherwise would be; or quality will be lower; or there will be less production and less employment than there otherwise would be. There are no other alternatives. It is vain to hope that only profits, and nothing else of interest to the community, will be affected by rigging the market in this manner. In a full-production economy, where productive capacity is already being strained, history has shown us how readily these monopolistic pressures for wage increases are immediately translated into price increases. In sluggish periods, when it is already difficult to sell at existing prices, the effect of a wage-cost increase (beyond that which free-market factors call for) can only have undesirable results of one kind or another—most probably reduced production or quality impairment.

Those who would insist at this point that the effect might be to compel employers to become more "efficient" overlook certain vital factors. Already under strong compulsion to efficiency, the employer is usually, in slow periods, as efficient as he can be under existing conditions of reduced production, or is in the process of becoming so. But, even more important, the blunt, massive, undiscriminating weapon of government seizure in order to compel wage increases not called for by market conditions is as ill-adapted to promoting business efficiency as one might expect a device to be when it was originally created for an entirely different purpose.

Government seizure is a device well adapted to compelling wage increases greater than those which, at the given time, the free operation of the market would afford. But increasing business efficiency is entirely another thing, calling for entirely different techniques. First of all, it takes money to buy efficiency. It takes money to buy the talent, the machines, the thought, without which greater efficiency is not to be expected. Greater efficiency calls, too, for a cooperative attitude on the part of workers and their unions; and unions have been more notable for their resistance to efficiency than they have been for their cooperation.[29]

In summary, it takes both motive and means to achieve greater efficiency, just as it does everything else. Government seizure does not provide motive; profits and the free market do that. Government seizure does not, on balance, increase motive, either; for, like high taxes and excessive government regulation, it tends on the whole to limit the efficacy of the great, central, motivating influence, profits, as much as it tends to accentuate the desire to increase efficiency. And government seizure during depressed periods is certainly not very helpful in providing the *means* necessary to achieving greater efficiency. Entirely the contrary. It takes from hard-pressed businesses at a most crucial time such little margin as they may possess—the very margin which might have been used to increase efficiency and production at lower unit costs.

The case against government seizure, in good times or bad, is the case against all government interventionism designed to limit profits and to increase costs of production. These devices may serve certain purposes exceedingly well; politicians have found them useful for centuries. But no one has ever been able to demonstrate that they provide the things that everyone wants, that they increase the wealth of nations and the well-being of people generally.

In terms of the present discussion, government seizure is properly viewed as another species of the market manipulation which has been the real meaning of collective bargaining over the years for union leaders. Like boycotting techniques, government seizure is designed to bring to bear upon employers forces which have no relationship to the peaceable, productive activity of the free market. The real desires of the workers themselves, the productivity of workers, conditions on the market generally—all these factors are subordinated in the process of establishing wages; and political intervention is given the dominant role.

Basically, the demand for the use of government seizure amounts to a declaration on the part of union leaders that they are no longer satisfied with what they can gain through striking, or even through the boycotting and other monopolistic techniques which they have used so long. Where employees participate voluntarily, a strike is a form of action which indicates that employees are dissatisfied with the existing wage structure. Unless there are great numbers of other workers who think that the existing wage structure is adequate, the strike is by itself a bargaining technique which is likely to secure from employers all concessions which existing conditions on the market make possible. If employees are forbidden to strike, it is not quite so certain that all employers will give in wages every last cent which the market would permit. And that is why the right to strike should be maintained, and why, probably, the Taft-Hartley Act does not absolutely prohibit even those strikes which imperil the national health and safety, but only postpones them.

But in advocating government seizure, unions aim at securing without a strike everything that (and possibly more than) they could get through striking. A union leader no longer need worry about anything, the real desires of the workers and other market conditions least of all. A great problem for all union leaders during strikes is whether or not the union members will remain "loyal." Union members are likely to abandon the strike, to return to work, if the demands of their leaders seem unreasonable while the offers of the employer seem tolerably reasonable. They are especially likely to do so if it appears that other workers are accepting the wages offered by the employer. Besides being a valid and true technique of the free market, the successful voluntary strike is thus a sign that the union leaders have perceived correctly the temper of their own members and have analyzed other conditions on the market accurately.

Strikes fail when union leaders have not interpreted these market factors accurately. When a businessman sets a price too high for existing market conditions, he is compelled either to reduce the price or to go out of business. Union leaders would prefer to be free of these rigorous alternatives, and government seizure suggests itself to them as an ideal system of freeing themselves from all restraints emanating from either the market or their own members.

Government seizure, with its confiscation of profits, hurts employers in roughly the same way that a strike hurts them. It may even hurt employers a little less than a strike does, in some cases; but that point is not important. The important point is that it obviates the necessity of striking and thus frees union leaders of all controls. They no longer need worry about the real desires or the loyalty of their members; there being no strike, the members continue to receive their wages and will be willing to back up indefinitely any demands made by the leaders. Only the employers and the consumers are hurt by the seizure, not the union or the employees. Nor need union leaders fear the conditions on the labor market; thousands of able men may be unemployed and willing to take jobs at the wages spurned by the union leaders, but since there is no strike those men have no possibility of making their existence felt.

Thus, government seizure and confiscation of profits represent utopia for union leaders. They can make the wildest of economic demands and insist upon them indefinitely. Or they can settle for less and then in a little while, for any or no reason at all, ask for additional concessions. If denied, they can again threaten to strike, and government seizure will be re-instituted, and the whole spectacle will be reproduced. No wonder unions scorn compulsory arbitration. After all, the arbitrators are often influenced, many times by express mandate of the law, to take market-factors into consideration. And unions cannot always be sure that their wishes will be respected in the selection of the arbitrators. But government seizure is different. It virtually removes market and political hazards. The advantage to the union is a fixed and unremovable feature of the system. No matter what the political climate, if government seizure is part of the law, the cards are stacked against the public, unemployed workers, and the employer, in the union's favor. Government seizure is interventionist politics domesticated to the will of union leaders.

The same observation holds true for many features of the law applicable to the process of collective bargaining. The law declares that employers must bargain collectively in good faith with unions representing a majority of their employees. The law also declares that the duty to bargain in good faith does not impose the duty to reach agreement, and from this declaration it may be inferred that employers have no duty to reach any particular agreement of any kind. This is the basic legal framework of the negotiation or "talking" features of collective bargaining.[30]

Whether or not the current rules relating to negotiations between employers and unions properly implement the basic legislative plan is something of a problem, for there are elements of ambiguity even in the basic plan. If an employer is under no duty to reach any particular agreement with a union, may the employer refuse to grant during negotiations with the union the same increase in wages which it later gives directly to the employees? The current rule applied by the National Labor Relations Board and the courts is that such conduct is unlawful.[31] This rule is probably a correct application of the present statutory law; such conduct on the part of the employer suggests bad faith. Furthermore, it might be considered a form of economic coercion, under current views. It is similar to the offering of a benefit, conditioned on abandonment of the union; its effect is to say to employees that the employer will give them directly what he will not give them through their union. The same is true of all so-called "unilateral" acts of the employer, and the current rule condemning such acts is probably by and large an accurate development of the "good faith" concept established by the basic legislative structure.

Real problems arise, however, in the situation where the employer absolutely refuses to make any concession whatsoever to the union. Take the case, for example, where an employer says to the union leaders during negotiations: "I am perfectly willing to discuss with you frankly and sincerely all matters of interest to you and the employees; but my judgment and experience convince me that this business can be operated effectively only if I continue to have the complete control of it which I now have. Therefore, the only agreement I will sign is one which declares that the level of wages, the conditions of work, the hours, the promotion or disciplining of employees, and all other employment factors remain subject to my exclusive control."

Unions and the National Labor Relations Board insist that an employer who takes such a position is guilty of an unlawful refusal to bargain in good faith, and some courts and analysts agree with them. They reason along the following lines: The Act created the obligation to bargain in good faith concerning wages, hours, and other terms and conditions of employment; this means that unions were intended to participate in the process of determining such matters; by insisting upon exclusive control of all employment factors, the employer is frustrating the national collective-bargaining policy.[32]

Some analysts, a few courts, and perhaps even the Supreme Court itself take a different view. They emphasize the fact that the law expressly declares that employers are under no duty to reach any agreement. For them, the fundamental intent of Congress in establishing the duty to bargain in good faith was one of inducing the opposing parties to meet and treat honestly and fairly and in a peaceful environment. They imply that the precise terms of agreement are to be fixed, not by law, but by the respective economic positions of the parties; ultimately the terms of the collective agreement are to be influenced by conditions on the market; if dissatisfied with the employer's offer the employees and the union are free to strike or to engage in such other market operations as the law permits.[33]

There can be little doubt of the fundamental soundness, economic and legal, of the latter point of view. The written words of the law itself are definitive. The law states as clearly as words can that employers are under no duty to reach any agreement whatsoever. For the NLRB to say that employers violate national policy in steadfastly refusing to make any concession at all is equivalent to saying that the law requires certain concessions, when this is manifestly not so. A similar conclusion is indicated when one departs from the abstract legal plane of analysis to the real facts of economic life. If it be true, as the NLRB and some courts insist, that the employer must make certain concessions, who is to determine the exact character of the concessions? Neither law nor policy affords an answer to this question. Certainly not the union; and equally certainly not the NLRB.

The fact is that the NLRB attitude, as unsound as it may be in terms of the law, amounts to another market-manipulating device of the general type already encountered here. It is designed to weaken the employer; to give the union a political-juridical advantage extraneous to economic, market considerations. While some courts, including the Supreme Court, seem to be dimly aware of these facts, it must be acknowledged that the view of the NLRB tends to prevail today. It is true that the Supreme Court has held recently that an employer may absolutely refuse to permit the union to participate in the process of hiring, promoting, discharging, or disciplining employees.[34]

But in so holding, the Court was compelled to reverse the NLRB's previous decision in the same case.[35] And the fact that the NLRB had previously held to the contrary is sufficient to indicate the position it takes. There is no doubt, furthermore, that the NLRB and most courts would hold it unlawful for an employer to assert unqualifiedly that he will sign no agreement other than one vesting in him all the authority which he previously had, including the authority to change wages when and as he sees fit.

As a result, few if any employers today will approach collective bargaining with such an orientation. Practically all employers confine themselves to calculations designed to keep at a minimum the concessions which they feel that the law compels them to make, whether or not they themselves think it advisable to make any concession at all at the given time. Obviously, even in such circumstances the market ultimately controls; unions will not insist upon concessions which the employer absolutely cannot make; nor will they insist upon concessions fantastically out of all proportion. But here, as in so many other features of labor relations law in the United States, the fact is that the market has been rigged by political forces in favor of the unions.

We end as we began the discussion of collective bargaining. The market controls ultimately in the determination of wages and working conditions; the law as written so states the matter; but the law as interpreted tends to rig the market in favor of unions.

Chapter 16

COLLECTIVE BARGAINING AND THE
INDIVIDUAL EMPLOYEE

A desire to safeguard and to promote the interests of individual workers must necessarily constitute the basis of collective-bargaining law and policy. We do not view unions and collective bargaining as ends in themselves, any more than we regard business corporations and freedom of contract as ends in themselves. Even though union leaders may sometimes act as though the institutional interests of their organizations are superior or antecedent to the interests of workers, this fact must not be allowed to distort the true view of the situation: that such privileges or powers as society and the law allocate to unions are conditioned upon the assumption that they are necessary if we are to have consistent rules and if unions are effectively to represent workers.[1]

The interests of individual workers are critically engaged in two phases of the collective-bargaining process. The first is the point at which union and employer discuss and come to agreement upon the terms and conditions of employment which are to prevail in the employment unit; at this phase the individual worker's concern is that the agreement reflect his interests as favorably and equitably as it does those of all other employees in the bargaining unit. The second crucial phase is that of administration and enforcement of the collective agreement; the individual worker is concerned here lest the agreement be administered and enforced, by either union or employer or both, in a manner prejudicial to his equal rights.

The Pacific Intermountain Express Company and the Teamsters' Union have provided a good example of the way in which the interests of individual workers may be critically affected at the two levels of collective bargaining just described.[2] In 1949 the company agreed to permit the union to dispose of all seniority disputes. This meant that the union had the power to decide which employees should be laid off first, or rehired first after a lay-off, or given first choice as to available positions. No one should be surprised to learn that, given such power, the union abused it; for, under all the circumstances, the Teamsters' Union could do nothing other than abuse the power. The Constitution of the Teamsters' Union has always considered length of union membership a "better" seniority claim than length of service with the particular employer. And in this case, according to the National Labor Relations Board report, the union "established the seniority dates of employees who were not members of the union when hired as of the date upon which they became members of the union rather than as of the date of their employment."[3] Thus a man hired in 1950 might be accorded seniority inferior to that given a man who began his employment in 1951, if the latter happened to belong to the union when he was hired, or if he speedily joined upon being hired, while the former failed to join the union at all or joined only at a later date.

Whether or not the Teamsters' Union's conception of seniority is the "sound" or "true" view is far less important for present purposes than the fact that employees prejudiced by the union practice might naturally (and did actually) feel aggrieved and mistreated. On the theory that the law is designed for the benefit of individual employees rather than of unions as institutions, it would seem that the sense of grievance of the prejudiced employees was one entitled to social consideration. For there is nothing beneficial to the employee as such in the Teamsters' conception of seniority. That conception essentially promotes the union, and in fact amounts to a kind of economic coercion to immediate union membership. Some employee or other is of course advantaged under any concept of seniority; but the advantage under the Teamster concept derives not from an employee's ability, not from his experience, and not from his actual length of service. It derives only from his tenure of union membership. To use the approach of the National Labor Relations Act, the Teamsters' seniority method constitutes discrimination between employees which is designed to promote union membership.[4]

Whether or not the union had in addition violated the implicit duty, as exclusive bargaining representative of all employees in the unit, to represent all employees fairly and without discrimination is uncertain; but, leaving that matter for the moment, we may note that the NLRB found the employer and the union both guilty of unlawful discrimination.[5]

The second phase of the case illustrates the point that the interests of employees may be seriously involved in the manner in which unions prosecute grievances. Among those employees prejudiced by the Teamsters' Union's seniority practices was one Sanders, who let it be known that he felt himself victimized. The union administration, disapproving Sanders' position, took action when it appeared that he intended to continue to insist that seniority be conceived in terms of length of service with the employer. Among other things, Sanders was beaten up. Shortly thereafter the employer discharged him, allegedly because he had been exceeding the speed limit. Feeling absolutely certain that the discharge was collusive, "rigged," and wrongful, Sanders filed with the union a formal grievance in which he questioned the truth of the speeding charge. The union assigned to the prosecution of Sanders' grievance the same person who had been fined and convicted for assaulting him. Discouraged, Sanders did not attend the grievance hearing. But he did file an unfair practice charge with the NLRB, and in that agency's hearing he relied upon a tachograph chart to disprove the employer's speeding accusation. Accepting this chart as satisfactory proof that Sanders had not in fact violated any speed limit, the NLRB held that he had been unlawfully discharged.[6] The discharge appeared to be, then, under all the circumstances, an act in appeasement of the union.

If the employer does not wish to or is in no position to defend the rights and equities of individual employees, and if there is reason to fear prejudicial conduct from unions at times, it seems plain that devices are needed which will protect individual employees from arbitrary treatment at the two levels of collective bargaining in which we are interested, the negotiation level and the grievance-processing level. We turn now to a systematic investigation of actual and potential checks upon arbitrary treatment of employees.

The Collective-Bargaining Level

Perhaps the best-known check upon arbitrary conduct by union negotiators in the collective-bargaining process is the requirement, established by the Supreme Court in the famous Steele case,[7] that a union must bargain fairly and nondiscriminatorily on behalf of all employees in the bargaining unit represented exclusively by that union. We know very little more about this broad rule than the foregoing very generalized statement suggests. Indeed, about all we *know* is that where a union proposes or accepts measures which will discriminate against certain employees on the basis of race, color, or creed, it has violated the legal duty implicit in its position as exclusive bargaining agent.

As presently formulated, the rule prohibiting arbitrary discrimination by unions is too broad to be of any real use. Except in those instances of bargaining in which the union represents an absolutely homogeneous group of employees, the collective-bargaining process inherently requires some discrimination. Indeed, there is more reason to fear that unions will fail to discriminate properly as among different categories of workers than there is that they will discriminate too much. This is true especially among complex industrial unions which represent many different categories of workers. During the summer of 1955, for example, in the negotiations between the Ford Motor Company and the United Automobile Workers, tool-and-diemakers represented by the UAW showed considerable dissatisfaction with the collective agreement finally reached, despite the enthusiasm with which that agreement was generally greeted, because it paid insufficient attention to their employment category and allegedly did not maintain suitable rate differentials for their highly skilled work.

Small, highly skilled groups in large and complex industrial unions will very likely find themselves neglected with some frequency—and in circumstances in which it will be impossible to make out a case of arbitrary discrimination against them by their union. After all, how can anyone say that a union has discriminated unfairly in negotiating a ten-cent increase for employees in category A and an eight-cent increase for employees in category B? This type of case, which is likely to recur with much greater frequency than the case of racial discrimination, must be dealt with on the basis of some technique other than the rule prohibiting discrimination by unions.

The principle of free employee choice of bargaining representatives, which underlies so much of current labor policy, is the technique which must be relied mainly upon, ultimately, to protect employees against arbitrary treatment in collective bargaining. In the case of the small minority of craftsmen in a complex industrial union, the principle of free employee choice finds expression in the Taft-Hartley rule liberalizing the circumstances in which craft units may be carved out of large industrial units.[8] If the NLRB is seriously concerned with promoting free employee choice and combating arbitrary discrimination by unions against minority groups, it will adopt liberal policies in regard to such minorities. Both employers and industrial unions may complain about this; but labor policy should not be designed for the convenience of employers and labor unions.[9]

On the other hand, it should be noted that if bargaining units are to be fractionalized and multiplied even more than they are at present, the harmful potentialities of strikes may be greatly increased; and it may therefore be argued that the rules of the game should be adjusted accordingly. The law might provide either that all collective agreements in a company composed of multiple bargaining units be negotiated simultaneously or that a strike in one bargaining unit be confined to that unit. It is about time that there be introduced into the law the principle that employees in unit A of a given company may not lawfully refrain from working simply because employees in unit B are on strike. Such "sympathetic" action ought to be viewed accurately; it amounts to a secondary boycott or a combination in restraint of trade, and ought to fall within the legal condemnations which cover conduct of that kind.

As demonstrated by the Pacific Intermountain Express case, arbitrary discrimination by unions is not necessarily limited to instances in which the bargaining unit comprehends employees in different work-categories. In that case, it will be remembered, all the employees were truckdrivers; and seniority privileges were geared to length of union membership rather than to length of service with the employer involved.

As it happens, the basic principle of free employee choice proves adequate to resolving the problem posed by that particular type of discrimination. Revolving about the principle of free employee choice, the Taft-Hartley Act, manifesting inherent integrity in this respect, forbids discrimination by either union or employer where such discrimination tends to encourage or discourage union membership. Such a provision logically comprehends a prohibition of one of the two or three greatest menaces to free employee choice, namely, compulsory unionism. And thus the law as it exists at present, inasmuch as it prohibits all the extreme forms of compulsory unionism, is adequate to the task of preventing unions from engaging in the type of thing evident in the Pacific Intermountain Express case. For all cases of that type involve more or less specious attempts to perpetuate unlawful compulsory-unionism conditions.

But there is a type of collective-bargaining discrimination with which no rule of law or principle has yet dealt adequately. This type may be generally described as one in which a union provides for less favorable treatment of one group than of others, but not on the basis of either union membership or race, creed, or color. An example is provided by the Hartley case,[10] where a union negotiated an agreement to the effect that, quite regardless of skill, seniority, etc., women workers were to be laid off before men when the employer found it necessary to reduce the working staff. It is easy to think of variations of such a rule— for example, a requirement that unmarried men be discharged before married men, regardless of seniority.

The court which decided the Hartley case held that the union acted lawfully in agreeing to such a provision.[11] Although no decision to the contrary has been found, the case becomes the more troublesome the more one thinks about it. Surely the decision in the Hartley litigation would have to be different under the Supreme Court's ruling in the Steele case, if Negroes were involved instead of women. Now, is discrimination any the less arbitrary when it involves white women and white men than when it involves colored men and white men? Justice Halpern, who decided *Wilson* v. *Hacker* in 1950,[12] would probably find such disadvantaging of women to be unlawfully arbitrary discrimination; for he held in that case that a union might not lawfully picket to take away the jobs of barmaids and give them to members of the Bartenders' Union, to which union the barmaids would not be admitted. Still, the argument to the effect that it is the job of the union to reconcile the frictions among its membership and to reach a solution which is in the interest of the most numerous class will certainly carry weight with many persons. It may be assumed that if the union submitted the rule involved in the Hartley case to a membership-referendum, a substantial majority would be registered in its favor. Furthermore, the United States Supreme Court has cited the Hartley decision with approval.[13]

For those who hold to the view that the political principle of majority rule should be controlling in labor relations and other social affairs, decisions like the one in the Hartley case are likely to create no problems. However, the fact is that the law has long since rejected the monolithic majority-rule conception. It forbids discrimination against nonunion men even in units where a majority of employees are union members; it prohibits discrimination against colored men by unions whose membership is preponderantly white; and, as is widely known, it protects "minority rights" in a number of other ways.

The question in every case of protecting minority rights against the clear desire of a majority is whether the interest of the minority is in some way socially superior to the principle of majority rule. In pursuing this analysis it may be taken for granted that if an employer discharges A rather than B, he does so because in some sense or other A is less valuable in the enterprise than B. We are all aware, of course, that in some instances the employer's valuation may be erroneous or prejudiced, or that it may even reflect anti-union animus, with A discharged primarily because he is an active union member, while B is not. But in a well-run company errors and prejudices will be kept to a minimum. Continued emphasis upon and study of the science and arts involved in running a business enterprise well may be suggested as the best means of eliminating errors and prejudices in personnel relations; furthermore, insistence upon careful review of questionable lay-offs and discharges is an entirely proper and desirable function of collective bargaining. And as to discharges and lay-offs motivated by anti-union considerations, the law forbidding them is now effectively enforced, and there is no indication that it will be repealed or that enforcement will be relaxed.

We may therefore return to the assumption that lay-offs and discharges will usually be based by the employer upon an evaluation of the relative worth to the enterprise of the employees involved. It goes without saying that, in terms of sheer efficiency, women or unmarried men will in some instances be worth more to a business than married men. And so, if sheer efficiency were the only criterion in lay-offs and discharges, employers would, if permitted, sometimes prefer to retain women and unmarried men. The quite evident fact is, however, that sheer efficiency is by no means a universally acceptable criterion for employers. An informal kind of seniority program, geared to length of service and "loyalty" to the employer, in fact prevails widely. Special circumstances usually obtain whenever an older employee is "passed over," and a younger one, in point of length of service, is preferred.

The attitude generally prevailing among employers is probably accurately reflected in the common type of collective agreement in which the union and the employer agree that where skill and ability are equal, preferment in regard to promotions, lay-offs, rehiring, etc., is to be based upon length of service in the company. That this type of seniority agreement should prevail widely is a fact of no small significance to the present discussion. For this prevalence tends to suggest that even though unions at times insist upon seniority privileges which put minority groups at a special disadvantage, such "unfair" treatment of minorities— whether they be Negroes, women, or unmarried men—is by no means a vital or essential or organic feature of trade-union activity. To put the matter another way, no union can intelligently and in good faith take the position that the power to discriminate against minorities as such is inherently necessary if trade unionism is to survive.

The analysis begins to shape up, then, somewhat as follows. On behalf of permitting unions to discriminate against such minority groups as unmarried men or women, two principles may be advanced: (1) the principle of majority rule; (2) the principle of collective bargaining, which means in this context that unions should be allowed to negotiate freely in accordance with their own policy decisions and that restrictions on collective bargaining should be as few as possible. Against such discrimination one might argue that (1) it represents too great an imposition upon persons who find themselves in a minority and (2) it would unduly frustrate certain profoundly important social processes.

The present problem, it may be suggested, is not one which is solved most intelligently by applying the principle of majority rule. We do not normally allow a majority of producers in any given field to decide which producers shall survive and which shall be discarded; in such areas we rely upon economic rather than political processes. Again, we do not tolerate the destruction of opinions and other intellectual conceptions on a mere nose-counting basis. The problem with which we are immediately concerned is very much like the two just mentioned. Whether or not, in a lay-off, married men should be given preference over single men or women is, from society's point of view, best determined in largely the same way that we decide which businesses are to survive under rigorous competitive conditions. There are certainly those who will interpose at this point that the social interest is plainly pre-empted by the married man with his family responsibilities. But this is too near-sighted a view of the social interest. The deepest of all social interests is in the progression and perfection of social productivity, in the smooth and effective functioning of the process whereby each individual fits himself into the position in society to which he is best suited and in which he best serves. It is untenable to assert that the social interest begins and ends with the advantaging of some men over others simply because those men have married and begotten. Every man can think of cases in which begetting has done very little for society.

And on the other hand it is not even true that the "equities" are always with the married man as against the single man or the woman. These latter, too, may have exigent personal responsibilities and hopes and dreams. To take the position that the "equities" are always with the married man is simply to be doctrinaire and dogmatic, and very often in error.

As to the contention that the interest in free collective bargaining requires that unions be permitted freely to negotiate the kinds of agreements under discussion, not a great deal of reflection is needed to uncover the deficiency. This is really something like the contention that no interference with freedom of contract should ever be permitted—a contention the inadequacies of which have already been discussed. There is nothing any more sacred about collective bargaining than there is in private property or freedom of contract or any other social institution. The problem in regard to the scope to be accorded all these institutions can never be permanently solved; the solution turns on the merits of each case. In terms of the present discussion, the problem, narrowly framed, is whether the social gain is greater if free collective bargaining be upheld than if, instead, one establish the rule that collective bargaining may not extend to the point where it prejudices minority groups arbitrarily.

Putting the matter this way naturally focuses attention on the problem of defining "arbitrary" conduct by the union. Now, one's conception of "arbitrary" action by unions is of course determined largely by one's idea of the proper role of the union. If the union be regarded as a miniature "welfare state," its role is a wide, practically limitless, one. Just as the welfare state is permitted the power to discriminate limitlessly among citizens on the basis of the conclusion that practically any conceivable "social goal" is appropriately attained through state action, so too the union, conceived as a welfare state in miniature, will be permitted a relatively wide range of action.

On the other hand, if the union be viewed as an institution with rather narrowly limited functions, the tendency will be to limit accordingly the grounds upon which it may discriminate among the employees it exclusively represents in collective bargaining. One will be inclined to say that the union's power in collective bargaining is exhausted when it has participated with the employer in establishing rules which apply equally to all the *human beings,* as such, for whom it bargains exclusively. Thus, seniority privileges, or even wage increases, geared to length of service in the particular production unit, would be acceptable subjects of collective bargaining under this approach; whereas the power to require a special advantage to A because he has been a union member longer, because he is a member of the white race, because he is married and has five children, or because he is light-haired and blue-eyed—such a power would have to be denied.

The need for conceiving the role of the union as a substantially limited one is very great, it seems to me. If the free society is to survive, it is in fact tautological to emphasize that the undifferentiated individual person must be put in the most favorable possible position. In the area under discussion this means that he should not be subordinated to the collective group pressures which must necessarily be largely the determinants of union policies. If the free society is to survive, again, it must be constantly concerned with preserving and promoting its productivity. The need for a rigorously conceived role for the union is perhaps most conclusively established by this concern; for the potential effects upon productivity to be expected from accepting a broad view of the role of the union are not encouraging if past performances are any criterion.

The Processing of Individual Grievances[14]

The individual employee is no less interested in the administration and enforcement of the collective agreement than he is in its negotiation. He is justified in regarding the most elaborate collective agreement as a mere scrap of paper—a "snare and a delusion," to use a fresh phrase—if it is not administered fairly and equitably. One of the two or three outstanding, constructive functions which unions perform, or which they can perform when well run, is that of "policing" the collective agreement, of taking every effective step necessary to make employers abide by their agreements. On the other hand, the individual employee must not be thrust into a position where he is obliged to depend upon unions and employers entirely for effective and equitable enforcement of the collective agreement. There is a need here, too, of social support to the individual employee who, without such support, is in a decidedly disadvantageous position in relation to the power aggregates, the large unions and employers,

which surround him. One needs only recall the plight of Mr.
Sanders in the Pacific Intermountain Express case when he took
the position that the union and the employer had colluded in
arranging for his discharge.

The probability is that, with certain relatively minor exceptions presently to be noted, the legal structure in relation to the
enforcement of the collective agreement is developing in tolerably good order. Certainly nothing works out perfectly in this
world, but it may be noted that at least the theoretical structure
in regard to the enforcement of the collective agreement is comprehensive and coherent. For one thing, the collective agreement
is practically universally regarded as an enforceable contract.
For another, while an employee may not as a general rule compel a union to prosecute his grievance, it is increasingly recognized that individual employees may bring their contract grievances to the courts when unions refuse to prosecute them. And,
according to most labor relations statutes, employees may bring
their grievances directly to their employers' attention.

The defects in this legal structure are what may be called in-
cidental and fragmentary. Perhaps the most important of the
current defects is the one recently created by the United States
Supreme Court in the Westinghouse case.[15] In that case a union
brought an action in its own name to recover damages on behalf
of employees against an employer allegedly because the employer had, contrary to a collective agreement, refused to compensate the employees for a certain holiday.[16] The action was
brought under the Taft-Hartley Act, which provides in Section
301(a) that "Suits for violation of contracts between an employer and a labor organization . . . may be brought in any
district court of the United States." According to a majority of
the Supreme Court, this statutory provision, on its face, is merely
procedural and, what is more important, does not establish a
right in unions to sue employers for violations of those provisions
of collective agreements which run in favor of individual employees. According to Justice Frankfurter, who wrote the opinion of the Court, remedies for such violations must be pursued by
individual employees, either singly or by means of such devices
as the class action, in the state courts. It should be noted that, in
Justice Frankfurter's opinion, suits by individual employees on

collective agreements are everywhere accepted by the common-law courts—an assumption not entirely unquestionable.

The decision in the Westinghouse case is difficult to understand on any basis, whether of law or policy. Whatever Justice Frankfurter may say to the contrary, it is impossible to see how the statute's express terms *compel* the conclusions (1) that no "federal law" of contracts was intended and (2) that unions may not sue for violations of collective agreements, or of those parts of such agreements which relate to the terms and conditions of employment of individual employees.[17]   The thing which really seems to have bothered Justice Frankfurter is that the statute, as drafted, gives the federal judiciary jurisdiction over legal problems, namely, contract violations, which have been traditionally handled by the state courts. The Justice insists that any decision other than the one reached in the Westinghouse case would raise "grave constitutional issues." But this conclusion is valid only on the assumption that the statute may not be read as establishing the substantive enforceability of collective agreements —an assumption open to question.[18]

As to the policy aspect of the Westinghouse case, it need only be noted that there is simply no practical reason *against* permitting unions to prosecute employee claims under collective agreements, and every practical reason in favor of permitting unions to act in such cases. This seems so obvious as to make further discussion superfluous.

In fact, one of the minor problems in the area under discussion is that of insuring effective prosecution of employee grievances by unions. Few, probably, would insist that unions be obliged to prosecute *every* employee grievance. Such a rule would certainly place intolerable burdens upon union administrations; the chronic "griever" is a well-known character in labor relations. Still, some measures are necessary to cover the situation in which a union arbitrarily refuses to prosecute employee grievances.[19]

The procedures obtaining under the Wisconsin Employment Peace Act may be cited in this connection as a good example of one fairly sensible way of handling the problem which arises when a union refuses to prosecute a grievance. That statute makes the violation of a collective agreement an unfair practice. Where a union "has unreasonably refused to process a grievance on behalf of the individual," the Wisconsin Employment Relations Board will entertain a complaint for violation of the agreement.[20]

An even more commendable method of dealing with the problem is that which seems to be evolving in New York, where the courts by and large hold themselves open to contract actions by individual employees in cases where unions have refused to process their grievances. New York courts have refused to compel unions to prosecute grievances,[21] but they seem quite rightly to be holding that the whole drift of labor relations policy requires that individual employees be allowed to seek their own enforcement where the union fails to act.[22] A recent decision of the Seventh Circuit Court of Appeals agrees in theory with the New York view although it dismisses an employee action on the ground that it was prematurely brought.[23]

Justice Frankfurter's assumption to the contrary notwithstanding, not all courts will accept actions brought by individual employees on collective agreements. A federal court sitting in Arkansas, for example, has refused such an action on the theory that there is no mutuality of obligation between the employer and the individual employees, as required by Arkansas law.[24] This decision overlooks the fact, of course, that the collective agreement has achieved legal status largely on the basis of third-party-beneficiary thinking, and that in sanctioning collective bargaining the law has negated the extremely significant right of individuals to bargain for themselves. These factors should be sufficient to supply "mutuality" on any equitable basis.

There does not seem to be any solid consideration militating against opening the courts to suits brought by individual employees. The rule ought to be that employees may sue in any case where (a) the union refuses to prosecute the grievance or (b) there is substantial reason to believe that the union will not prosecute the grievance fairly and seriously. Certainly none of the objections which unions normally use against progressive proposals are applicable here. Unions will not be "undermined" if employees are allowed to bring their grievances to court only after the unions themselves have refused to process them or have indicated that they will not process them fairly, nor is there reason to believe an undue amount of litigation will ensue.

Perhaps the most important of available legal techniques relating to the individual processing of grievances is that embodied in the current labor-relations statutes, of which Section 9(a) of the National Labor Relations Act is the best-known example. After establishing the exclusive bargaining status of the majority union in any bargaining unit, this section declares that "any individual employee or a group of employees shall have the right at any time to present grievances to their employer and to have such grievances adjusted, without the intervention of the bargaining representative, as long as the adjustment is not inconsistent with the terms of a collective-bargaining contract or agreement then in effect . . ."

I shall spend very little time on this phase of the law, despite its importance, because it has been worked over in considerable detail, and because, aside from questions of emphasis, I have virtually nothing to add to the excellent recent analysis by Professor Summers and his associates on the Committe on Improvement of Administration of Union-Management Agreements, 1954.[25] The committee takes the position that the Taft-Hartley Act quite properly preserves the right of individuals to prosecute their own grievances, without going through the union. They urge that the Section 9(a) proviso be read as prohibiting the preclusion of this right by union-management agreement; that unfair practice sanctions be imposed upon employers who refuse to entertain individual grievances; and that the individual right be construed as including the right to bring grievances all the way to arbitration if the collective agreement goes that far.

I find myself largely in agreement with the conclusions reached by the committee and with its analysis of the Taft-Hartley Act, an analysis that is especially notable for the respect it pays to Congressional intent as expressed in the language chosen. Legitimate statutory interpretation seems to be repugnant to most of the administrative agents, judges, and students who deal with the statute. To find Professor Summers and his associates giving due respect to the normal rules of statutory construction is encouraging and lends strength to the hope for a scientific jurisprudence, as opposed to the chaos to which abandonment of the carefully wrought rules of interpretation must necessarily lead.

Part III

A LABOR POLICY FOR THE UNITED STATES

The United States will have the honor of proving ... that true policy goes hand in hand with moderation and humanity.
—Jean Baptiste Say

Chapter 17

UNIONS OF THEIR OWN CHOOSING

It is a remarkable fact that labor policy has evolved in the United States much along the lines that the theory of the free society would have laid down, had it been in control of events. Free employee choice, the central principle of modern labor relations policy in the United States, is a corollary of freedom of association; and free association is implicit in the principles of private property and freedom of contract, the basic operating principles of the free society. The correspondence between the actual evolution of labor policy in this country and the theory of the free society is thus very close: free employee choice figures prominently in both.

Yet, the survey in Part II of this book demonstrates that, however central the principle of free employee choice may be in the labor policy of the United States, the current status of both policy and principle leaves much to be desired. This is so mainly because the principle is neither rigorously and coherently conceived nor effectively enforced in the United States today. Important forms of coercion of employees go unrecognized as such, and it is no exaggeration to say that the most drastic types of trade-union coercion, even when recognized as such, enjoy a virtual privilege owing to lack of effective juridical prevention techniques.[1] The resulting situation can be desirable only to those who favor compulsion and coercion as standard operating methods in labor relations.

Disinterested persons familiar with conditions in labor relations can scarcely approve. For a sound and workable principle, commended by both theoretical considerations and the felt needs of a people, is being frustrated by deficiencies in the authoritative legal institutions. The consequence has been, if the analysis in an earlier part of this book is correct, the perversion and distortion of trade-unionism, to the general harm of society.[2] Internal corruption in some trade unions and the external dangers to society posed by many trade unions can all be traced directly to compulsory, coercive practices. Besides presenting the gravest kind of social threat, these practices drain the vitality of the principle of free employee choice and pose a biting challenge to the integrity of our principles and policies generally. More is involved than the deprivations of human freedom which characterize our labor relations, more even than the corrupt and uneconomic practices which compulsion and coercion in labor relations are breeding. At stake, too, are the simple honesty, humanity, good sense, and integrity of the United States, and its ideals as an intelligently conducted, enduring free society.

A basic necessity at this time, therefore, is to secure to employees the right to have unions of their own choosing. Rigorous conception and enforcement of the principle of free employee choice will rid us of coercive deprivations of the freedom of workingmen and provide a stout functional check to corruption within unions; at the same time it will go far toward extirpating antisocial, monopolistic trade-union practices. More than that, it will achieve those results consistently with the theory of the free society—something that no other measure can promise. For, in order to secure free employee choice, it is necessary only to prevent coercive conduct; it is not necessary to impair the social rights of any one concerned. The theoretical soundness, the essential "rightness," and the organically emergent dominance of the principle of free employee choice are all implicit in that fact. The principle of free employee choice has evolved naturally in the United States in much the same way that its parent principles, private property and freedom of contract, emerged from more primitive methods of organizing human relations. It has seemed the only intelligent, humane way to solve labor-relations problems without sacrificing the great goals of the free society: freedom, well-being, and security.

Securing the free choice of employees is a matter today largely of recognizing the coercive character of certain common trade-union practices. Prohibiting trade-union coercion in general will not suffice; for the law already does that. Yet, on the other hand, no startling new insights are needed. It is necessary only that the insights of some leading legal authorities in the country be shared by all. In addition, certain phases of the rules covering employer conduct vis à vis employees need to be clarified. Finally, some basic problems concerning the bargaining choices available to small groups of employees within larger groups must be solved. These are the subject of the present chapter. Procedural devices necessary to implement free employee choice are considered in Chapter 19.

Union Coercion of Free Employee Choice

By express statute or by common-law development, the federal government and the governments of every state in the Union guarantee to employees the right of free choice in trade-union membership. In addition, the federal government and a large number of states expressly prohibit restraint or coercion of free employee choice by employers or labor organizations. Notwithstanding these facts, some of the most common methods of union coercion of free employee choice are largely permitted under federal law. Moreover, owing to the fact that federal law is today regarded as pre-empting state law in labor relations, the privilege of coercion which trade unions enjoy under federal law has tended to become universal.

Organizational Picketing. As was pointed out in Chapters 10 and 11, the most common forms of union coercion of employees are stranger-picketing for organizational or recognition purposes, compulsory unionism, and the several types of secondary action in which unions frequently engage. The writer of this book is by no means alone in characterizing as coercive the foregoing types of union action. Indeed, as reference to the chapters just cited will show, a good many authorities agree with the characterization. As regards organizational and recognition picketing, for example, many state courts of last resort share the opinion expressed here.[3] The Supreme Court of the United States has suggested that it is inclined to view organizational picketing as coercive,[4] and at least one other high federal court has taken the same position.[5] Finally, disinterested

scholars have insisted that organizational picketing is unlawfully coercive of free employee choice.[6]

If the truth be known, indeed, the view that organizational
picketing is *not* coercive seems to be held rigidly by only one
judicial agency. A number of state courts have refused to enjoin organizational picketing, it is true. But when the cases are
examined, it appears that they do so, not because they consider
organizational picketing inherently noncoercive and lawful, but
because they feel that they are prevented by superior authority
from holding otherwise. Thus, some state courts refuse to enjoin because they consider themselves bound by anti-injunction
statutes;[7] some because the Supreme Court's old picketing–free-
speech doctrine seems to them to preclude injunctive relief;[8] and
some because they feel that organizational picketing violates the
National Labor Relations Act and is therefore not subject to
their jurisdiction.[9] Each such decision directly implies, of course,
that if the court were free to decide on the merits it might well
hold organizational picketing coercive, unlawful, and enjoinable. And that is probably true in respect of a great many courts
in this country.

The one judicial agency which holds organizational picketing noncoercive is the National Labor Relations Board.[10] Now
many are sure to think that since only the NLRB holds such
picketing noncoercive, the matter is not very serious. Nothing,
however, could be further from the truth. For the NLRB is in
a position to frustrate the entire juridical activity of the nation
in labor relations law, owing to certain decisions of the Supreme
Court of the United States, with which we shall deal in Chapter 19. Suffice it to say here, that the NLRB's attitude toward
organizational picketing largely determines the status of such
picketing in this country. The National Labor Relations Act
at present makes it an unfair labor practice for a trade union to
restrain or coerce employees in the exercise of their right to join
or not to join unions. When the NLRB holds, even though
contrary to all reason and authority, that organizational picketing does *not* restrain or coerce employees within the meaning of
the NLRA, its holding effectively precludes a contrary holding
by any other court under current conditions of legal procedure
in the United States.

The best way to solve the problem posed by the intransigence of the NLRB is for Congress to amend the present law. As it now reads, the law simply prohibits union "restraint or coercion" of the exercise by employees of their right to join or not to join a union. It should be amended so that it prohibits union "restraint or coercion, *whether by peaceful picketing or otherwise.*" With the law so drafted it ought to be impossible even for the NLRB to misconstrue its meaning. There is no need to fear that the Supreme Court will hold such a prohibition of picketing unconstitutional under the picketing–free-speech theory. For the Court has already held that peaceful picketing may be prohibited where it is designed to reach an unlawful objective, and of course organizational picketing which coerces free employee choice has an unlawful objective.[11]

Compulsory-Unionism Contracts. Compulsory unionism presents a somewhat different problem. Seventeen states now prohibit all forms of compulsory unionism,[12] and current federal law prohibits the most extended forms.[13] The states which prohibit all compulsory unionism leave little to be desired. They are doing all they can to insure the basic rights of free workingmen in a free society. As regards the states which permit compulsory unionism—and these, it might be noted, include a good many of the highly industrialized states—one can only point out that their legal structures lack inherent integrity, since all these states broadly declare a right of free choice in employees. As regards the federal government, the problem is for the most part one of *enforcement* of the present prohibition of compulsory unionism, a matter with which we deal in Chapter 19. However, even the federal law is not entirely unexceptionable as it now stands. It accepts the principle that unions may in certain circumstances compel the discharge of employees who refuse to pay union dues.[14] Complete integrity of the principle of free employee choice requires the rejection of even such a quasi compulsory-unionism principle. The present law should be amended to provide broadly and simply that a union commits an unfair labor practice whenever it "causes or attempts to cause an employer to encourage or discourage union membership by discrimination in hire or in tenure, terms, or conditions of employment."[15]

Secondary Action. The central problem in regard to secondary action arises from the present lack of general agreement concerning the proper characterization of such action by trade unions. A subordinate problem is posed by the fact that trade unions use secondary action in order to gain a number of diverse objectives. If everyone were to agree that secondary action is a form of economic coercion, essentially monopolistic in nature, and if secondary actions were utilized always to compel unwilling employees to become union members, the problem of drafting appropriate preventive legislation would be simplified considerably. Indeed, the proposal already offered would suffice. The prohibition of union "restraint or coercion [of free employee choice], whether by peaceful picketing or otherwise," would cover secondary strikes and all the known forms of secondary boycotts described in Chapter 10, such as "hot-cargo" agreements and blacklisting.

In regard to the current lack of agreement concerning the characterization of secondary action, not much can be added here to what has already been said above and in Chapters 10 and 11. As stated there, the present writer is of the opinion that all forms of secondary union action for organizational purposes are economically coercive in character. They are designed to impose unionization upon unwilling employees, not through peaceable persuasion and solicitation, but through economic pressure, usually in the form of a threat to the unwilling workers' livelihood. Furthermore, secondary action is monopolistic in the sense that, unless prohibited, it must necessarily result ultimately in the coerced unionization of all employees which unions wish to organize.

A union which achieves the total unionization of a craft or an industry through noncoercive methods cannot be accused of monopolistic conduct, any more than a business firm can be accused of monopolistic conduct simply because it emerges as the only business in an industry owing to its superior efficiency. Monopolistic conduct means, in short, coercive conduct; it means achieving monopoly by means of coercive devices, as contrasted to superior excellence in service or performance or to the volitional activity of the relevant participants.

If, in a social group, one person does all the talking, it is not accurate to say that that person has "monopolized the conversation," unless he has aggressively suppressed all others who might wish to talk. If one person does all the talking because by common consent he is the one whom the others most wish to hear, one may say that he has had a monopoly of the conversation; but it would be inaccurate to say that he "monopolized." So too when all employees in a certain trade, craft, or industry freely choose to join a given union, one cannot say that the union has monopolized; but when people join because the union has threatened their livelihood, coercive monopolization is present.

To repeat, if widespread agreement to this analysis existed, the simple prohibition of *all forms* of trade-union economic coercion would suffice. However, since such agreement is not assured, a more detailed prohibition of secondary economic coercion of free employee choice seems required. In addition to the provisions already set forth, the NLRA should be amended to provide that:

It shall be an unfair labor practice for a labor organization or its agents, directly or indirectly, to induce or to attempt to induce the cessation or interruption of any economic relationship, or any work-stoppage, temporary or prolonged, by one or more employees, of the whole or any part of the duties of such employees, whether by means of another work-stoppage, a contractual arrangement, picketing, or otherwise: *Provided that* nothing in this subsection shall be construed as prohibiting a peaceful, primary strike concerning wages or working conditions in an appropriate bargaining unit, called or ratified against an employer by the labor organization representing a majority of the employer's employees in such bargaining unit: *Provided further* that nothing in this subsection shall be construed as prohibiting appeals by a labor organization or its agents to the general public which contain no threats of reprisal or force and which are not combined with or a part of activities violative of this or any other law.[16]

The purpose of the foregoing proposal is to prohibit all forms of coercive union action, while at the same time preserving the right to strike and to make noncoercive appeals to the general public. The provision is complicated. But, it should be remembered, the complications are owing to the confusion which prevails now and has long prevailed as to the proper characterization of secondary trade-union conduct. If one could rely upon consistency in the application of the term "coercion," so lengthy a provision would not be necessary. For it will be remembered that when the Wagner Act quite simply and straightforwardly outlawed "interference, restraint, and coercion" by *employers,* the ruling authorities held that *all* forms of economic coercion by employers were prohibited. Had the authorities been consistent,[17] the identical prohibition of union coercion would have been similarly applied. The complexity of the provision just offered is therefore caused by the refusal of the NLRB and of other legal authorities to be consistent. A basic rule of statutory interpretation, and a basic rule of good reasoning, too, requires that the same words be given equivalent meaning when used in different parts of a single document, unless the context strongly suggests that the words were used in different senses. Rejection of this rule produces chaos, and dispelling chaos can be a complicated job. Those inclined to criticize the provision offered here because it is complicated must keep these considerations in mind.

Employer Coercion

While the authorities have been inordinately restrictive in applying the term "coercive" to union activities, they have at one time or another held that almost every kind of *employer* activity is "coercive," whether or not a meaningful conception of the term would cover the employer conduct in question. Thus employers have been held guilty of unlawful "coercion" if they criticized unions sharply, calling them such names as "communists";[18] if they withheld or threatened to withhold benefits from employees as a means of discouraging unionization;[19] if they induced or encouraged outsiders, such as local civic associations, to discourage unionization;[20] if they suggested that they would shut down their businesses in order to frustrate union organization;[21] and, indeed, even if they offered special wage increases or other benefits at a time when a union began organizational efforts.[22]

Attention to the foregoing decisions will demonstrate that the authorities had no such difficulties in regard to employer coercion as they have had in regard to union coercion. Employers were held to have violated the law's ban on coercion whether their conduct was "primary" or "secondary." It made no difference that an employer enlisted the aid of outsiders. An agreement among employers to blacklist strikers was regarded simply as economic coercion of employees.[23]

With respect to most of the activities just mentioned little need be said here. A meaningful conception of coercion quite reasonably covers most of them, as it would cover, if the concept were applied fairly, the types of union action we have been discussing. But two of the types of activity just mentioned come within no reasonable conception of coercion. The first of these is the employer speech critical of unions. For this, however, the current law has provided a corrective. As now written, the law privileges employer statements of opinion which contain no threats of reprisal or force or promise of benefit.[24] An important question, however, is whether or not the current law should not be amended in order to permit employers more freely to offer benefits directly to their employees.

For it should never be forgotten that *employees and their choice* are the primary concern of modern labor relations law. To forbid employers to offer benefits directly to employees is to lose sight of that fact. In the first place, it is very difficult to see how a reasonable conception of coercion would prohibit an offer of benefit. Of course, if employers condition a benefit to employees upon an indefinite renunciation of unionization,[25] one might reasonably argue that the policy of safeguarding the right of self-organization is frustrated. On the other hand, if it is the free choice of employees which counts, we must rid ourselves of any suggestion that national policy somehow favors unionization over nonunionization. We are concerned with the well-being of employees. If they can secure greater benefits from employers directly than indirectly through union action, the direct method should be preferred.

The law should therefore be amended to prohibit only employer threats of reprisal or force. Statements promising benefits should be privileged, except where conditioned upon a renunciation of the right of self-organization. A provision of this kind would make it lawful for an employer, during an organizational drive, to offer benefits directly to employees. There is no need to fear that employers will offer benefits, only to withdraw them after employees have voted against union representation. If employers should do so, they would only be breeding a great deal of trouble for themselves. They would provide irrefutable arguments to union organizers in subsequent election campaigns. With their right of self-organization guaranteed, employees would be induced by duplicitous employer conduct to see in unions their only real safeguard; and, after choosing union representation, they would be inclined to give the employer a much harder time of it than would otherwise be the case.

Employers, therefore, understanding these things, would be induced to extend themselves in providing *and maintaining* benefits to their employees. To consider this a form of coercion of free employee choice is as untenable as it would be to insist that consumers are coerced by businessmen who secure their patronage by offering them products of the highest quality at the lowest price. Indeed, acquiring the high regard of employees through the extension of benefits to them is the very contrary of coercion. That our law should confuse a concept with its contrary is an unhealthy and dangerous thing. While the problem under discussion is not very great in itself, it becomes important when considered together with the total confusion surrounding the conception of coercion. If we hope ever to attain a satisfactory understanding of the meaning of coercion, we should not omit any opportunity to correct misconceptions.

It should be added, however, that the employer privilege to offer benefits directly to employees ought to be confined to the organizational stage. After employees have selected a union and the union is bargaining for them, the law should not permit an employer to make more attractive offers directly to employees than he is making to the union. This prohibition should be based, however, not on the anticoercion policy, but on the policy promoting orderly and efficient collective bargaining. There is no mere quibble or word-play here. It is always important to have a clear understanding of the policy intended to be promoted by particular measures. For if the policy orientation is not clear, there is a tendency to err in establishing the proper characterization of particular measures. This kind of confusion probably accounted in the first place for the general prohibition of all offers of benefits by employers.

Representation of Small Groups

If the national labor policy is to be oriented in terms of free employee choice rather than in terms of the convenience of unions or employers, allowance must be made for a good deal of fractional representation. Insistence upon single, large bargaining units in production organizations including diverse skills may simplify collective bargaining in a superficial sense; but at the same time it tends to multiply minority groups and thus the occasions for unfair treatment. For there can be no doubt that unions, like all other agencies of representation, have a natural tendency to favor majorities.

Under its present rules, the National Labor Relations Board makes some allowance for this problem. It will permit the severance of a small craft unit from a larger unit of production and maintenance employees in certain circumstances.[26] As consideration of a recent decision will demonstrate, however, the Board does not go nearly far enough, and it follows a standard which must necessarily result frequently in the frustration of the free choice of highly skilled workers. The case in question involved a small number of tool-and-die-makers employed by the Elgin National Watch Company.[27] These men had formed a social group which they called the Harmony Club. When a large union asked the NLRB to certify it as exclusive bargaining representative of all Elgin production and maintenance workers, the tool-and-die-makers asked that they be allowed to form a separate bargaining unit, with the Harmony Club as their bargaining representative. The NLRB rejected this request. It ruled that the Harmony Club might have a place on the election ballot, but only in competition with the large national union as the exclusive bargaining representative of *all* Elgin production and maintenance employees; it refused to declare the tool-and-die-makers a separate bargaining unit. Of course, it must have been obvious to the Board that the Harmony Club would have no chance in a general election, since the rank-and-file workers greatly outnumbered the tool-and-die-makers. Yet it had to refuse the tool-

and-die-makers' request, it said, because the Harmony Club had
not acted "traditionally" as a collective bargaining representative.

The criterion of "traditionality"—a creation of the NLRB, not
of Congress—clearly means that nothing new in the form of employee representation of small minority groups is ever to be
allowed; only unions which have acted in the past are to represent
such employees in the future. It is difficult to imagine a standard
which more effectively frustrates the free employee choice of bargaining representatives. A necessary consequence of the decision
in the Elgin case is the prejudicing of small, highly skilled craft
groups, since it is to be expected that a union representing both
rank-and-file workers and highly skilled craftsmen will not be
overly solicitous of the latter. Indeed, some unionists seem to take
pride in emphasizing as one of their goals the reduction of the
spread between the wages of skilled and unskilled workers.

Representation proceedings—including the determination of
appropriate bargaining units, the timing of elections, and voting
rules—today compose one of the most challenging and most un-
explored areas of labor policy. If Congress is really concerned
with promoting the free choice of employees, it must undertake
an exhaustive study of the issues raised in representation proceedings. There has been a great deal of experience in this area
during the last twenty years. On the basis of that experience, it
should be possible for Congress to set forth clear-cut and exhaustive legislative rules for representation proceedings. When it has
done so, it may utilize the National Labor Relations Board as a
strictly administrative agency to conduct those proceedings strictly
in accordance with the legislative rules. Appeals to the federal
courts should then be made available to any employee, union, or
employer which feels that the administrative agency has exceeded
its authority. Taking the Elgin case as an example under the
proposed procedure, the tool-and-die-makers would be allowed
to appeal directly to the courts when the NLRB refused to allow
them a separate bargaining unit.

An important point to remember in connection with the Elgin
case is that frustrations of free employee choice by the NLRB in
representation proceedings cannot be cured by recourse to the
courts, for at present such recourse is unavailable.[28] To put the
matter another way, an important right specifically stated in a

notable federal law is in actuality unsecured. It is that most unfortunate of all concepts in the law: a right for the deprivation of which there is no judicial remedy. When one considers that the Constitution of the United States expressly declares that the federal courts must have jurisdiction of all cases arising under statutes of the United States,[29] the whole situation becomes even more remarkable. For then, to the lack of wisdom and the unfairness, must be added the unconstitutionality of the deprivation of an appeal to the courts in instances such as that involved in the Elgin case. But this is another matter which will be discussed further in Chapter 19.

Chapter 18

FREE COLLECTIVE BARGAINING

Some economists have taken the position that collective bargaining is inconsistent with and potentially destructive of any free market.[1] This may be a sound view if the reference is to collective bargaining characterized by violent interference with the market, coercion of free employee choice, monopolistic control, and, ultimately, thoroughgoing governmental intervention.[2] But if the reference is to genuinely free collective bargaining, the judgment and the prediction lack merit.[3] Free collective bargaining is a principle inherent in the theory of the free society and differs in no material way from other institutions of the free market. Far from clashing with the free society, it is a product of one of the basic rights in such a society, the right of free association.[4]

On no subject in labor relations, indeed, is there as widespread agreement as there is in regard to the desirability of free collective bargaining. Union officers, employers, and labor relations specialists have all repeatedly announced allegiance to this principle; and labor law itself has long been evolving naturally toward according it a prominent role. Despite the agreement in principle and the long-run evolutionary trend, however, the current status of collective-bargaining law and practice leaves a great deal to be desired. Not every one means the same thing when he advocates "free collective bargaining." Moreover, a number of prevailing legal rules are inconsistent with "free collective bargaining."

This chapter is designed to offer a meaningful conception of free collective bargaining, to describe the more important departures from that conception in current law and practice, and to indicate the kinds of measures necessary to effectuate a policy of genuinely free collective bargaining. The thesis is, quite simply, that there are no insuperable problems in the creation and enforcement of a collective-bargaining policy in all respects consistent with the theory of the free society. The basic rules necessary to such a policy are simple, clear, and workable. Only understanding and will are needed to make collective bargaining a vital, fruitful institution of the free society.

Employer and Union Restraints

A free market is the essential prerequisite to free collective bargaining. In an environment other than that of the free market, the term "free collective bargaining" is an idle and even deceptive abstraction, useful only to distort and misrepresent issues. Although achievement of a free market in labor relations depends to some extent upon the elimination of governmental intervention in collective bargaining, it depends mainly and more immediately upon the prevention of employer and trade-union interference with the market.

The free market can provide the means of civilized settlement of even the most complicated industrial disputes. If it is to do so, however, all violent, coercive, and monopolistic interference in its operation, whether by unions or employers, must be eliminated.

The economic issues in labor disputes can be satisfactorily solved only in a peaceful environment, for a satisfactory solution is one which accords with the wishes and desires of the employer and the employees immediately involved. If the employer is privileged to use force and violence as means of compelling the employees to work under terms unsatisfactory to them, it must be perfectly obvious to all that the underlying dispute has not been resolved in any enduring and satisfying way and that there has been no free collective bargaining. Hence every effort must be bent toward the elimination of employer compulsion and coercion in labor disputes.

The free market and free collective bargaining are no less sabotaged by intimidatory and violent union action. The will and desires of persons are frustrated as effectively by union violence, by the violence of organized workers, as they are by physical intimidation on the part of employers or nonunion employees. It is a matter of common understanding that unions

picket in numbers in order to block access to struck premises.[5]
The object is to prevent by intimidation and physical coercion
the employment of workers, whether union members or not, who
are out of sympathy with the economic objectives of the striking
union. Only an extraordinary obtuseness can account for the
rather common failure to realize that such conduct by unions is
fundamentally responsible for most of the violence which occurs
in labor disputes. Only an equally extraordinary stubbornness
can account for the refusal to admit that no free market can
exist in labor relations as long as unions are allowed to picket in
numbers.

As already shown, law in the United States *formally* prohibits
all violent interference with the market.[6] However, as we have
also seen, the formal prohibition is rarely effective. In the area
of federal law the prohibition is almost completely ineffective.
The National Labor Relations Board will not issue a cease-and-
desist order until long after the damage has been done, until
long after the free market has been destroyed, in any particular
labor dispute. To speak of a deterrent effect produced by such
an order would be merely foolish. Moreover, the NLRB insists
that it has no power to make unions pay for the damage they do.[7]
And thus the efforts of the NLRB, so far as violence is concerned,
have no deterrent effect at all.

Conditions in some states are more consistent with the requirements of the free market and civilization. In others, where
injunctions against violent picketing carefully preserve the right
of the union to continue picketing in numbers, the situation is
substantially the one which prevails under the federal law. But
nowhere, not even in the states where the courts sometimes
prohibit all picketing after violence has occurred, can it be said
that an intelligent and effective method of *preventing* violent
interference with the free market prevails. The solution is, of
course, a law clearly and straightforwardly proscribing all picketing in numbers, faithful administration of such law, and accurate
judicial application and interpretation of the law.[8]

No tenable argument can be advanced in support of a "right"
in organized workers to picket in numbers. Such picketing can
be designed only to frighten people. If the union and the organized workers wish to advise, observe, and persuade only, they

should welcome a law which proscribes all picketing in numbers, for such picketing only interferes with and confuses advice, observation, and persuasion. One or two persons, or even a large sign, posted at each entrance to struck premises will not frighten anyone or obscure the events which are to be observed. Observation and persuasion proceed satisfactorily in a calm and peaceful atmosphere; they are impossible in an atmosphere of turbulence and fright.

Perhaps we as a nation will never take the steps necessary to establish civilization in labor disputes. But if we fail in this it will not be to our credit. Failure in this project will not be a glowing tribute to our "sympathy for the underdog"; for the underdog in picket-line violence is always the man who is frightened, hurt, or killed. That man, if he understands the situation accurately, will know that his society has failed him by its refusal effectively to prevent so atavistic an enemy of civilization as the picket line. With respect to the members of society as a whole, the refusal must reflect itself in all the undesirable consequences which flow from the absence of a free market and free collective bargaining.

Economically coercive, monopolistic restraints on the market may hamper free collective bargaining even more seriously than violent restraints do.[9] If, during a strike against one employer, all employers in the surrounding area should join together in refusing to deal with or to give jobs to the strikers, the ability to maintain the work-stoppage must certainly be impaired. The strikers will scarcely be able to hold out as effectively as they might if all other opportunities available in a free market remained available during the strike.

Merchants commonly extend credit to strikers; perhaps even more commonly, strikers take other jobs for the period of a work-stoppage; and one union or group of unions will frequently give financial aid to the striking members of another union. These are all normal incidents of the exercise of the property and contract rights of which a free market is composed. If employers were privileged in labor disputes to blacklist strikers, so that merchants and other employers would not deal with them, the market would be hampered. Blacklisting combinations by employers should therefore be prohibited, and it is a source of some satisfaction to report that such employer conduct has for a long time been prohibited by law in this country.[10]

The equivalent of the strikers' access to a free market is the access of employers to all alternatives available in a free market during a strike. When an employer seeks replacements for strikers, or when he asks another employer to take over services or production interrupted by a strike, he is exercising exactly the same right which strikers do in seeking other employment during a strike. The replacements who seek the work vacated by the strikers are also exercising the same basic property right. And the businessmen who agree to take over functions from the struck employer are likewise exercising the property right which is the basis of the free market. To permit a union to block the access of a struck employer to these free-market alternatives is to give that union the privilege of destroying the free market—the privilege, in short, of expropriating the struck employer, the striker-replacements, and the outside businessmen who are strangers to the labor dispute.

No reasonable theory of law can justify the extension of such a privilege to one party to a dispute while it is denied to the other party. If this privilege is to be available to unions, it must also be made available to employers. But if the objective is the promotion of free collective bargaining, then the privilege must be denied to both union and employer. As a matter of fact, current federal law, straightforwardly read and applied, does forbid secondary action of the kind under consideration to both union and employer.[11] So far as the employer is concerned, the law is enforced. But as regards secondary *union* action, the tendency in the courts has been to refuse to apply the law in accordance with its plain terms. Courts have held that a union may, during a strike, extend its coercive pressures to secondary employers who take over work from the struck employer.[12]

These decisions, since they are wrong in terms of both general principle and law, should of course be abandoned. Once the federal courts understand that the limitation of union coercion of outsiders is balanced by the proscription of employer coercion or blacklisting of strikers, they may well abandon their erroneous interpretation on their own motion. In any event, the proposal already made in Chapter 17 is designed to correct this misapplication of law and principle.

As to the state courts, the problem is more complicated. Some state courts, under either common-law principles or statutes, prohibit almost all forms of secondary union action. Others prohibit very few forms.[13] The most clean-cut solution would be to accept a federal statute of the kind offered here as applicable to all labor disputes, whether "intrastate" or "interstate" in character. Failing this, a uniform state law forbidding all secondary union action would seem the best alternative. Since there is little chance of either of the foregoing being accepted, the only hope is that state courts will come to the realization that secondary union action flagrantly violates the property rights which it is the duty of the common law to defend. One or another of these alternatives must fructify if there is to be genuinely free collective bargaining.

Governmental Restraints

All interventionism affects labor relations and collective bargaining to some degree. High, discriminatory corporate and personal income taxes impede capital formation, industrial growth, and competition. They thus influence the general environment of collective bargaining by limiting the alternatives available to workers; and the consequent tendency for wages to be lower than they otherwise might be tends to reduce standards of living. Tariffs and other subsidies tend likewise to impoverish everyone, and often bear intimately upon labor relations problems. The maritime industry offers a significant example. There, subsidies of one kind and another to American shipowners have weakened their resistance to the antisocial, coercive, and monopolistic pressures exerted by the maritime trade unions. The result has been a wage structure for maritime workers which bears no relationship to reality, which has made competition between American and foreign shipowners a joke, and which, in normal and expectable fashion, has continuously evoked more and ever more tortuous forms of interventionism. Another obvious result has been the underemployment of American seamen.

We must confine ourselves here, however, to interventionism as it relates directly to labor relations and collective bargaining; for that type of interventionism presents difficulties and complexities enough. As has been shown in Chapters 12-15, governmental intervention in the collective-bargaining process takes an extreme variety of forms. It has tended to give large, affiliated unions advantages over smaller, independent unions; and the effect of complex and detailed regulations of the negotiation aspects of the bargaining process has been to hamper the resistance of employers to union pressures.

The general objective should be, if the goal is free collective bargaining, to eliminate all political pressures from negotiations between unions and employers. Political pressures have worked their way into collective bargaining most extensively by way of the requirement that bargaining be in "good faith." On the basis of this requirement, the National Labor Relations Board and the courts have come very close to repealing the statutory declaration to the effect that the duty to bargain does *not* imply any duty to make a concession or to reach an agreement.[14] Some decisions imply that employers must make counterproposals if they do not want their "good faith" doubted.[15] The Board and some courts have insisted that employers must give extensive wage and other information to unions, on the theory that "effective" collective bargaining requires such assistance to unions.[16] The Board has quite clearly indicated its displeasure with employers who take an adamant stand on certain employment matters and who insist that they will not share with unions any authority over hiring, firing, promoting, demoting, and so on.[17]

A reasonably effective method of avoiding such complex political pressures is to require employers only to *meet with* unions representing a majority of employees in an appropriate bargaining unit. Under such a definition of the duty to bargain (the duty, incidentally, which the Congress thought it was imposing in the original Wagner Act),[18] the employer would not be required to do anything more than confer with the union, as to any matters which the latter wished to raise. Moreover, conferring with the union could not be stretched into anything further than its plain meaning. It would mean, to take an extreme case, that an employer satisfied the legal duty if he did no more than listen to everything that the union negotiators had to say, and replied to every suggestion or proposal with an unqualified "no."

There is no need to fear that a duty to bargain so narrowly defined would tend to undermine collective bargaining. On the contrary, it would tend to make collective bargaining a freer and more flexible institution. Like all interpersonal relationships, those involved in collective bargaining tend to become complicated. A collective agreement represents an intricate series of intersecting and overlapping compromises.[19] Political intervention into such a complex tends only to confuse and inhibit. If the parties (the union and employer negotiators) are left completely alone, the agreement ultimately reached is far more likely to represent a mutually satisfactory compromise of the conflicting interests than is to be expected from a bargaining process hampered by political interventionism.

Fundamentally, terms and conditions of employment are a resultant of the combined effect of general market factors: the desires of and alternatives available to employees, prevailing fashions and trends as regards employment terms and conditions, the market position of the employer, and the productivity of the employer and his employees. Political interventionism, unless it goes so far as to subsidize the employer or the employees directly, can have no very great substantive effect upon employment terms or conditions. It serves mainly to confuse and to debilitate collective bargaining and employer-union-employee relations.

There is no reason to conclude, either, that the position of employees and their unions will be unduly weakened by imposing upon employers only a duty to meet with employee representatives. A protected right of self-organization and a guaranteed right to strike are sufficient to bring home to employers the inadvisability of arbitrary conduct in negotiations with employee representatives. What really counts is not whether an employer has to bargain "in good faith" in respect to, say, a complicated welfare-plan proposed by the union negotiators, but whether the employer feels that he can afford it, that the employees want it badly enough to strike if they do not get it, and that the employer will be worse off if there is a strike than he will be if he makes the concession sought by the union. The same is true, except in an infinitely more complicated sense, in respect of the totality of matters covered in negotiations. A duty to meet with union negotiators is all that is necessary. Indeed, the law need not even set forth that much of a duty. Any employer who fails to meet with the union representing a majority of his employees is only inviting a great deal of trouble for himself, whether or not he has a legal obligation to meet. If, notwithstanding the penalties which the employees and their union can impose, the employer still refuses to confer, the chances are very great that his being forced by the law to meet with the union will not be very productive. Still, on the possibility that a mere physical meeting will upon occasion avert a strike or other kind of a dispute, it is probably desirable that the law impose the minimal obligation of a meeting.[20]

A consequence reasonably to be expected of a limited bargaining requirement is that the institution of collective bargaining will develop more naturally, and that it will become a more effective instrument of establishing wages and working conditions, than under a regime of governmental intervention.

It need scarcely be added here, after the discussion in Chapter 15, that collective bargaining should be left free of governmental intervention even in industry-wide labor disputes. The present law, providing for "cooling-off" periods, involves about as much governmental regulation as is consistent with free collective bargaining. To go any further would be to supplant the free market with a rigged market—rigged against employers in most cases, probably, but quite possibly against organized workers when political conditions are propitious. Industry-wide strikes can cause a great deal of inconvenience and even tragic harm. Yet these are less to be dreaded than the consequences of governmental intervention.

A habit of political interventionism in economic disputes can result only in the substitution of the edicts of politicians for the freedom of action of employers, employees, and union officers. Consider the dispute in the steel industry during 1951 and 1952. Of this dispute, Mr. Harry S. Truman, then President of the United States, says in his memoirs: "The demands of the steel workers did not seem out of line to me."[21] A few paragraphs later, he observes that the "profits of the steel companies were constantly rising." The steel companies had not instituted action for price increases. They had only declared that, if the union representing the steel workers insisted upon wage increases, price increases would be necessary. Referring to the companies' attitude, Mr. Truman notes that the "nation was drafting its men to serve on the field of battle." In the circumstances, he says, "I thought that the ammunition and arms manufacturers and their raw materials producers ought not to use the emergency to insist on extra profits." When, notwithstanding these opinions, the steel workers' union and the companies insisted upon "extra profits," Mr. Truman took over the control of the steel companies, manifestly with a view to establishing the exact terms and conditions of employment which were to prevail. This action, he writes, should not be confused with "expropriation of private property."

Mr. Truman's insistence that his conduct did not amount to expropriation must of course not be allowed to modify the facts. His conduct, whatever he might say about it, may be fairly defined as an attempt at expropriation. For an integral aspect of the right of private property is the ability to put a value upon one's goods or services and to control the disposition of the objects of one's property rights; and thus when Mr. Truman "seized" the steel companies, he intended to exercise the control which the right of private property vests in the owners of goods, services, and means of production.

Mr. Truman's analysis of the facts and circumstances may tend to divert attention from the real problems and consequences involved in governmental intervention in the collective-bargaining process. But a firm grip on the main point will emphasize the fact that in the steel dispute an attempt was made to impose prices, wages, and working conditions by political fiat. That the political force then in power happened to find the union's position the more attractive one is interesting; but in terms of the larger analysis, it is only a relatively unimportant detail. The important consideration lies in the expropriation inherent in the abrogation of free collective bargaining. Intervention into the collective-bargaining process means both expropriation and the end of free collective bargaining.

The current structure of unionization and the current deficiencies in the controls over abuse of power by union leaders lead to industry-wide labor disputes and create great temptations to political intervention. These temptations must be resisted if we are to have a viable collective-bargaining policy. The only satisfactory long-run solution is a structure of unionism which reflects more the desires and interests of workers and less the power motivations of union officials. The hope for such a structure rests essentially in vigorous promotion of the principle of free employee choice.

This principle can play, and under present law does play, an important role in collective bargaining. The law at present provides that strikers who have been replaced are not entitled to vote in representation elections conducted after the strike is no longer current.[22] Under the present law, only the persons currently employed in a bargaining unit are eligible to vote in elections involving the selection of bargaining representatives for that unit. The theory is that the principle of free employee choice would be violated if persons not employed in a given bargaining unit were given a voice in the selection of representatives for that unit.

Quite plainly the current law is correctly oriented. To depart from it would be like permitting residents of Chicago to vote for candidates for the mayoralty of New York. Yet, precisely such a condition existed in labor relations at one time, under the Wagner Act; and, more important, there is strong pressure today in favor of returning to that anomalous rule.[23]

Anyone who correctly understands the consequences reasonably to be expected of a departure from the current rule must resist these pressures if he is in favor of free collective bargaining. The proposed revision would tend to make union leaders even more careless than they are now in calling strikes. Under the current rule, a union leader takes a real risk of losing his own influence if he errs too badly in his leadership. It is true that union leaders never suffer as badly during strikes as the strikers themselves do; the union leader's salary usually continues. Still, the current rule does tend to impose a functional, structural check upon union leadership. The union leader may lose his representative status if he errs too badly in calling a strike when many are unemployed, and if he persists in that error.

Objectors to this check upon the abuse of union power contend that it gives employers the power to defeat unionization. The argument is that since under current law an employer has the right to ask for a representative election whenever a controversy concerning the representation of his employees arises, employers will demand elections as soon as they have hired replacements for strikers. The replacements will naturally vote against the union which has called the strike, and, since the strikers will not be eligible to vote in the election, the striking union will be defeated.

This argument distorts the pattern of representation procedure under the current law. An employer may secure an election only when a genuine controversy concerning representation exists *among his employees*. Furthermore, there can be only one representation election a year in any bargaining unit. If a union calls a strike, and if during that strike the employer is able to replace a majority of the strikers, he may still not secure an election unless a year has elapsed since the last one.[24] If more than a year has elapsed since the preceding election, the striking union is still not arbitrarily denied a place on the ballot. It may compete for representative status among the employees. It will lose only if the employees do not want it to continue as their bargaining representative.[25]

This account of the character of representation proceedings reveals the true nature of the demand for a change in the present rules. The demand for a change is, properly understood, a demand for a special privilege. It is a demand by unions for the special privilege to make mistakes without incurring any penalties. More important than that, it is a demand for the special privilege of frustrating free employee choice. It is entirely accurate to say that unions, in seeking a revision of the current eligibility rules, are insisting that they should have the privilege of stuffing the ballot boxes in representation elections.

The current rule is vitally necessary to the integrity of the principle of free employee choice. Abandoning this rule will mean in effect that *employees* in a bargaining unit do not have the right of self-determination. Again, abandonment will tend to encourage stupid and arrogant conduct by union leaders; it will relieve them of a part of the responsibility to exercise with

260 A LABOR POLICY FOR THE UNITED STATES

care their power to call strikes. To do this would be the equivalent of saying to businessmen that they may carelessly raise prices without the fear that they will lose their positions on the market if they do so. The interests in free employee choice, in free collective bargaining, and in the encouragement of responsible union leadership all converge in favor of the present rule declaring strikers ineligible to vote in elections in bargaining units where they are not employed.

Respect for Collective Agreements

If collective bargaining is to occupy a respected status in the community, its most significant product, the collective agreement, must be scrupulously honored and enforced. Disrespect for collective agreements by the parties who make them, or a legal status shrouded in ambiguity, must necessarily redound in the long run to the disadvantage of the whole institution of collective bargaining. Those who are in favor of collective bargaining, therefore, must insist upon a status for the collective agreement comparable to the status of traditional contracts.

As has already been noted, the law is well on the way to achievement of these goals. The great problems of principle have been resolved. The collective agreement is generally regarded an enforceable contract, and suits may be brought in almost all courts, by unions, employers, or employees.[26] Only two deficiencies of any magnitude remain: first, the Supreme Court's narrow interpretation of the circumstances in which unions may bring legal actions based on collective agreements;[27] and second, the current uncertainty as to whether or not the federal courts may decree specific performance of collective agreements.[28]

A coherent collective-bargaining policy requires reversal of the Supreme Court's narrow construction. The Taft-Hartley Act should be amended to state clearly that the federal courts have jurisdiction to apply the general law of contracts to collective agreements, and that unions, employers, and employees may bring suit for any violation of a collective agreement. The law should be amended also to provide explicitly that the jurisdiction of the federal courts extends to the issuance of injunctive relief in appropriate cases involving the violation of collective agreements. These proposals would bring to collective bargaining the same rules and principles which the common law has been developing for centuries in regard to other contractual relationships. The law of labor relations has been a heavy loser as a result of its long divorcement from the general law. A sensible policy in the circumstances requires that the losses be cut—that, wherever possible, the law of labor relations become an integral part of the general law.

The parties to a collective agreement, like the parties to any other agreement, may terminate or modify their agreement, before the stipulated termination date, when both wish to do so. But neither party, under present law, may unilaterally terminate or modify the agreement *before* the stipulated termination date, or take aggressive action, such as a strike or lockout, in order to do so.[29] This provision, too, brings to collective bargaining one of the rudimentary principles of the general law of contracts and is manifestly a reasonable and proper rule for collective bargaining. As such, the only reason for mentioning it here is to reaffirm its desirability. The reaffirmation is necessary because, notwithstanding the plain import of the statute, there has been a tendency to permit unilateral attempts to modify collective agreements before the stipulated termination date.[30] Since the statute is already as clearly phrased as possible, one can only exhort the courts to continue to perform their judicial duty faithfully: to apply the law in accordance with its plain meaning.

Chapter 19

ENFORCEMENT OF LABOR POLICY: A SENSIBLE JURIDICAL STRUCTURE

Measured against the subject of this chapter, the matters considered in the preceding chapters may seem inconsequential. There we encountered errors, distortions, and perversions of law. Here we come face to face with a more portentous development: the destruction of law itself.

Let the reader consider what his reaction would be if he were seriously harmed by unlawful conduct but could find no justice under law, could not even find a court of law to hear his grievance. He will then accurately understand the situation which tends to prevail today in labor relations. A worker has his means of livelihood wrenched from him by the unlawful conduct of an employer or a trade union but can get no court to hear him. A union suffers harm through the unlawful conduct of an employer or another union but finds it impossible to get a hearing, let alone the relief which the law seems to promise. An employer spends a lifetime building a business upon which the livelihood of many depends but finds all courts of law closed to him when a union *unlawfully* injures or even threatens to destroy it.

Such is the situation which is emerging in the field misleadingly called "the law of labor relations."[1] There is, properly speaking, *no* law of labor relations today. It is not true in labor relations that "every man is entitled to his day in court," or that an effective remedy is available for every wrong. The rule of law indispensable to any free society simply does not exist. It has been destroyed in labor relations by a complex of developments which are implacably reactionary in character and profoundly at odds with the evolutionary processes of centuries of Anglo-American law.

The Great Tradition of Progressive Judicial Reform

Patiently and steadily, despite false turnings and setbacks, Anglo-American law has sought over the centuries the just and yet effective juridical institutions necessary to secure the personal rights which are the essential features of the free society. Progress has been measured in terms of achieving ready access to the courts, disinterested judges, fair hearings with the irreducible minimum of technicalities or surprises, an effective remedy for every legal wrong, the uniting in a single court of both common law and equity powers so that the best techniques of both might be available in every case, and, at the highest level, a single rule of law to cover the broadest possible area of human affairs.

The great reformers and reform movements in the law have taken such objectives as the substance of their plans. Common-law judges before the twelfth century increasingly liberalized the access of wronged persons to the courts, and when the common law thereafter became technical and restrictive, Maitland tells us, the English Chancellors began "driving the law through those accidental impediments which sometimes unfortunately beset its course."[2] Then a towering Chief Justice of England, Lord Mansfield, joined law and equity and with them what seemed to him the best rules of law, regardless of source.[3] Although negated for a while in England by retrograde successors, Mansfield's work took root in the American colonies and was to influence what is perhaps the greatest legal reform document in the history of the world: the Constitution of the United States.[4] Progress accelerated in that most progressive of all centuries, the nineteenth, stimulated by the zealous Bentham and culminating in the English Judicature Act of 1875 which wedded forever law and equity in England.[5]

Reform progressed in the United States during the nineteenth century on largely similar terms: liberalizing procedures, reducing technicalities to a minimum, unifying law and equity. But the United States during the twentieth century does not seem to have grasped the true measure and character of progress in the law. Direct access to the courts is ever more limited. While procedures have been formally liberalized, the ideal of "speedy justice" is foundering in the always exasperating and often tragic delays of crowded court dockets.[6] Many of the states persist in the penchant for elective judges and thus hamper progress toward a genuinely disinterested administration of justice. Law and equity have been formally merged, but anti-injunction legislation has made it impossible for equity to apply its direct and effective techniques in labor relations, a field where they are indispensable if injuried parties are to have any real relief. The once shining ideal of the rule of law flickers weakly; interventionist ideology threatens momentarily to engulf it in a welter of special interest legislation, offering a favorable rule for each politically significant voting bloc.

In terms of the great tradition of progressive legal reform, the twentieth century must be characterized, on balance, as retrogressive, even reactionary, with only Chief Justice Vanderbilt of New Jersey and a few others standing out in the tradition of Mansfield, the framers of the Constitution, Bentham, and the other great reformers of the administration of justice.[7] We have indeed in many ways gone backwards, in our ignorance repeating mistakes and following again false turnings which were explored in sixteenth- and seventeenth-century England and eighteenth-century America, only to be found dead ends. Instead of improving the administration of justice, we have abandoned it. This has happened in many areas of law; but in none so conclusively as in labor relations.

The purpose of this chapter is to document that charge, and to suggest changes which will set us once more on the route to the achievement, in labor relations at least, of effective justice under law for every person who has been wronged. I shall show in this chapter that the rule of law does not exist in labor relations; that there a man is *entitled* in only exceptional cases to a day in court, no matter how unlawfully he has been harmed; and that the relief available to persons harmed by unlawful conduct is more often than not inadequate. I shall show how this condition has come about, and how profoundly retrograde it is. I shall, finally, offer the simplest and best remedy consistent with the great tradition of progressive legal reform for a condition which must seem intolerable to every person who wishes to live in a free society.

Atavism: No Man Is Entitled to a Day in Court

We shall be concerned here with persons or organizations involved in interstate commerce. This category includes the overwhelming preponderance of workers, unions, and employers in the United States; for relatively few are engaged in strictly local activities, having no effect upon interstate commerce. In respect to those few, it would not be as accurate to say that access to the courts does not exist as it is in respect to the many more whose activities affect interstate commerce. For the remainder of this chapter, therefore, unless the contrary is indicated, we shall be referring to the latter.

When a worker, a union leader, or an employer suffers a wrong which he believes to be unlawfully inflicted, his legal counsel may consider four agencies as possible sources of redress. These four are: the National Labor Relations Board; a state labor relations board (if the state happens to have one); a federal court; or a state court. After having informed himself on the law, however, legal counsel will conclude that in all probability his client is *entitled* to no remedy—and not even to a hearing—no matter how clearly unlawful the harm done may be, unless it happens to be physical harm. And even then, the availability of an adequate, effective remedy will often seem questionable.[8]

If relief is sought from the National Labor Relations Board, the injured party will learn that he must file an "unfair practice charge" with the General Counsel of that agency. Having filed a charge, he must await the General Counsel's decision. If the General Counsel declines to prosecute the charge, the injured party has no further recourse, no way of compelling the General Counsel to entertain his charge. He has no way, indeed, even of knowing whether the charge was dismissed because it failed to spell out a violation of law, or because it was not within the jurisdiction of the NLRB, or because insufficient facts were set forth, or because the General Counsel or a subordinate simply did not like his looks or sympathize with his plight. There is, in short, no way in the world for the injured party to find out why his complaint was denied a hearing. The General Counsel may offer an explanation; but he is under no enforceable obligation to do so. Moreover, if the General Counsel does in fact issue a complaint, the National Labor Relations Board may then refuse to hear it, without giving any explanation of its refusal other than the arbitrary statement that, in the discretion of the Board, a hearing on the complaint would not be advisable.

Some will say, perhaps, that such a situation cannot be, that surely the courts are available to remedy such arbitrary denials of legal process. Nevertheless, the situation does exist. If the injured person goes to a federal court, he will be told that there is no appeal from a refusal by the General Counsel to issue a complaint.[9] The court will say to him, too, that whether or not the NLRB wishes to pass upon any unfair practice is entirely within its discretion.[10] Unless the NLRB and its General Counsel concur in giving an injured person a hearing on the merits of his complaint, therefore, he will get no hearing in the federal system. No federal court will command either the Board or the General Counsel to act.

Furthermore, the federal court itself will not act. It will not give a hearing on the merits of the case, unless it happens to involve conduct which has been declared by federal law to be unlawful as well as an unfair labor practice.[11] With respect to the few types of conduct falling into that category, moreover, the injured party will not be able to secure injunctive relief, the only effective form of relief against the prohibited practices; he may secure only money damages.[12] In summary, as regards the vast preponderance of unfair labor practices, relief in the federal system is available only if the NLRB and its General Counsel, in the exercise of their discretion, agree to provide a hearing.

If the injured party then turns to state courts or state administrative agencies, he will in most instances fare no better. Here, however, we face a vast, almost indescribable confusion.[13] Out of this confusion, the injured person may in some instances succeed ultimately in having his day in court; he may finally, if he is extraordinarily tenacious, force matters to a hearing on the merits although even then he will have suffered grievous, perhaps irreparable, injury before he secures any relief.[14] But in the preponderance of cases he will probably secure no hearing

on the merits and no relief at all. State courts and state administrative agencies will tell him that their jurisdiction has been
pre-empted, that they sympathize with his plight, but that federal law, as interpreted by the United States Supreme Court,
precludes a hearing in state courts on matters "covered by federal
law."[15]

It must be emphasized, lest we sacrifice accuracy to drama, that
the situation varies from one state and from one court to another.
Some state courts will give a hearing and ultimately relief to an
injured person who has not been able to get a hearing from the
NLRB or its General Counsel.[16] Some state courts go so far as
to grant a hearing to those few injured persons who, because of
the local nature of their activities, seem not to be engaged in
interstate commerce at all, or who, at any rate, do not fall within
the jurisdictional standards which the NLRB issues from time
to time.[17] But most state courts are now tending to conclude that
the Supreme Court has forbidden them to exercise any jurisdiction at all.[18] Moreover, those state judges who cannot bring
themselves willingly to acquiesce in this destruction of law find
themselves pretty consistently reversed by the Supreme Court,
and steadily bombarded by the NLRB and its General Counsel.[19]
Federal Judge Moore has put the situation well:

The General Counsel refuses to issue a Complaint on which an adjudication could be made, and then turns around and contends that the
State procedure is precluded. In effect, the General Counsel ... is contending ... that there should be no remedy at all.[20]

If the situation is to be remedied, complete understanding of
the causes which have brought it about is necessary. These
causes lie partly in Congressional action and partly in action of
the Supreme Court. Congress is responsible for the rule that the
refusal of the NLRB General Counsel to issue a complaint may
not be reviewed by any federal court. It is also responsible for
the creation of the National Labor Relations Board as a judicial
agency. Whether or not Congress intended the Board as distinct
from the General Counsel to have an unreviewable discretion to
dismiss complaints, this writer doubts.[21] But there can be no
doubt of Congressional responsibility for the other matters; they

are clearly and explicitly set forth in the National Labor Relations Act.[22]

They are equally clearly unconstitutional. The Constitution of the United States provides in Article III, Section 2, that "the judicial power [of the United States] shall extend to all cases, in law and equity, arising under this Constitution ... [and] the laws of the United States." As to what is meant by the "judicial power," the Constitution is perfectly clear. No one can read Section 1 of Article III of the Constitution without realizing that an administrative agency such as the NLRB, whose members are short-term political appointees, is not within the constitutional concept of judicial power:

The judicial Power of the United States, shall be vested in one supreme Court, and in such inferior Courts as the Congress may from time to time ordain and establish. The Judges, both of the supreme and inferior Courts, shall hold their offices during good behaviour, and shall, at stated Times, receive for their Services, a Compensation, which shall not be diminished during their Continuance in Office.

Congress did not act unconstitutionally in establishing rights and duties of employers, workers, and unions in the National Labor Relations Act. But it did violate the Constitution when it gave exclusive power to prosecute and adjudicate those rights and duties to the National Labor Relations Board and its General Counsel. For neither the General Counsel nor the personnel of the NLRB can be considered federal judges; neither has life tenure in office, nor any of the other characteristics of judicial office. Yet they are given judicial power which the Congress has expressly denied to the federal courts, the true repositories of the "judicial power of the United States."

When a person aggrieved by a violation of the NLRA is denied a hearing by the NLRB or its General Counsel, the fact that he may not then get a hearing from any federal court demonstrates beyond the shadow of any doubt that the judicial power of the United States is not extending to a case arising under a law of the United States. That this is unconstitutional should be evident to anyone who knows the language of Article III, Sections 1 and 2, of the Constitution.

Less evident, perhaps, is the unconstitutionality of the condition which prevails when the NLRB *has* granted a hearing.

Then, too, do NLRB members exercise judicial power without possessing the characteristics of judicial office plainly set forth in Article III, Section 1. The unconstitutionality is less evident because the NLRA gives the federal courts power to review NLRB decisions on the merits. If this were a power to pass completely upon the law and the facts as dealt with by the NLRB, the Constitution might not be violated. But the federal courts are held to have only a limited power to review conclusions of law and an even more limited power to review NLRB findings of fact.[23]

"Cases" are made up of legal issues and factual issues. Unless a court has full power to pass upon both the facts and the law of a case, its activity cannot be said to be coextensive with the "case."[24] The NLRA is a law of the United States; and a case involving the NLRA is a case arising under a law of the United States. As such, under the plain language of Article III, Section 2, of the Constitution, it is a case to which the true judicial power of the United States, vested only in the federal courts, must extend. In giving the federal courts only a limited power of review over decisions of the NLRB, therefore, the Congress acted unconstitutionally.

While the Congress has been responsible for the denial of the access of injured persons to the federal courts, the Supreme Court of the United States is essentially responsible for the denial of access to the state courts. The situation here, however, is far more complicated than the one just surveyed.

Grappling with the Supreme Court's pre-emption theory is a difficult project. The Court has never stated this theory exhaustively and unequivocally. It has never defined clearly either the statutory or constitutional basis of the theory, or its practical application. At times the Court seems to operate on the assumption that pre-emption is required by the Constitution; at times that it has a statutory basis. More frequently the two are mixed, with the Court saying that, in passing the NLRA, Congress intended to "occupy" the field of labor relations; so that any assumption of jurisdiction by a state court, whether the result of a decision by the state court would be consistent or inconsistent with the result intended by Congress, would clash with the will of Congress.[25]

The only possible constitutional basis for the Court's theory is to be found in the supremacy clause:

> This Constitution, and the Laws of the United States which shall be made in Pursuance thereof . . . shall be the Supreme Law of the Land; and the Judges in every State shall be bound thereby, any Thing in the Constitution or Laws of any State to the Contrary notwithstanding.

Perusal of this clause will demonstrate that only state-court decisions *in conflict* with federal laws are condemned. The supremacy clause cannot be read as forbidding state-court decisions *consistent* with federal law. Much less can it be read as forbidding all state-court jurisdiction over matters involving federal law or persons subject to federal jurisdiction. As a matter of fact there is implicit in the clause the assumption that state courts will take cases involving federal laws; otherwise there would be no point in requiring them to conform to federal law. Indeed, the framers of the Constitution took it for granted that state courts would participate in the enforcement of national law. So ardent a Federalist as Alexander Hamilton made this clear:

> The [Constitution] . . . by extending the authority of the federal head to the individual citizens of the several States, will enable the government to employ the ordinary magistracy of each, in the execution of its laws. . . . It merits particular attention . . . that the laws of the Confederacy . . . will become the SUPREME LAW of the land; to the observance of which all officers, legislative, executive, and judicial, in each State, will be bound by the sanctity of an oath. Thus the legislatures, courts, and magistrates, of the respective members, will be incorporated into the operations of the national government . . . and will be rendered auxiliary to the enforcement of its laws.[26]

If the Supreme Court's pre-emption theory held only that state courts may not hand down decisions in conflict with federal law, it would seem to be an accurate application of the supremacy clause. But in going much further, to hold that state courts may not assume jurisdiction at all over cases involving parties subject to federal power, the pre-emption theory finds no basis in the supremacy clause, or in any other provision of the Constitution, and flouts the clear understanding upon the basis of which the Constitution was approved and accepted. Nor can the Court claim for its unconstitutional theory the merit of "practicality." For denying the state courts a role in the enforcement of federal law is a most impractical and frustrating move. It hampers the enforcement of the national labor policy.[27]

The Court counters this argument by finding a Congressional intent in the Taft-Hartley Act to "occupy the field" to the exclusion of the state courts.[28] But extensive research and analysis have demonstrated that no such Congressional intent is evident in either the statute or the relevant legislative history of the statute.[29] The draftsmen of the Taft-Hartley Act, when they spoke at all of the possible effect of their legislation on the jurisdiction of state courts, talked as if they were adding to or supplementing remedies which state courts might afford, not as if they intended to exclude them.[30] Demonstrating the inaccuracy of the Supreme Court's reference to legislative intent, a bill now in Congress declares that:

No Act of Congress shall be construed as indicating an intent on the part of Congress to occupy the field in which such Act operates, to the exclusion of all state laws on the same subject matter, unless such Act contains an express provision to that effect.[31]

Two integrated considerations are relevant in connection with this bill. In the first place, it does nothing more than restate the rule which has always been thought applicable by the Supreme Court itself in cases of possible federal pre-emption.[32] Therefore, it demonstrates, in the second place, that in terms of the interpretive rules prevailing when it was drafted, the Taft-Hartley Act was never intended by Congress to oust state courts of their traditional jurisdiction. If this bill becomes law, the Supreme Court will have to reverse its decisions ousting the state courts of jurisdiction, unless it wishes to abandon completely the theory of legislative supremacy.

Sometimes a person subject to federal jurisdiction will go to a state court for relief from conduct which violates a state law but which does not violate the Taft-Hartley Act. The Supreme Court suggested in one case that even in such a situation the jurisdiction of the state courts is pre-empted.[33] Whatever Congress did not prohibit in the Taft-Hartley Act, the Supreme Court asserted, it intended absolutely to privilege.[34] Yet nothing could be easier to demonstrate than the error and fallacy of this proposition. Indeed the Supreme Court has itself emphasized the fallacy. It has held in case after case that conduct not declared unlawful in the Taft-Hartley Act is still entitled to no special privilege.[35] It has never been thought, and even now may not rationally be argued, that conduct is privileged against state regulation merely because it is not declared unlawful by federal law.[36] Throughout our history the states have been conceded and have exercised the power to regulate conduct left unregulated by federal law. The only limitations have been the ones found in the supremacy clause, striking down state laws *in conflict* with federal laws, and those direct and express prohibitions of state laws such as the contracts clause.[37] In the same bill which has already been referred to, Congress is seeking to drive home this point, too. The bill goes on to provide that:

> No Act of Congress shall be construed as invalidating a provision of State Law . . . unless there is a direct and positive conflict between an express provision of such Act and such provision of the State Law so that the two cannot be reconciled or consistently stand together.

This proposal does nothing more than reaffirm the Constitution, and the rule which the Supreme Court itself has applied for a good part of American history.[38] That it should be necessary for the Congress to instruct the Supreme Court on the Constitution and its own rules seems a strange thing.

The immediate causes of the denial of access to the courts in labor relations are thus to be seen in the combined action of the Congress and the Supreme Court. Congress has given the NLRB and its General Counsel arbitrary power to deny an injured person a hearing. Congress has closed the federal courts to persons injured by conduct forbidden under federal law. Congress did not, however, prevent unlawfully harmed persons from seeking whatever remedies they might find in the state courts. That blow to the ideal that every man is entitled to his day in court was struck by the Supreme Court.

Atavism in Equity

Retrogression in the twentieth century has not been confined to reducing access to the courts. It is to be seen also in the limitations which Congress and many state legislatures have imposed upon the use of equitable remedies (mainly injunctions) in labor disputes. Many "progressives" took an active part in the movement which resulted in the elimination of equity in labor relations, it is true. But it is for the reader to decide, when the relevant considerations are brought to attention, whether the movement is properly to be characterized as progressive.

The legal system of a dynamic, progressive society must be dynamic and progressive, too, in its own proper ways if it is to carry out the functions and the objectives allocated to it by a living and changing society. In many ways, equity has historically filled this role, has been the growing point in the Anglo-American juridical structure.[39] Sir Henry Maine went so far, indeed, as to generalize that equity and legislation are the devices which release the law from the anachronizing rigors of pure logic.[40] No a priori assumption against the virtue and utility of equity is therefore permissible. In Anglo-American law equity has historically served, on the contrary, to keep the real ends of law in prominent view: to circumvent when it could not directly eliminate the tendency of the common law to lose sight of main objectives in the labyrinth of intricate rules and distinctions which the mind of man often seems to revel in.[41] The great figures in Anglo-American legal history have in fact been great to a large degree because they have combined the best of law and equity. They have respected rules and distinctions—but with an eye always upon the main objectives. Their motto might well be: substantial and effective justice under law.[42]

One of the ancient deficiencies of the common law as an effective instrument of law enforcement was its incapacity as a rule to do anything more than give money damages to a person harmed by unlawful conduct. Yet in a great many instances a mere award of damages will not do effective justice. A money judgment can effectively remedy only such harm as can be measured with precision in terms of dollars and cents. It is a pale remedy for harm not measurable in money terms, an inadequate remedy for harm which, though economic in character, can still not be calculated with any certainty. A great deal of harm falls into one or the other of these categories, and this is true no less in labor relations than in other fields of human action. Unlawful trade-union conduct usually interferes with production and thus destroys an intricate web of relationships: between employers and employees, among employers and customers or suppliers, sometimes the infinitely complex interplay of a whole community. Harm of this kind can be measured with precision in money terms in only the rarest of cases. Even when it could be so measured, the common law had no way of making a trade union pay for the harm it did; the assets of trade unions could not be reached in common-law proceedings. Again, some types of unlawful harm are such that no *remedy* of any kind does any good. The law can perform its function adequately in such instances only by *preventing* the unlawful conduct.

To correct these deficiencies in the procedures of the common law has been one of the main historic functions of equity. And from a sound perception of this historic role has grown the formulation of the proper occasion for the issuance of equitable relief: *Equity will intervene to provide affirmative relief against unlawful conduct where no adequate remedy at law exists.*

This fundamental rule of equity has in no sense been developed particularly for use in labor disputes. It is a generic formulation held progressively applicable to all cases falling naturally within it. As one first-rate judge described equity's role in a case about as far removed from labor relations as can be imagined:

> ... the jurisdiction of equity is constantly growing and expanding, and relief is now granted in cases where formerly the courts would not have thought for a moment of so doing. From time immemorial it has been the rule not to grant equitable relief where a party praying for it had an adequate remedy at law; but modern ideas of what are adequate remedies are changing and expanding, and it is gradually coming to be understood that a system of law which will not prevent the doing of a wrong, but only affords redress after the wrong is committed, is not a complete system and is inadequate to the present needs of society.[43]

It is not necessary here to trace in detail the general course of equity's development in Anglo-American legal history. That job has been adequately and admirably done by others, who have shown clearly the progressive character of equity on the whole. Our interest is essentially in the role of equity in labor relations. However, we may note that in the opinion of many scholars, equity's role in labor relations was in no sense unique or anomalous. Roscoe Pound referred to labor and other cases indiscriminately, in tracing the course of developments in equity.[44]

Maitland, perhaps the most profound of all students of equity, tells us, with no particular reference to labor cases, that the "wrongs that the chancellor redressed were often wrongs of the simplest and most brutal kind: assaults, batteries, and forcible dispossessions."[45]

Although equity developed independently, its rules, its attitudes, its large-minded and sensible emphasis upon securing effective and substantial justice under law found in labor disputes appropriate occasion for the exercise of equitable powers and remedies. Here were problems with which only equity could adequately cope. Unlawful union action toward the end of the nineteenth century presented courts of equity in case after case with instances of harm done or threatened which could in no reasonable way be measured in money terms. And even if it could be measured in money terms, there was no way in which the injured parties could recover at law, since trade-union funds were not subject to legal process.[46] So, in numerous instances, equity enjoined unlawful strikes and boycotts;[47] most often it enjoined violent, intimidatory, and coercive interference by trade unionists with the relationships between employers and nonunion employees.[48] As noted in Chapter 14, however, peaceful strikes for higher wages were universally held privileged, lawful, and unenjoinable.

Trade unionists were nevertheless vastly irritated. At the turn of the century they launched a great crusade against "government by injunction." Politicians and others duly attended to the rumblings of the crusade, even when from it there emerged demands for the total abolition of equity.[49] They deceptively acknowledged the demands in 1914 by passing the Clayton Act; but the deception was revealed by an able Supreme Court, which demonstrated irrefutably that the Clayton Act, in regulating the issuance of injunctions in labor disputes, did nothing more than restate the best equity practice of the time.[50]

The best equity practice of the time was of course not enough for the trade unionists. They wanted no equity at all in labor relations. Indeed, if a statement frequently attributed to Samuel Gompers may be credited, the aim of trade unionists was to have no law at all, of any kind, applicable to their activities. They were to secure their wish before too many years had passed. The great crusade reached a high point in 1930, with the publication of one of the most influential law books ever written in this country, *The Labor Injunction*. Two years later the Congress passed the Norris-LaGuardia Act, which virtually wiped out the equity powers of the federal courts in labor disputes. Within ten years, most of the state legislatures followed Congress, although few went quite so far. Equity was pretty well taken care of; and, since equitable remedies were the only ones which had any tendency to check unlawful union conduct, one might as well say that the Gompers goal was substantially achieved.

Some may think that the success achieved by the trade unionists must have been well merited. If judgments of merit are to be based upon considerations other than strenuous effort, however, decision must be suspended until the arguments by or on behalf of the trade unionists are examined.

The central and most persistent contention was that courts defeated "strikes" by issuing injunctions in labor disputes. The exact form in which this contention was sometimes cast should be considered with care. *The Labor Injunction* put the case like this:

> The suspension of activities [by an injunction] affects only the strikers; the employer resumes his efforts to defeat the strike, and resumes them free from the interdicted interferences. Moreover, the suspension of strike activities, even temporarily, may defeat the strike for practical purposes and foredoom its resumption, even if the injunction is later lifted.[51]

This statement creates a clear general impression that strikes themselves were frequently enjoined, and thus defeated. Reference is made to "activities," "interdicted interferences," and "strike activities." And the writers are thus in a position to say that they did not contend that strikes themselves were being enjoined. Yet most persons hearing or reading such an argument will surely gain the impression that strikes as such were being enjoined. For there can be no question of "resumption" of a strike which has never been enjoined. And when the writers declare that resumption of a strike may be foredoomed after an injunction, they are surely implying that the strike has been enjoined.

Whether intended or not, this is the impression which such arguments conveyed. Indeed, it is also the view held today by many, who are still inflamed by the old battle-cry, "government by injunction." The view is, of course, erroneous. Courts are not now, were not then, and had not been enjoining simple peaceful strikes for higher wages or better working conditions.[52] But nothing of this shows in *The Labor Injunction*. That book is copiously documented with many extensive charts setting forth all sorts of details about labor injunctions. Yet one looks in vain among these charts for information concerning the number of instances in which *strikes* were enjoined.

In fact, the courts had been enjoining the violent, intimidatory, coercive activity of trade unions, not strikes for higher wages and better working conditions.[53] In many cases there were no strikes at all to enjoin—but only violent attempts by trade unionists to interfere with employees and employers who wanted only to go peaceably about their business. *The Labor Injunction* cites the famous Tri-City case sixteen times,[54] suggesting, at the very least, a suspect character for it.[55] But there was no strike in that case. Upon resuming operations after a shutdown caused by lack of business, an employer had managed to get a substantial number of employees back to work. Dissatisfied with the wages offered by the employer, a group of unions, although apparently not representing the views of any employees, declared a "strike" and established squads of pickets who were guilty of numerous acts of violence in their attempt to prevent the workers from carrying on. Only two of the several hundred persons actually employed joined in the picketing. To say that the Tri-City case essentially involved a strike would therefore be stretching things pretty far. Moreover, regardless of one's conclusion on that matter, the fact is that the Supreme Court issued no "strike injunction" in that case. It prohibited only picketing in numbers and violent interference with the undoubted right of the employer and the nonunion employees to enter into an employment contract. It did not prohibit any strike.[56]

We must examine, too, the implication of the statement, "the employer resumes his efforts to defeat the strike, and resumes them free from the interdicted interferences." The suggestion here is that employers derived undue advantages from injunctions. But the truth is that the injunctions only preserved the right of employers and prospective employees to come into contact without violent or intimidatory interference by others. How this may with any integrity be viewed as an undue advantage is impossible to see. It gives the employer and the nonunion employees no more advantage than the union men derive from their right to strike. The bitter complaints about "government by injunctions" can be pretty well judged on the basis of these considerations. Trade unionists and their supporters were not seeking fair play; they were *objecting* to it. Most contentions put forward in the great crusade were of that character.

Protagonists of anti-injunction legislation have always made much of the allegedly unprecedented character of the opinion of equity courts that one's business is a "property right" which equity ought to defend against unlawful interference.[57] One student of labor relations reflects this point of view when he says:

Of course it was easy to see that strikers who broke windows and damaged buildings, machinery and rolling stock, or threatened to do so, were harming or threatening to harm property. But it was not so obvious that the purely economic pressures of unions which caused great monetary losses to employers and sometimes to nonunion labor, were harmful to property. If they were, it was certainly in a different sense. For the harm to intangible interests of employers and nonunion labor, such as loss of production, of customers and business, and of profitable relationships, did not touch anything theretofore conventionally thought of as property.[58]

This view of "property right," when measured in the light of progressive, liberal legal views, can only be characterized as highly restrictive. Judges had long since brought the concept of "property" to a much higher level of generality.[59] Injunctions were first issued in labor disputes in the United States toward the end of the nineteenth century.[60] Long before then English and American courts had evolved an extensive conception of "property right." Indeed, a famous British Vice-Chancellor created no stir when, in 1869, he spoke thus of property rights:

What is property? One man has property in lands, another in goods, another in a business, another in skill, another in reputation; and whatever may have the effect of destroying property in any one of these things (even in a man's good name) is, in my opinion, destroying property of a most valuable description. . . .

Now the business of a merchant is about the most valuable kind of property that he can well have. Here it is the source of his fortune, and therefore to be injured in his business is to be injured in his property. But I go further, and say if it had only injured his reputation, it is within the jurisdiction of this Court to stop the publication of a libel of this description which goes to destroy ... his reputation, which is his property, and, if possible, more valuable than other property.[61]

We have now surveyed the main arguments in the campaign for the abolition of equity in labor disputes. But there were, of course, others. It was contended that preliminary restraining orders were often issued *ex parte,* that is, without notice and hearing to the union officers and men whose activities were temporarily restrained. This was held to be vicious and unjust because thus too were "strikes" defeated without even affording the defendants a hearing. But since the restraining orders, like the injunctions themselves, never prohibited lawful, peaceful strikes for higher wages, it is difficult to give any more weight to this contention than to the others already considered. Furthermore, it is impossible to see how the mission of equity can be accomplished at all unless judges are authorized to issue *ex parte* restraining orders in some instances, when irreparable injury is threatened. So long as such orders restrain only unlawful conduct, and so long as the complaining party is required to swear under oath that unlawful conduct threatens irreparable injury to him, there can be no persuasive argument against the issuance of such orders. The argument then is transformed into an indirect challenge to equity itself. If equity is to survive, the *ex parte* restraining order in appropriate cases must survive with it.[62]

The one clearly solid argument put forward in the great crusade was that the substantive law of labor relations—at that time better described as the law regulating union conduct—was not carefully and precisely enough defined. Professor Sayre, writing in 1930, quite accurately portrayed the confusion which existed in the law, and he quite justifiably argued that the campaign for anti-injunction legislation should be subordinated to the clarification of the substantive law.[63] Had this proposal been followed, things might have been different. The equity powers as such would not have had to be destroyed; they would merely have become inapplicable, to the degree that conduct formerly considered unlawful was straightforwardly legalized; for equity may, as a general rule, enjoin only *unlawful* conduct which threatens irreparable harm.

But this was not to be the method. Instead of defining legal boundaries for union conduct, Congress chose to make practically all union conduct unenjoinable.[64] Why this method was followed it is, of course, impossible to say with certainty. Perhaps the reason is that neither Congress nor public opinion would have tolerated then, as it will not now, a straightforward declaration that all types of union activities are lawful. The expropriatory, coercive, and oppressive character of many types of union conduct is evident to every one. That being true, the tendency of judges to limit union action, when they are left free to apply to unions the same laws applicable to everyone else, is properly viewed as a simple reflection of general opinion and of the logical structure of the human mind.[65] These influences work upon legislators, as well as judges; and quite possibly account for the decision to make all union conduct unenjoinable, rather than to legalize union conduct generally, and straightforwardly.

There can, incidently, be no doubt that the Norris-LaGuardia Act was intended to work no change in the substantive law. This point is repeatedly emphasized in *The Labor Injunction*: ". . . the immunity accorded is circumscribed: it is not immunity from legal as distinguished from equitable remedies—hitherto unlawful conduct remains unlawful."[66] One of the writers of *The Labor Injunction* was later to hold, as a member of the Supreme Court, that the conduct made unenjoinable by the Norris Act was also legalized.[67] But, notwithstanding this contradiction, there is really no substantial basis for discrediting the earlier statement, as puzzling as the later contradiction may seem to some. Justice Roberts, who dissented from the latter decision, summed up its character tolerably well: "I venture to say that no court has ever undertaken so radically to legislate where Congress has refused so to do."[68]

*   *   *

So much for the destruction of equity in labor relations. Determined to secure immunity in one way or another for unlawful conduct, trade unionists in the United States were ultimately about as successful, for a time, as their British colleagues had been in 1906. Everywhere unable to establish the merits of straightforwardly legalizing conduct which clearly threatens the destruction of law, if not of civilization itself, trade unionists nevertheless succeeded indirectly in reaching the same result. Congress and the state legislatures withdrew equity. They declined, however, to modify the substantive law. The Supreme Court of the United States later did what Congress and the state legislatures had declined to do. These aids were apparently not enough, however.

Congress also contributed the Wagner Act, with its one-sided emphasis upon only employer unfair practices; and it took away all possibility of direct access to the federal courts, as noted in the preceding section of this chapter. But Congressional benefits accorded to trade unions were only negative in character, and many state courts were not as compliant as they might have been. So the Supreme Court accorded another positive privilege in holding picketing entitled to constitutional protection as a form of freedom of speech, immune to any form of state control.

Then, changing its course, Congress in the Taft-Hartley Act expressly declared that most of the types of conduct legalized by the Supreme Court were unlawful. Enforcement, however, left largely to a National Labor Relations Board appointed by a President completely out of sympathy with the law, was not very vigorous. When the picketing–free-speech identification proved less serviceable than expected, and when the state courts seemed inclined to enforce the national labor policy more vigorously than the National Labor Relations Board, the Supreme Court conceived the theory of federal pre-emption.

And there we now stand. Two things are prominent: deviousness and an unutterable confusion. The deviousness is accounted for by the overwhelming *fact* that trade unionists have never been able directly to convince the nation at large and its courts of the merits of their demands for special privilege. The confusion is accounted for as the necessary consequence of a devious method of securing privileges which could not be gained in any straightforward way.

The pressure in a largely free society for a just and equal rule of law, effectively and equitably enforced, is not unlike the power of a mighty river. Attempts to block it may succeed momentarily;

but before long it will seek and find new channels, perhaps creating chaos and destruction in the process. Such has been the history of labor relations law for the past generation: tortured, frustrated, destructive, chaotic, senseless. If reason, good sense, and effective administration of justice are to prevail, the regressive policies which produced the present senseless chaos must be rejected.

A Fair and Sensible Juridical Structure

The Norris-LaGuardia Act ought to be repealed. The National Labor Relations Board should be abolished. The regular constitutional courts should be given full jurisdiction, in law and equity, in all cases arising under the National Labor Relations Act. The state courts should be given clear authority to participate in the enforcement of the national labor policy, with their decisions subject to the unifying review of the Supreme Court of the United States. And all persons should be granted direct access to the courts for disinterested decisions on the merits in every instance in which they feel that they have been injured by unlawful conduct.

Thus alone can we resume progress toward the ideals of a day in court for every man who seeks justice, of fair hearings on the merits, of an effective remedy for every legal wrong, and of the prevention of irreparable injury. If we do these things we shall be in a good way to achieving the juridical structure and techniques which accord with good sense, the Constitution of the United States, and the liberal, progressive spirit which has animated the great tradition of judicial reform.

*　　*　　*

The only convincing argument brought forth in the campaign for anti-injunction legislation is no longer applicable. A detailed, coherent code of substantive law for labor relations exists already in large measure and can be realized in full with no trouble. Suggestions to this end have been made in the preceding two chapters. With the substantive law in good order, there is no reason to abandon equitable remedies in labor relations, any more than there is in any other field of law. Labor relations indeed represent the area par excellence in which equitable remedies are needed, if irreparable injury by unlawful conduct is to be prevented.

The Norris-LaGuardia Act should therefore be repealed, and the best rules of equity, the best equity practice, should be held applicable in labor relations, just as they are in all other fields of federal jurisdiction. The reflection upon the fairness and the impartiality of federal judges implicit in the Norris Act is an affront to a group of judges who are on the whole, in the common opinion of the lawyers of the country, the fairest, most liberal, and best instructed judges in the land. If the federal judges had not already proved their stature in a thousand other ways previously, they certainly did so in their scrupulous acceptance of the rigorous and even insulting limitations imposed upon them by the Norris Act.

*   *   *

All relevant considerations point to the desirability of making a place for the state courts in the enforcement of national labor policy. Far from sacrificing the goal of a uniform policy, such a step appears upon examination to be indispensable to that goal. State judges must become accustomed to and familiar with the national labor policy if we are to have a uniform rule of law throughout the nation. The "dividing line" between federal and state power, between "interstate" and "local" affairs, is a chimera; it exists only in fevered imagination, not in the realities of life and commerce. This fact does not suggest that the state courts ought to be denied all jurisdiction in labor cases; that would be both impossible and undesirable. Even those who argue in favor of federal pre-emption recognize this. They suggest that the state courts be left with power to handle "local" cases, under no obligation to conform decisions in such cases to national law.[69]

Such a suggestion rests upon an inadequate conception of reality. It assumes as stable and real that which is neither real nor stable: a distinction between "interstate" and "local." Its product has been, is now, and always will be chaos in both judicial administration and substantive rules of law. State courts will always be handling cases "on the borderline" between interstate and local. If we want a sensible, coherent, uniform rule of law in this country, we must frankly face and accept that fact. The thing to do is to grant jurisdiction straightforwardly to the state courts over cases involving federal law. There is every reason to believe that state judges who become accustomed to applying federal law will do so in all cases in which the possibility is open to them.

We have a single judicial head of the country, the United States Supreme Court. Appeals lie to that Court from the decisions of all the other courts of the country in matters of national concern or national law. With such appeals available from decisions of state courts, there is no reason to believe that we shall not get a much more uniform national labor policy from a deliberate program of enlisting the aid of the state courts than we are getting at present in the hopelessly confused situation which now prevails. We shall also have taken a long-needed step toward creating a single rule of law. Uniformity is an unattractive quality in many areas of human action. But to law it is an essential necessity; there is no law except uniform law. We can at the same time preserve the positive values inherent in the states' rights position if we secure to the state courts a permanent role in the national scheme of law.

* * *

Abolishing the National Labor Relations Board is not the radical or extreme proposal which some may think it. The infatuation with "quasi-judicial" administrative tribunals characteristic of past decades has long been on the wane in the United States. Statistics and the vivid experience of many persons have demonstrated that the "speedy justice," the liberal procedures, and the *expertise* at first associated with administrative tribunals are, in practice, conspicuous mainly by their absence.[70]

Trading ready access to real courts of law for these promised benefits has proved a very bad bargain. We have given up something precious, the *right* to a day in court, and have received nothing, even less than nothing, in return. Administrative tribunals have only added substantially to the law's delays,[71] and instead of liberal *expertise* they have given us a wooden, pettifogging kind of mechanical jurisprudence.[72] Never, in any administrative agency, has there emerged a figure fit to carry the boots of any of the numerous great chancellors and judges. More often than not the personnel of the quasi-judicial administrative tribunals, with their short, political tenure of office, have acted the narrow, doctrinaire bureaucrat, which, after all is said and done, they really are.

The great fact established during the past generation is that we as a nation now realize that we have made a bad bargain.[73] We have come to the conclusion that the things we have given up are worth much more than what we have received from that contradiction in terms, "administrative law." We have found that "speedy justice" means, more often than we are prepared to tolerate, no justice at all. Moved by this conclusion, we proceed step-by-step away from "administrative law." We deny to administrative agencies in most cases the power to make completely binding and completely irreversible decisions, or the power to issue immediately enforcible judgments and decrees. This withdrawal from the logic of administrative tribunals signals the first recognition of the visionary character of the goal of "speedy justice" through "administrative law."

Not too long after we gained some real experience with administrative tribunals, we came to the additional conclusion that there was something radically wrong in the assumption that they would better satisfy our desires for liberal procedures than the courts had been doing. Investigation after investigation demonstrated that the "liberality" of administrative procedures was of a most illiberal character. The procedures of the federal courts began to appear to be sensible, flexible, and liberal in an elevated degree. Then began that slow process of evolution which was to produce, in the Taft-Hartley Act, the direction to the National Labor Relations Board that it follow the rules of procedure of the federal courts "so far as practicable."[74] Similarly, the functions of prosecutor and judge, at first united in the NLRB, were ordered separated in accordance with a great and treasured tradition. We were not prepared to abandon fair hearings.[75]

We are now at an uneasy, unstable, wasteful, and dilatory midpoint. The modifications dictated by unfavorable experience have made the "administrative process" the slowest process of justice in the country. Suspicious of administrative tribunals, we insist that the real courts of law exercise extensive surveillance over them. The scope of judicial review, not yet complete as to either facts or law, yet increases steadily.[76] Thus, administrative agents compile interminable records which the courts in their turn are then required to review "on the whole."

Many experienced practitioners suspect that administrative hearings have become a gigantic make-work program. The truth probably is, however, that the inordinate size of the records often made in such hearings comes about owing to a mixture of ignorance and caution. Not always being experts in the rules of logic and careful reasoning known as the law of evidence, administrative hearing officers sometimes admit reams of irrelevant testimony. At the same time, less fuss is likely to be created by a reviewing court if too much evidence is admitted rather than too little; and so the hearing officers let everything in, thus establishing a semblance of "fairness."

But fairness is not established by the mere admission of testimony. It requires a liberal, undoctrinaire, wholesome, open-minded evaluation of all the relevant testimony. It matters very little that all offered testimony is admitted—if the hearing officer is less open-minded about the evidence on one side than on the other. Yet reviewing courts cannot possibly take the position that unfairness is established by a mere one-sided crediting of conflicting testimony. They must adhere to the rule that the function of evaluating conflicting testimony is properly within the province of the person who observes the witnesses, and cannot be assumed by a reviewing court except in cases of plain abuse and prejudice. But crediting all witnesses on one side and discrediting all those on the other side is not itself a sign of abuse or prejudice. It is possible that all the witnesses on one side are liars. So, in many cases, reviewing courts uphold such accreditations. Their adherence to rules of law and sensible procedure requires them to do so.[77]

But whether all this produces a fair hearing is another matter. All that we know beyond doubt is that the administrative process becomes ever slower, more prolix, and more cumbersome. Persons threatened by irreparable harm make every effort to bypass the excruciatingly dilatory processes of the NLRB. These efforts are often frustrated by the pre-emption theory and the theory of the exclusive original jurisdiction of the NLRB.[78] Yet there can be no doubt that the unfortunate results produced by these theories are widely known and that a change is in the offing.

The Hoover Commission has recommended the creation of a specialized administrative court, of largely constitutional stature, with exclusive jurisdiction in the labor and some commercial fields.[79] This proposal deserves serious consideration. It has a solid, evolutionary basis, and carries along the trend we have been noting. And yet, one may ask, why should the labor and commercial fields be thus separated from the other fields of law? Simplicity, uniformity, universality are marks of advancement in many areas of science and of action. This is true, too, of the administration of justice, as Roscoe Pound has observed: "Legal history shows the general course of development to be a setting up of a multitude of specialized tribunals, and then a gradual consolidation of them into a simple unified system."[80] Why then take a step in the direction of proliferation of tribunals and of complication of the legal system?

Some will say that the Hoover Commission proposal is at least another step in the right direction and should be adopted for that reason. But is there, at this point in development, any real justification for insistence upon a step-by-step mode of procedure? We are not experimenting here in the great unknown. It is not as though the regular federal courts are an unknown quantity. They have been handling labor and commercial cases for almost a century, and their record over the long years has been outstanding. They are, by common consent, the best courts in the country.

Another consideration put forth by those who favor the creation of specialized courts is that such courts develop a valuable *expertise* in their field of action. The problem presented by this view lies less in its admiration of *expertise,* however, than it does in its uncritical assumptions concerning the "field of action." Certainly *expertise* is desirable. No one wants decisions made by persons who do not know a lot about the field in which they operate. But it must never be forgotten that the field of action with which we are concerned is *law.*

For anyone who has a proper, comprehensive understanding of law and of the functions of courts in a legal system, the considerations concerning *expertise* add up to an overwhelming argument in favor of the courts of general jurisdiction. The law of a country is a seamless web of integrating rights and duties and policy considerations. No one sees this seamless web in its entirety, in its full complexity, as does a court of general jurisdiction. Only the judges of such courts see all the ramifications of law and of legal problems. The fallacy of the *expertise* position as it is ordinarily stated has been demonstrated time and again in the labor relations field, where the federal courts have frequently exposed the narrow, specialistic errors of the National Labor Relations Board.[81] The field with which we are concerned is *law*. Your true experts in *law* are the judges who sit on the courts of general jurisdiction.[82] The *expertise* argument is one of the strongest arguments for giving original jurisdiction in labor and all other cases to the federal district courts and to the comparable state courts of general jurisdiction. I know of nothing in the decisions of administrative tribunals equal to the broadminded *expertise* demonstrated in this statement by the Wisconsin Supreme Court:

> We have concluded that we were in error in our original determination of the issues in this case. . . . We are convinced that in our study of the issues presented we gave too little consideration to the fact that there are limitations upon the right of free speech, and that the prohibition of action against free speech is not intended to give immunity for every use or abuse of language. We gave insufficient notice to the fact that free speech is not the only right secured by our fundamental law, and that it must be weighed . . . against the equally important right to engage in a legitimate business free from dictation by an outside group, and the right to protection against the unlawful conduct which will or may result in the destruction of a business; that both the right to labor and the right to carry on business are liberty and property.[83]

*   *   *

It has been suggested recently in a thoughtful article that giving the federal courts the full jurisdiction that the Constitution meant them to have would be to "turn back the clock."[84] Strangely enough it is also suggested in the same article that "the ideal development of our administrative law would be for it to follow the pattern of the executive tribunals of three centuries ago."[85]

Chronological reasoning is not always conclusive. In many areas of science and in material production we are further along in the twentieth century than men were, say, in the eighteenth century, when the Constitution of the United States was drafted. But in the arts and sciences of government and law there is really very little to indicate that we have gone forward in this century. Many, including the great Albert Schweitzer, are of the opinion that this century has not distinguished itself in those fields;[86] and the state of affairs of the world today tends to bear them out. In many ways we may have gone backward. We do not see some things as clearly today as they were seen by the best men of politics and law in the eighteenth century. I do not think that we would be setting back the clock if we were to create the juridical structure which they planned and set forth in the Constitution. On the contrary, such an operation would in my opinion require us to adjust the clock, and our minds, forward.

NOTES

CHAPTER 1

1. Charles Darwin, quoting Sir John Lubbock, in *The Origin of Species and the Descent of Man* (Modern Library; New York: Random House, Inc.), p. 470.

CHAPTER 2

1. "In the Silesian region taken over from the Germans there is a colony of Polish miners who used to live in France. There they always voted Communist. Now they want to go back—and can't. Recently a group of them was asked: 'What do you miss most? The countryside? French wine? The people?' 'Liberty,' they replied." The account is C. L. Sulzberger's, in *The New York Times*, February 27, 1956, p. 22, col. 5.

CHAPTER 3

1. "A barbarian speaks in terms of power. He dreams of the super-man with the mailed fist. He may plaster his lust with sentimental morality of Carlyle's type. But ultimately his final good is conceived as one will imposing itself upon other wills. This is intellectual barbarism. The Periclean ideal is action weaving itself into a texture of persuasive beauty analogous to the delicate splendor of nature." Alfred North Whitehead, *Adventures of Ideas* (Mentor Book; New York: The New American Library, 1955), pp. 58-59. Cf. Friedrich A. Hayek, *The Political Ideal of the Rule of Law* (Cairo, Egypt: 1955), pp. 29-32, and *Individualism and Economic Order* (Chicago: University of Chicago Press, 1949); Michael Polanyi, *The Logic of Liberty* (London: Routledge & Kegan Paul, Ltd., 1951), pp. 114 ff. Ludwig von Mises refers to the same idea as "the harmony of the 'rightly understood' interests" in *Human Action* (New Haven: Yale University Press, 1949), pp. 669 ff.

2. The biologist sees this point perhaps more vividly than other students of man and nature. Roger J. Williams has said: "There is no genetic advantage in being born under affluent circumstances. Human worth and even potential greatness may appear anywhere. A backwoods baby born to unprosperous parents, possessing nothing of what we call

culture, may turn out to be an Abraham Lincoln. A puny, sickly one, born in an obscure village and having a threadbare hold on life, may result in a Mark Twain. An infant who loses sight and hearing during babyhood may turn out to be the magnificent specimen of humanity that Helen Keller is. Actually human worth resides not only in those whom we regard as great, but in all of us, and we should provide an environment which will give everyone an *equal chance* to develop his potentialities in the way best suited to him individually." *Free and Unequal: The Biological Basis of Individual Liberty* (Austin: University of Texas Press, 1953), p. 12.

3. Cf. Friedrich A. Hayek, "Progressive Taxation Reconsidered," in M. H. Sennholz (ed.), *On Freedom and Free Enterprise* (Princeton: D. Van Nostrand Co., Inc., 1956), pp. 265 ff.; Walter J. Blum and Harry Kalven, Jr., *The Uneasy Case for Progressive Taxation* (Chicago: University of Chicago Press, 1951); *Facing the Issue of Income Tax Discrimination* (New York: National Association of Manufacturers, 1955).

4. *Ibid.* And see David McCord Wright, *Democracy and Progress* (New York: Macmillan Co., 1948), pp. 95 ff.

"One of the great illusions about the individual income tax, which tenaciously persists, is that the progressive rates are necessary from the revenue standpoint. The thinking goes that heavy revenue reliance on the tax makes substantial progression inevitable even if not desirable.

"The fallacy of this thinking is shown by the data . . . The entire progressive superstructure produces only 16 per cent of the total revenue derived from the individual tax, or $4.7 billion. The remainder, $24.7 billion, or 84 per cent, is derived from the basic tax rate paid by all income taxpayers on all of their taxable income. It will be noted that half of the revenue from progression ($2,343 million) is taken from the taxable income brackets up through $16,000–$18,000, where the tax rate reaches 50 per cent, and that the other half comes from all higher brackets and rates." *Facing the Issue of Income Tax Discrimination* (New York: National Association of Manufacturers, 1955), p. 12.

5. "An even more paradoxical and socially grave effect of progressive taxation . . . is that this instrument, intended to decrease inequality, in effect helps to perpetuate existing inequalities and eliminates one of the most important compensations for the kind of inequality which is inevitable in a free enterprise society. It does this by greatly reducing vertical mobility because it diminishes the chances of rising from one class to another." Hayek, "Progressive Taxation Reconsidered," p. 280.

6. *Human Action*, pp. 804–5. The reader might find interesting the whole of Mises' discussion of confiscatory taxation.

7. No one, perhaps, has ever brought to bear upon the problems of man and society so extensive and profound a perspective as has Charles Darwin. Unlike some present natural scientists, Darwin saw in private

property and in the accumulation of private wealth factors relevant to the whole future of man as a species:

"Man accumulates property and bequeaths it to his children, so that the children of the rich have an advantage over the poor in the race for success, independently of bodily or mental superiority. On the other hand, the children of parents who are short-lived, and are therefore on an average deficient in health and vigour, come into their property sooner than other children, and will be likely to marry earlier, and leave a larger number of offspring to inherit their inferior constitutions. But the inheritance of property by itself is very far from an evil; for without the accumulation of capital the arts could not progress; and it is chiefly through their power that the civilised races have extended, and are now everywhere extending their range, so as to take the place of the lower races. Nor does the moderate accumulation of wealth interfere with the process of selection. When a poor man becomes moderately rich, his children enter trades or professions in which there is struggle enough, so that the able in body and mind succeed best. The presence of a body of well-instructed men, who have not to labour for their daily bread, is important to a degree which cannot be overestimated; as all high intellectual work is carried on by them, and on such work, material progress of all kinds mainly depends, not to mention other and higher advantages. No doubt wealth when very great tends to convert men into useless drones, but their number is never large; and some degree of elimination here occurs, for we daily see rich men, who happen to be fools or profligate, squandering away their wealth." Charles Darwin, *The Origin of Species and the Descent of Man* (Modern Library; New York: Random House, Inc.), p. 502.

8. "The essence of freedom is the practicability of purpose. Mankind has chiefly suffered from the frustration of its prevalent purposes. . . . The literary exposition of freedom deals mainly with the frills. The Greek myth was more to the point. Prometheus did not bring to mankind freedom of the press. He procured fire, which obediently to human purpose cooks and gives warmth. In fact, freedom of action is a primary human need." Whitehead, *op. cit.*, p. 73.

CHAPTER 4

1. Cf. Ludwig von Mises, *Human Action* (New Haven: Yale University Press, 1949), pp. 279-80.

2. While the analysis in this chapter does not purport to be formally legal in character, it may be well to note that it is broadly shaped by and consistent with legal analysis in its conception of property rights. Most courts and a good many students of law would agree with it. This is demonstrated in an interesting way by a Massachusetts statute passed in 1914. That statute declared that "the right to enter into the relation of

employer and employee . . . and to . . . carry on business . . . or to work and labor as an employee, shall be held and construed to be a personal and not a property right." The statute was, of course, designed to create a special privilege for labor unions to interfere with and coerce employers and employees. But it would not have been necessary unless the common law and equity had created a conception of property rights of the kind developed in this book. The statute is thus to be characterized as inconsistent with the general development of Anglo-American law. On this, see A. V. Dicey, *The Law of the Constitution* (7th ed.; London: Macmillan & Co., Ltd., 1908), pp. 191 ff., who suggests that declarations such as those contained in the Massachusetts statute turn upside-down the normal course of Anglo-American juridical development. Incidentally, the statute was declared unconstitutional in Bogni v. Perotti, 224 Mass. 152 (1916). And for those who think that the views expressed by Dicey, by the Massachusetts court in 1916, and here are "obsolete," reference may be made to a very recent decision of the Wisconsin Supreme Court, where it was said that "both the right to labor and the right to carry on business are liberty and property." Vogt v. Teamsters, 29 CCH Lab. Cas. ¶ 69,747 (1956). It does not matter what particular word is used in order to denote personal autonomy or personal liberty. What matters is that all facets integrally parts of those concepts be recognized as such and be called by the same name, in order to avoid distinctions where there are no differences. "Property right" is used here only because it has tended historically in the law to develop as the appropriate term. When all rights proper to the person are called by the same name, judges and others will be less likely to err in evaluating and balancing disputes between persons. Either "liberty" or "property" would do equally well. The use of both terms by the Wisconsin Court is thus very suggestive. See, further, pages 278-79 in Chapter 19.

3. *Ibid.* And see Adair v. United States, 208 U.S. 161 (1908); Hitchman Coal & Coke Co. v. Mitchell, 245 U.S. 229 (1917); American Steel Foundries v. Tri-City Central Trades Council, 257 U.S. 184 (1921).

4. Cf. Morris R. Cohen, "The Place of Logic in the Law," 29 *Harvard Law Review* 622, 631 ff. (1916).

5. Cf. Felix Frankfurter and Nathan Greene, *The Labor Injunction* (New York: Macmillan Co., 1930), pp. 212-14.

6. Cited in note 3, above.

7. Cf. *The Case Against the "Right to Work" Laws* (Washington, D. C.: Congress of Industrial Organizations, 1955) and other references in note 13 of Chapter 10, below.

8. Cf. Francis B. Sayre, "Labor and the Courts," 39 *Yale Law Journal* 682, 696 (1930). Conversely, those who argue against statutes forbidding the closed shop are required by the rules of straight reasoning to uphold the right of employers to discriminate against union members. Cf. Percy L. Greaves, Jr., "Is Further Intervention a Cure for Prior

Intervention," in M. H. Sennholz (ed.), *On Freedom and Free Enter-prise* (Princeton: D. Van Nostrand Co., Inc., 1956), pp. 285-307.

9. See Chapter 7 and Part II of this book.

CHAPTER 5

1. Cf. A. V. Dicey, *The Law of the Constitution* (7th ed.; London: Macmillan & Co., Ltd., 1908), pp. 179 ff.

2. "Unfortunately the notion of freedom has been eviscerated by the literary treatment devoted to it. . . . The concept of freedom has been narrowed to the picture of contemplative people shocking their genera-tion. When we think of freedom, we are apt to confine ourselves to freedom of thought, freedom of the press, freedom for religious opinions. . . . This is a thorough mistake. . . . The literary exposition of freedom deals mainly with the frills. . . . Prometheus did not bring to mankind freedom of the press. He procured fire, . . ." A. N. Whitehead, *Adven-tures of Ideas* (Mentor Book; New York: The New American Library, 1955), p. 73.

3. Cf. J. D. Glover, *The Attack on Big Business* (Cambridge: Har-vard University Press, 1954), especially the bibliography at pp. 358 ff.

4. Cf. Friedrich A. Hayek (ed.), *Capitalism and the Historians* (Chicago: University of Chicago Press, 1954); Ralph W. Hidy and Muriel E. Hidy, *Pioneering in Big Business* (New York: Harper & Bros., 1956); Herrymon Maurer, *Great Enterprise: Growth and Behavior of the Big Corporation* (New York: Macmillan Co., 1956). For the most pointed and most trenchant view of the general problem, one must go again to the writings of Ludwig von Mises. See *Human Action* (New Haven: Yale University Press, 1949), pp. 613-19.

5. (New York: Fredrick A. Praeger, 1955).

6. Cf. Ludwig von Mises, *The Theory of Money and Credit* (Lon-don: Jonathan Cape, 1934), pp. 14-22, 216-61.

7. See the reference to the "pernicious abstractions regarding 'free-dom' and 'equality'" in Felix Frankfurter and Nathan Greene, *The Labor Injunction* (New York: Macmillan Co., 1930), p. 228.

8. Cf. Glover, *op. cit., passim.*

9. Morris R. Cohen, "The Place of Logic in the Law," 29 *Harvard Law Review* 622 (1916).

10. *Ibid.*, p. 631.

11. Cf. Roger J. Williams, *Free and Unequal: The Biological Basis of Individual Liberty* (Austin: University of Texas Press, 1953), p. 12.

12. For an analytical demonstration that the problem of abusive monopoly is kept at a minimum in the unhampered market economy, see Mises, *Human Action*, pp. 354 ff., especially pp. 362-68.

13. See generally Marquis W. Childs and Douglass Cater, *Ethics in a Business Society* (Mentor Book; New York: The New American

Library, 1954), pp. 101 ff. These authors refer to the most recent researches and the other relevant literature. Unfortunately, no reference is made to one of the most significant of all recent studies, that of Professor Warren Nutter, *The Extent of Enterprise Monopoly in the United States, 1899-1939* (Chicago: University of Chicago Press, 1951).

14. The hope that the "democratic controls" of parliaments or legislatures can provide a check upon the powers of the industrial "managers" of a socialist state must be dismissed as illusory. Cf. Hayek, *The Road to Serfdom* (Chicago: University of Chicago Press, 1944), pp. 56-71, 106 ff., where this point is implacably demonstrated and documented; cf. especially note 2, p. 63. For Americans, one may refer to the attitude of Mr. Robert Moses when the New York State Legislature had the audacity to consider checking up on the activities undertaken by Mr. Moses with public funds and public authority. Mr. Moses is reported to have said: "Do you think I am going to defer to the clerk of the Budget Bureau? Don't make me laugh." Mr. Moses also asserted that the legislative proposal would require "officers of the department to waste unbelievable amounts of time and energy justifying their plans to persons without competence to pass upon them." *The New York Times,* January 26, 1956, p. 22, col. 8. This happened at about the same time that almost all the top officers of the General Motors Corporation were required to appear before a Congressional committee and to bare the most intimate affairs and policies of that corporation. Those officers were not belligerent at all; were, indeed, most compliant, and made many concessions to the committee. Mr. Moses operates with public funds and public authority. General Motors is a private enterprise. Yet democratic controls seem to work better in respect to the latter than the former. Perhaps this is so because Mr. Moses has much less to lose than the owners and officers of General Motors.

CHAPTER 6

1. Cf. Chapter 1, pages 6-8.

2. All the current arguments for state ownership and operation of productive or service facilities are pretty old and have been repeatedly exposed as inadequate. See Yves Guyot, *Where and Why Public Ownership Has Failed* (New York: Macmillan Co., 1914); Ludwig von Mises, *Socialism* (New Haven: Yale University Press, 1951), pp. 487 ff.

3. Cf. Chapter 17, page 239.

4. Chapter 7, pages 109-19.

5. International Union, UAW-AFL v. Wisconsin Employee Relations Board, 336 U.S. 245 (1949).

6. See, for example, National Protective Assn. v. Cumming, 170 N.Y. 315, 321 (1902).

7. Vegelahn v. Guntner, 167 Mass. 92 (1896).

8. Cf. A. V. Dicey, *Law and Opinion in England* (2d ed.; London: Macmillan & Co., Ltd., 1930), pp. 150-58.

9. The loose and somewhat unsatisfactory formulation which prevails today is reflected by Mr. Justice Reed's statement: "lawful acts may become unlawful when taken in concert." United States v. U. S. Gypsum Co., 333 U.S. 364, 401 (1948).

10. "Freedom from arbitrary arrest, the right to express one's opinion . . . and the right to enjoy one's own property, seem to Englishmen all to rest upon the same basis, namely, on the law of the land. To say that the 'Constitution guaranteed' one class of rights more than the other would be to an Englishman an unnatural or a senseless form of speech." A. V. Dicey, *The Law of the Constitution* (7th ed.; London: Macmillan & Co., Ltd., 1908), pp. 196-97. How Englishmen would react today, under welfare-state ideology, I do not know. But a good many people in the United States are still of the view that Dicey expressed. The Wisconsin Supreme Court has just said, in 1956, that "free speech is not the only right secured by fundamental law . . . it must be weighed . . . against the equally important right to engage in a legitimate business free from dictation by an outside group, and the right to protection against unlawful conduct which will or may result in the destruction of a business; . . . both the right to labor and the right to carry on business are liberty and property." Vogt v. Teamsters, 29 CCH Lab. Cas. ¶ 69,747 (1956).

11. For a classic analysis of the right of self-defense, see Dicey, *The Law of the Constitution*, pp. 489 ff.

12. As, for example, a strike called to compel an employer to commit an unlawful act. Cf. NLRB v. National Maritime Union, 175 F. 2d 686 (2d Cir. 1949).

13. Ludwig von Mises, *Human Action* (New Haven: Yale University Press, 1949), pp. 149-50.

14. *Ibid.*, p. 150.

15. The libertarians are a realistic breed. "[P]hilosophy is not there just to be overwhelmed by the kind of reality which is apprehended by unbalanced and confused imaginings. Thus philosophy, when it inquires and interprets, knowing well that the man who enslaves another wakes in him awareness of himself and enlivens him to seek for liberty, observes with serenity how periods of increased or reduced liberty follow upon each other and how a liberal order, the more it is established and undisputed, the more surely decays into habit, and thereby its vigilant self-awareness and readiness for defence is weakened, which opens the way for a 'recourse' . . . to all of those things which seemed to have vanished from the world, and which themselves, in their turn, open a new 'course.' " Benedetto Croce, *History as the Story of Liberty* (New York: Meridian Books, 1955), pp. 58-59. The liberals know that they must take their joy in the struggle for freedom; cf. *Human Action*, pp. 145-57, 177-94. Only the zealous *étatist* finds the defeat of, or even the

failure completely to consummate, large interventionist plans an intolerable frustration; cf. Eric Hoffer, *The True Believer* (New York: Harper & Bros., 1951).

16. *The Wealth of Nations* (Modern Library; New York: Random House, Inc.), pp. 3-29.

17. Cf. David Ricardo, *The Principles of Political Economy and Taxation* (Everyman's Library; London: J. M. Dent & Sons, Ltd.), pp. 77-94, 253 ff.

18. Cf. Friedrich A. Hayek, *The Road to Serfdom* (Chicago: University of Chicago Press, 1944), pp. 61 ff.

19. We have recently been told by Mr. Harry S. Truman, who ought to know, that the Presidency of the United States is a job for "six men in the best of health." If this is true, then no single man can ever fill the job adequately, no matter how good his health. What is to be done? Are we now required to elect six presidents at once? Or can it be, perhaps, that the only decent alternative is to conceive the function of government more rigorously and more narrowly?

20. Cf. A. T. Vanderbilt, *The Challenge of Law Reform* (Princeton: Princeton University Press, 1955), pp. 76 ff.

21. The federal budget for 1956-57 was summarized in *The New York Times* for January 17, 1956. The *Times* of March 17, 1956, p. 1, col. 8, announced "2.4 billion total voted by Senate for farm relief." That is more than the government takes by its confiscatory tax rates.

CHAPTER 7

1. It would be difficult to exaggerate the significance of the fact that before the advent of interventionist labor legislation in the United States, injunctions against peacefully conducted strikes for higher wages were virtually unknown (see Chapters 14 and 19). Since such legislation (dating roughly from the Railway Labor Act of 1926), injunctions against peaceful, though large-scale, strikes for higher wages have been sought and granted in a number of cases. The petitioning party is in each instance the government—usually the federal government, but sometimes a state government. See R. A. Smith (ed.), *Labor Law,* 2 vols. (2d ed.; Indianapolis: Bobbs-Merrill Co., 1953-54), I, 557 ff.

2. Cf. *ibid.,* II, 129 ff., especially pp. 132-45. This section of Professor's Smith's book is contributed by the distinguished British scholar, Professor Otto Kahn-Freund. It is curious to note the diffident and circumspect manner adopted by Professor Kahn-Freund when dealing with the approach of the welfare state to wage problems. The obvious fact is that such a state cannot "afford" to leave wages to the free interplay among employees, unions, and employers; cannot, in short, afford to have free collective bargaining "interfering" with its careful plans for

the economy. And this, of course, is the ultimate, albeit indirectly stated, burden of Professor Kahn-Freund's discussion.

3. See Leonard A. Lecht, *Experience under Railway Labor Legislation* (New York: Columbia University Press, 1955), pp. 188-202. There is a great deal to be learned from the careful historical researches which Mr. Lecht undertook in this book, concerning the fate of trade unionism under collectivism.

4. See generally, for the statistics cited in this chapter, W. S. Woytinsky and Associates, *Employment and Wages in the United States* (New York: Twentieth Century Fund, 1953); David McCord Wright (ed.), *The Impact of the Union* (New York: Harcourt, Brace and Co., Inc., 1951); Albert Rees, "Labor Unions and the Price System," 58 *Journal of Political Economy* 254-63 (June, 1950); Arthur M. Ross, "Collective Bargaining and Common Sense," 2 *Labor Law Jounral*, 435 (1951).

5. U. S. Department of Labor, Bureau of Labor Statistics, *Handbook of Labor Statistics* (Washington, D. C.: Government Printing Office, 1950), p. 139.

6. Ross, "Collective Bargaining and Common Sense," p. 442. See also Harry A. Millis and Royal E. Montgomery, *Organized Labor* (New York: McGraw-Hill Book Co., Inc., 1945), chaps. viii-x.

7. *Human Action* (New Haven: Yale University Press, 1949), p. 749.

8. Cf. Sir Henry Sumner Maine, *Popular Government* (New York: Henry Holt & Co., Inc., 1886), pp. 196 ff., especially p. 247; and see the remarks of Mr. Justice Jackson in Hood & Sons, Inc. v. DuMond, 336 U.S. 525 (1949).

9. Some labor relations students take a pretty dim view of the marginal-productivity theory; see, for example, Neil W. Chamberlain, *Collective Bargaining* (New York: McGraw-Hill Book Co., Inc., 1951), pp. 340 ff. That is probably because they either do not understand it, or expect more of it than can reasonably be expected from a theoretical explanation of the tendency in a market economy. Cf. the attitude taken by the economists who contributed to the Wright (ed.) *The Impact of the Union;* and see Woytinsky, *op. cit.,* pp. 3-13.

10. I take no pleasure in making these charges and wish that the demands of accurate analysis could be satisfied in some other way. Documentation of the charges would certainly result in the most gargantuan note of all time, and so there is a necessity of distribution. The reader is referred to the books, articles, court decisions, newspaper reports, and Congressional investigations cited throughout this chapter and Parts II and III of this book. As a beginning, consult the *Hearings before the Committee on Education and Labor of the House of Representatives on Bills to Amend and Repeal the National Labor Relations Act, and for Other Purposes* (Washington D. C.: Government Printing Office, 1947); *Hearings before the Committee on Banking and Currency*

of the Senate on the Economic Power of Labor Organizations (Washington, D. C.: Government Printing Office, 1949); *Hearings Before the Committee on Education and Labor on Matters Relating to the Labor Management Relations Act* (Washington, D. C.: Government Printing Office, 1953); also Herbert R. Northrup, *Organized Labor and the Negro* (New York: Harper & Bros., 1944). The charges in some respects involve matters of common knowledge. In other respects they can be appreciated only by those who have had the personal experience of membership in trade unions or intimate enough familiarity with union members to understand events in their true significance. The present writer has had both.

11. See Chapters 10 and 14.

12. This is a point which seems always to elude those students of labor relations who wish to leave with unions the power to control employment but who still do not like the results which come about when unions have such power. The ablest of the representatives of that point of view, Professor Clyde Summers, starts with the assumption that employers once had the dictatorial powers which closed-shop unions now possess, and apparently does not realize that that is an assumption, rather than a fact. Operating on such an erroneous assumption, it is no wonder that his conclusions, while logically derived, are erroneous. See Clyde Summers, "Union Powers and Workers' Rights," in *The Law and Labor-Management Relations* (Ann Arbor: University of Michigan Press, 1951) pp. 364, 376: "The employer's word was law. The worker retained full freedom—to submit or starve. The advent of unions has not changed the inescapable character of modern industry that an individual's economic life is governed by forces beyond himself." But the employer, too, and everyone else, is "governed by forces beyond himself." The employer is subject to the market, the consumers, competitors, and all the other influences which affect the actions of men. He is no freer than anyone else, no matter how rich he may be. Professor Summers is guilty here of uncritical acceptance of a superficial cliché. For an accurate exposition of the real state of affairs, see Mises, *Human Action*, pp. 270-72, 592-630.

13. J. Henry Richardson, *An Introduction to the Study of Industrial Relations* (London: George Allen and Unwin, Ltd., 1954), pp. 187-88.

14. *Ibid.*, p. 188. These observations should correct the error of those who, like Professor Summers, feel that the thing to do is to make unions "more democratic," not to deny them compulsory-unionism privileges.

15. Cf. Chapters 10 and 11.

16. Cf. Summers, *op. cit.*

17. Leonard Sayles and George Strauss, *The Local Union: Its Place in the Industrial Plant* (New York: Harper & Bros., 1953).

18. Indeed, it is questionable whether a union needs to do more than *threaten* a strike in most cases, when its demands are reasonably

justified by market conditions. This speculation cannot be considered a wild one when one considers that in the vast majority of cases (probably more than 75 per cent) union-management disputes are settled without any strike at all. For the strange case of a union which declares in its constitution that it will give up its bargaining authority rather than call a strike, see Culinary Alliance v. Beasley, 286 P.2d 844 (Calif. 1955).

19. Scarcely a better example could be cited than the Westinghouse strike of 1955-56. For a resumé of that dispute (after 104 days), see the *New York Times,* January 29, 1956, p. 51, col. 1.

20. For the authorities, see S. Petro, "Job-Seeking Aggression, the National Labor Relations Act, and the Free Market," 50 *Michigan Law Review* 521-28, notes 73 and 74 (1952).

21. See Leo Wolman, "Wages in the United States Since 1914," *Proceedings of the Sixth Annual Meeting, Industrial Relations Research Association,* pp. 1-7.

22. For an excellent example of the way coercive unions destroy small unions, see the editorial "Big and Little Unions," *The New York Times,* March 16, 1956, p. 22, col. 3.

23. There are still in this country a number of small, independent unions. Of these, the best known is perhaps the Chicago Truck Drivers Union, Local 705. It is a model of clean, effective employee representation, and the excellent wages and working conditions it has negotiated for its members should help to emphasize the fallacy of the assumption that unions need to sabotage the free market if they are to serve their members effectively. For an interesting description of this union, see Madelyn Vieth, "An Honest Union," *National Review,* March 21, 1956, p. 17.

24. See Chapters 11, 13-15.

25. Notes 1-3, above.

26. Cf. Henry Simons, "Some Reflections on Syndicalism," 52 *Journal of Political Economy* 1-25, reprinted in Henry Simons, *Economic Policy for a Free Society* (Chicago: University of Chicago Press, 1948), pp. 121 ff.; Charles Lindblom, *Unions and Capitalism* (New Haven: Yale University Press, 1949).

27. See notes 1-3, above.

CHAPTER 8

1. U. S. Department of Labor, Bureau of Labor Statistics, *Handbook of Labor Statistics* (Washington, D. C.: Government Printing Office, 1950), pp. 137 ff.

2. See Chapters 14 and 17.

3. Cf. Hitchman Coal & Coke Co. v. Mitchell, 245 U.S. 229 (1917), where the Supreme Court of the United States said that an employer has a legal and constitutional right to exclude union men from its employ."

4. This movement gained some success in that it secured the enactment of the Clayton Act, 38 Stat. 730, 28 U.S. Code §§ 381–383, 386–390; 29 U.S. Code § 52. Section 20 of the Clayton Act purported to limit the issuance of injunctions against many forms of union action.

5. Cf. the Declaration of Policy of the Wagner Act of 1935, 49 Stat. 449, § 1.

6. 47 Stat. 70, 29 U.S. Code §§ 101–115.

7. 49 Stat. 449, 29 U.S. Code §§ 151–168.

8. For a comprehensive history of trade unionism in the United States, see H. A. Millis and R. E. Montgomery, *Organized Labor* (New York: McGraw-Hill Book Co., Inc., 1945).

9. Cf. Charles O. Gregory, *Labor and the Law* (New York: W. W. Norton & Co., Inc., 1946), pp. 269 ff.

10. *Ibid.*, at 334 ff. Cf. Thornhill v. Alabama, 310 U.S. 88 (1940); Swing v. A.F.L., 309 U.S. 659 (1940).

11. Cf. Universal Camera Corp. v. NLRB, 340 U.S. 474 (1951); Ward, "Proof of 'Discrimination' Under the National Labor Relations Act," 7 *George Washington Law Review* 797 (1939).

12. See Chapters 10, 11, and 17.

13. See Chapter 16.

14. Chapters 10-11.

15. The leading case is NLRB v. Mackay Radio & Telegraph Co., 304 U.S. 333 (1938).

16. For only one of literally countless instances of extreme violence by trade unionists, see the trial examiner's report in United Mine Workers of America, District 31, 95 N.L.R.B. 546, at 556-67 (1951). For even more egregious conduct by the same union, see 92 N.L.R.B. 916, at 931 ff. (1950). For current examples, see your daily newspaper, or read the labor law reporters.

17. See Chapter 11, pages 165-69.

18. See generally Willcox and Landis, "Government Seizures in Labor Disputes," 34 *Cornell Law Quarterly* 155 (1948); Teller, "Government Seizure in Labor Disputes," 40 *Harvard Law Review* 1017 (1947).

19. Cf. United States v. United Mine Workers of America, 330 U.S. 258 (1947).

20. Sections 201–210 of the Taft-Hartley Act, 61 Stat. 136, 29 U.S.C. §§ 141–150.

21. See, for example, the approach of New Jersey, as described in New Jersey Bell Telephone Co. v. Communications Workers of America, 5 N.J. 354, 75 A.2d 721 (1950).

22. See Chapter 15, pages 207-17.

23. Cf. Kurt Braun, *The Right to Organize and Its Limits* (Washington, D. C.: The Brookings Institution, 1950), pp. 13-15.

CHAPTER 9

1. Cf. Vegelahn v. Guntner, 167 Mass. 92, 44 N.E. 1077 (1896);
Commonwealth v. Hunt, 4 Metcalf 111 (Mass. Sup. Jud. Court 1842);
Commonwealth v. Moore, Mayor's Court of Philadelphia (1827), in
John R. Commons *et al.* (eds.), *A Documentary History of American
Industrial Society* (Cleveland: A. H. Clark Co., 1910-11), IV, 99, 255.
For analysis of a case apparently to the contrary, the often-cited Phila-
delphia Cordwainers case, see Chapter 14.

2. NLRB v. Jones & Laughlin Steel Corp., 301 U.S. 1 (1937).

3. Hitchman Coal & Coke Co. v. Mitchell, 245 U.S. 229 (1917).

4. As of 1901, total union membership has been estimated at more
than a million; as of 1910, well over two million. U. S. Department of
Labor, Bureau of Labor Statistics, *Handbook of Labor Statistics* (Washington, D. C.: Government Printing Office, 1950), p. 139.

5. Cf. Cornellier v. Haverhill Shoe Manufacturers' Assn., 221 Mass.
554, 109 N.E. 643 (1915).

6. Authorities cited in notes 1 and 2, above; see further Chapter 14.

7. Chapters 10, 14, and 16.

8. American Steel Foundries v. Tri-City Central Trades Council, 257
U.S. 184 (1921).

9. 44 Stat. 577, 45 U.S.C. §§ 151 ff.

10. 47 Stat. 70, 29 U.S.C. §§ 101-115.

11. 49 Stat. 449, 29 U.S.C. §§ 151 ff.

12. *Ibid.,* § 7.

13. *Ibid.,* § 8 (1)-(5).

14. Cf. "Administrative Discretion v. Rule of Law," 1 *Labor Law
Journal* 579 (1950).

15. Section 8(4), Wagner Act; § 8(a)(4), Taft-Hartley Act.

16. Section 8(a)(1).

17. Section 8(a)(2).

18. Section 8(a)(3).

19. Section 8(a)(4).

20. Section 8(a)(5).

21. Republic Aviation Corp. v. NLRB, 324 U.S. 793 (1945).

22. NLRB v. Lake Superior Lumber Corp., 166 F.2d 147 (6th Cir.
1948); NLRB v. Waterman S.S. Corp., 309 U.S. 206 (1940).

23. NLRB v. Stowe Spinning Co., 336 U.S. 226 (1949).

24. Cf. NLRB v. Ranco, Inc., 28 CCH Lab. Cas. ¶ 69,188 (6th
Cir. 1955). Compare NLRB v. Babcock & Wilcox Co., 30 CCH Lab.
Cas. ¶ 69,911 (U.S. Sup. Ct. 1956); NLRB v. Monsanto Chemical Co.,
28 CCH Lab. Cas. ¶ 69,389 (9th Cir. 1955).

25. Cf. NLRB v. Edinburg Citrus Assn., 147 F.2d 353 (5th Cir.
1945).

26. Marshall Field & Co. v. NLRB, 200 F.2d 375 (7th Cir. 1952).

27. NLRB v. Jones & Laughlin Steel Corp., 301 U.S. 1 (1937); NLRB v. Citizens-News Co., 134 F.2d 970 (9th Cir. 1943); NLRB v. Shen-Valley Meat Packers, 211 F.2d 289 (4th Cir. 1954).

28. Radio Officers' Union v. NLRB, 347 U.S. 17 (1954).

29. Union Starch & Refining Co. v. NLRB, 186 F.2d 1008 (7th Cir. 1951).

30. Section 8(c), Taft-Hartley Act. For a brief but excellent analysis of this provision, see "Developments in the Law: The Taft-Hartley Act," 64 *Harvard Law Review,* 781, 812 (1951).

31. For interesting and revealing cases involving the employer right of free speech, see NLRB v. Armco Drainage & Metal Products, Inc., 220 F.2d 573 (6th Cir. 1955); Lux Clock Co., 113 N.L.R.B. No. 117 (1955).

32. *Ibid.*

33. For an extended discussion of this matter, see S. Petro, "Job-Seeking Aggression, the NLRA, and the Free Market," 50 *Michigan Law Review* 497 (1952).

34. *Ibid.*

35. Cf. Schwab v. Motion Picture Machine Operators, 165 Ore. 602, 109 P.2d 602 (1941).

36. Petro, *op. cit.*

Chapter 10

1. The federal government and a large number of states have in recent years enacted statutes declaring the right of employees to refuse to join unions and prohibiting union coercion of the exercise of that right. For the authorities, see Chapters 11 and 17.

2. Compare the facts recounted in the Philadelphia Cordwainers case of 1806, John R. Commons *et al.* (eds.), *A Documentary History of American Industrial Society* (Cleveland: A. H. Clark Co., 1910-11) III, 60, with the facts of such recent cases as Local 450, Operating Engineers, 112 N.L.R.B. No. 60 (1955); Local 449, Plumbers, 112 N.L.R.B. No. 85 (1955); Morgan Painting Contractor, 111 N.L.R.B. No. 66. (1955); NLRB v. Denver Building & Construction Trades Council, 219 F.2d 870 (10th Cir. 1955).

3. For an extensive analysis of these characteristics of picketing, see S. Petro, "Picketing and Labor Strategy," 2 *Labor Law Journal* 247 (1951), and "Effects and Purposes of Picketing," *ibid.* at 323. See also Charles O. Gregory, *Labor and the Law* (New York: W. W. Norton & Co., Inc., 1946), pp. 334 ff., especially pp. 347 ff.

4. A well-known student of labor law has said: "The International Brotherhood of Teamsters has made wide use of its ability to shut off the flow of supplies into an establishment, or to stop the movement of its products, merely by posting a single picket at each driveway normally used by incoming or outgoing trucks. Other unions exercise simila

power not by appealing to the public but because of the discipline of their members. The truck driver who crosses a teamsters' picket line is subject not only to union fines but also to expulsion, and in the trucking industry suspension or expulsion from the union carries with it loss of employment—the capital punishment of the industrial world. The constitutions and by-laws of other unions provide similar sanctions and while reliable statistics are not available, it seems plain that whenever the union is strong enough to exercise its power, the power will be invoked if necessary. In such cases the picket line is not a method of securing publicity nor are the pickets seeking to secure adherence by persuading others of the truth of what they say. The pickets' reliance in such a case is on the sanctions inherent in the discipline and organized economic power of their union." Cox, "The Influence of Mr. Justice Murphy on Labor Law," 48 *Michigan Law Review* 767 (1950).

5. Section 8(a)(5) of the NLRA so provides. For a typical decision applying that section, see NLRB v. Stow Mfg. Co., 217 F.2d 900 (2d Cir. 1954).

6. See Dennis, "The Boycott Under the Taft-Hartley Act," *N.Y.U. Third Annual Conference on Labor* (1950), pp. 367-460.

7. For an example of the rigor of such pressures, see Tidewater-Shaver Barge Lines v. Dobson, 195 Ore. 533, 245 P.2d 903 (1952).

8. For example, see Climax Machinery Co., 86 N.L.R.B. No. 142 (1949).

9. The terminological difficulty is discussed by Hellerstein, "Secondary Boycotts in Labor Disputes," 47 *Yale Law Journal* 341 (1938). See also Leo Wolman, *The Boycott in American Trade Unions* (Baltimore: Johns Hopkins Press, 1916).

10. Cf. Loewe v. Lawlor, 208 U.S. 274 (1908); Elliott v. Amalgamated Meat Cutters, 91 F. Supp. 690 (D.C. Mo. 1950); Denver Building & Construction Trades Council, 87 N.L.R.B. No. 136 (1949).

11. Cf. Paducah Newspapers, Inc. v. Wise, 247 S.W.2d 989 (1951), 269 S.W.2d 721 (1954); Venturelli v. Trovero, 346 Ill. App. 429, 105 N.E.2d 306 (1952); Howard v. Haven, 281 S.W.2d 480 (Tenn. 1955).

12. For recent cases involving "hot cargo" agreements, see Douds v. Milk Drivers, 28 CCH Lab. Cas. ¶ 69,379 (D.C. N.J. 1955); Graham v. International Woodworkers, 28 CCH Lab. Cas. ¶ 69,300 (D.C. Ore. 1955); United Brotherhood of Carpenters & Joiners, Local 1976, 113 N.L.R.B. No. 123 (1955); McAllister Transfer, Inc., 110 N.L.R.B. No. 124 (1954).

13. The literature on compulsory unionism is voluminous. For a brief analysis of the issues, with references to other works, see S. Petro, "The External Significance of Internal Union Affairs," *N.Y.U. Fourth Annual Conference on Labor* (1951), pp. 339, 346-55. See also *The Case Against the "Right to Work" Laws* (Washington, D. C.: Congress of Industrial Organizations, 1955) and the reviews of that work by Selwyn H. Torff, "The Case for Voluntary Union Membership," and Lee

Loevinger, "The Case Against 'Anti-Union Security' Legislation," in 40 *Iowa Law Review* 621, 627 (1955).

14. Consider the discussion in Chapter 4, pages 50-52; Chapter 6, pages 76-78; and Chapter 7, pages 109-17.

15. See further Chapter 14.

16. Cited above, note 2.

17. 167 Mass. 92.

18. 257 U.S. 184.

19. A conservative estimate would put the number of cases involving union violence which have been reported in opinions of appellate courts in this country well into the hundreds. And these would amount to only a fraction of the decisions, reported and unreported, of courts of first instance, or trial courts. Any kind of estimate of the number of instances of union violence which never reach the courts would be too rough to be of any use. The documented reports establish clearly, however, that union violence occurs so frequently as to pose real problems for any society aiming toward civilized status.

20. Authorities cited in notes 17 and 18, above. And see the examples of injunctive decrees reprinted in the appendices to Felix Frankfurter and Nathan Greene, *The Labor Injunction* (New York: Macmillan Co., 1930).

CHAPTER 11

1. This point is developed in Chapter 19.

2. For an extensive analysis of Massachusetts decisions on picketing, see S. Petro, "Picketing as Persuasion in Massachusetts," 2 *Labor Law Journal* 643 (1951). See also Charles O. Gregory, *Labor and the Law* (New York: W. W. Norton & Co. Inc., 1946), pp. 52 ff.

3. 167 Mass. 92, 44 N.E. 1077 (1896), analyzed in 2 *Labor Law Journal* 403 (1951).

4. American Steel Foundries v. Tri-City Central Trades Council, 257 U.S. 184 (1921).

5. Cornellier v. Haverhill Shoe Manufacturers' Assn., 221 Mass. 554, 109 N.E. 643 (1915).

6. See generally, as to the development of the New York view of picketing, S. Petro, "Picketing as Persuasion: Early New York Cases," 2 *Labor Law Journal* 563 (1951).

7. National Protective Assn. v. Cumming, 170 N.Y. 315 (1902); Stillwell Theatre, Inc. v. Kaplan, 259 N.Y. 405 (1932).

8. Exchange Bakery v. Rifkin, 245 N.Y. 260 (1927).

9. Cf. Gregory, *Labor and the Law*, pp. 76 ff.

10. Florsheim Shoe Store Co., Inc. v. Retail Shoe Salesmen's Union, 288 N.Y. 188, 42 N.E.2d 480 (1942); Dinny & Robbins, Inc. v. Davis, 290 N.Y. 101, 48 N.E.2d 280 (1943).

11. Goodwins, Inc. v. Hagedorn, 303 N.Y. 300, 101 N.E.2d 697 (1951).

12. The New York Court of Appeals seems hesitant to take the last logical step. Cf. Wood v. O'Grady, 307 N.Y. 532, 122 N.E.2d 386 (1954), where a bare majority of the Court refused to enjoin stranger picketing for organizational purposes. The decision does not stand for the proposition, however, that such picketing is always privileged. See the analysis in 30 *N.Y.U. Law Review* 388, at 397–98 (1955).

13. Section 8(b)(1)(A), Taft-Hartley Act.

14. Chapter 10.

15. Perry Norvell Co., 80 N.L.R.B. 225 (1948). For evidence that the NLRB will have little opportunity to reverse its decision, see the NLRB General Counsel's refusal to act upon charges involving organizational picketing. Administrative Decision of the General Counsel, Case No. 1069, Dec. 3, 1954, reported in CCH *Labor Law Reports,* V, ¶ 52,493 (1954). For criticisms of the NLRB position, see 20 *University of Chicago Law Review* 109 (1952), *Washington University Law Quarterly* 183 (1955).

16. NLRB v. Capital Service, Inc., 204 F.2d 848 (9th Cir. 1953).

17. Garner v. Teamsters Union, 346 U.S. 485 (1953).

18. Lane v. NLRB, 186 F.2d 671 (10th Cir. 1951); Eclipse Lumber Co., 95 N.L.R.B. 464 (1951); Mundet Cork Corp., 96 N.L.R.B. 1142 (1951); Roadway Express Co., 108 N.L.R.B. No. 123 (1954).

19. Colonial Hardwood Flooring Co., 84 N.L.R.B. 563 (1949); Progressive Mine Workers of America v. NLRB, 187 F.2d 298 (7th Cir. 1951).

20. Irrefutable criticisms of the NLRB position are to be found in 1 *Columbia Law Review* 83 (1951) and 2 *Labor Law Journal* 83 (1951).

21. The trend in the state courts can be detected most efficiently perhaps by reference to the labor law articles in the *Annual Survey of American Law* (New York: New York University Press) for the past four or five years.

22. See Chapter 19, pages 269-72.

23. See generally Gregory, *Labor and the Law* (index references under "Boycott").

24. *Ibid.* And see: Hellerstein, "Secondary Boycotts in Labor Disputes," 47 *Yale Law Journal* 341 (1938); Ludwig Teller, *The Law Governing Labor Disputes and Collective Bargaining,* (New York: Baker, Voorhis & Co., Inc., 1940), II, chap. ix.

25. Cf. Cox, "Labor and the Antitrust Laws: A Preliminary Analysis," 104 *University of Pennsylvania Law Review* 252 (1955); Gregory, *op. cit.,* chaps. viii, x.

26. See, for example, National Fireproofing Co. v. Mason Builders' Assn., 169 Fed. 259 (2d Cir. 1909).

27. For a sarcastic and destructive criticism of the use of this theory by the courts, see Holmes, "Privilege, Malice, and Intent," 8 *Harvard Law Review* 1 (1894).

28. Cf. Bossert v. Dhuy, 221 N.Y. 342, 117 N.E. 582 (1917).

29. As does Gregory, *Labor and the Law,* chaps. iii-vi.

30. Every legal system in the world has a doctrine more or less to the effect that the deliberate infliction of temporal harm is actionable unless justified. A characteristic of progressively civilized man is to resent and to react to the deliberate infliction of harm, and to wish to punish such conduct unless some superior ground for justification may be advanced. Abandoning the prima-facie tort theory is therefore not the sensible thing to do. It makes much more sense to formulate clear-cut rules concerning the grounds of justification—a job for legislatures—and then to have the courts apply those rules to the multitudinous controversies which come before them. Cf. Holmes, "Privilege, Malice, and Intent."

31. Cox, "Labor and the Antitrust Laws: A Preliminary Analysis," pp. 262-66. See also Chapter 19, page 280.

32. Gregory, *Labor and the Law,* chaps. vii, xii.

33. The analogy to the situation prevailing in England after unions had been relieved of all legal responsibility by the Trade Disputes Act of 1906 ought to be noted. See K. Braun, *The Right to Organize and Its Limits* (Washington, D. C.: The Brookings Institution, 1950), pp 38-39. See also A. V. Dicey, *Law and Opinion in England* (2d ed. London: Macmillan and Co., Ltd., 1930), chaps. xliv-xlvii. For further discussion of the situation in the United States from 1930 to 1947, see Chapter 13, below.

34. For detailed analysis of the statutory terms and the process whereby those terms were deprived of their plain meanings, see my articles in 1 *Labor Law Journal* 339, 835, 1075 (1950). For an opposing view, see Tower, "The Puzzling Proviso," *ibid.,* p. 1019 (1950).

35. *Ibid.*

36. See the observations of Professor Cox, quoted in note 4 to Chapter 10, above.

37. NLRB v. International Rice Milling Co., 341 U.S. 665 (1951) discussed at length in *New York University 1951 Annual Survey of American Law* (New York: New York University Press, 1952), pp 305-11.

38. Cf. Cox, "Federalism in the Law of Labor Relations," 67 *Harvard Law Review* 1297 (1954); Petro, "Participation by the States in the Enforcement and Development of National Labor Policy," 28 *Notre Dame Lawyer* 1 (1952).

39. Garner v. Teamsters, 346 U.S. 485 (1953); Anheuser-Busch, Inc. v. Weber, 348 U.S. 593 (1955). See Chapter 19, pages 269-7

40. See further Chapter 19.

41. Section 14(b), NLRA. Cf. State v. Whitaker, 228 N.C. 35 45 S.E.2d 860 (1947).

42. See generally 2 CCH *Labor Law Reports* ¶¶ 4500-4540.

43. This is an inference based on the adamant refusal of union spokesmen to accept any limitation at all on the types of compulsory unionism they seek.

44. Sections 8(a)(3) and 8(b)(2), NLRA. See Radio Officers' Union v. NLRB, 347 U.S. 17 (1954); Union Starch & Refining Co. v. NLRB, 186 F.2d 1008 (7th Cir. 1951).

45. NLRB v. Electric Auto-Lite Co., 196 F.2d 500 (6th Cir. 1952); Pen and Pencil Workers Union, 91 N.L.R.B. 883 (1950).

46. Special Machine & Engineering Co., 109 N.L.R.B. No. 125 (1954); Victor Metal Products Corp., 106 N.L.R.B. 1361 (1953); International Brotherhood of Teamsters, 112 N.L.R.B. No. 168 (1955); International Assn. of Iron Workers, 112 N.L.R.B. No. 137 (1955).

47. See note 41, above.

48. For a list of these states, see Chapter 17, note 12, below.

49. See "Closed Shops and Closed Unions," 1 *Labor Law Journal* 163, 259 (December 1949 and January 1950).

50. This fact undoubtedly accounts for the rigor of the current union campaign for repeal of state anti-compulsory union statutes. See the works cited in note 13, Chapter 10, above. See also the position taken by President George Meany of the AFL–CIO, as reported in *The New York Times,* February 24, 1956, p. 52, col. 3. Mr. Meany argues as though the only problem involved is that of the right of union workers to work or not to work with nonunion employees at will. The real problem of course is whether employee free choice is to prevail over pro-union coercion by unions as well as anti-union coercion by employers. See Chapter 4, pages 50-52.

CHAPTER 12

1. NLRB v. American National Insurance Co., 343 U.S. 395 (1952).

2. For an argument to the effect that the "new" NLRB has been violating the "will of Congress" in reversing the (mis)interpretations of its predecessor, see Ratner, "Recent Changes in National Labor Relations Board Policies," *N.Y.U. Eighth Annual Conference on Labor* (1955), 143-76. For another view of what has been going on, see the article on labor relations law in the *N.Y.U. 1955 Annual Survey of American Law* (1956), pp. 199 ff.

3. The definitive works comparing the theories of the free market with those of the hampered market are the massive treatises by Ludwig von Mises, *Human Action* (New Haven: Yale University Press, 1949) and *Socialism* (New Haven: Yale University Press, 1951). This chapter and Part I of this book owe much to those works.

4. *Human Action,* p. 83.

5. Ludwig von Mises, *The Theory of Money and Credit* (London: Jonathan Cape, Ltd., 1934), pp. 14-22, 216-61.

CHAPTER 13

1. E. M. Dangel and I. R. Shriber, *The Law of Labor Unions* (Boston: National Law Publishers, 1941), pp. 530 ff; Ludwig Teller, *The Law Governing Labor Disputes and Collective Bargaining*, 3 vols. (New York: Baker, Voorhis & Co., Inc., 1940), II, § 462.

2. When the highest British court, the House of Lords, held that damages might be assessed against union funds for unlawful union action, in Taff Vale Railway Co. v. Amalgamated Society of Railway Servants, A.C. 426 (1901), the "unions immediately began a vigorous campaign against this doctrine arguing that they could not perform their legitimate functions without occasionally causing damage to employers." K. Braun, *The Right to Organize and Its Limits* (Washington, D. C.: The Brookings Institution, 1950), p. 37. A Royal Commission appointed to investigate the problem declared that "When Trade Unions . . . wrong . . . outsiders, there can be no more reason that they should be beyond the reach of the law than any other individual partnership or institution." The unions nevertheless secured their immunity in England, with the Trade Disputes Act of 1906. Braun, pp. 38-39.

3. Cf. *Senate Report* No. 105, 80th Cong., 1st Sess., pp. 15-18 (1947).

4. See note 2, above. Braun, *op. cit.*, p. 39, remarks of the British situation that "unions thus attained all the immunities they had sought."

5. Section 9(a), Wagner Act.

6. Sections 7 and 9, Wagner Act.

7. Chapters 8 and 11.

8. Cf. *Senate Report* No. 105, 80th Cong., 1st Sess., pp. 418-19 (1947); *House Conference Report* No. 510, 80th Cong., 1st Sess., pp. 54-55 (1947), where it is said that "in the past the Board has made findings of violation [of the Wagner Act] in cases involving independent unions . . . upon much weaker evidence than it has required in cases involving affiliated unions, and it has ordered employers to take far more drastic action with respect to independent organizations than with respect to affiliated organizations."

9. The absence of any restraint upon union coercion of free employee choice is greatly emphasized by the fact that the law positively forbade the federal courts to enjoin such union conduct. Cf. Yoerg Brewing Co. v. Brennan, 59 F. Supp. 625 (D.C. Minn. 1945) and the general discussion in Petro, "Job-Seeking Aggression," 52 *Michigan Law Review* 497, 506-8 and authorities cited there (1952).

10. Yoerg case, note 9.

11. *Ibid.*, and see Chapter 19, pages 272-82.

12. Authorities cited in note 1 above, and see Charles O. Gregory, *Labor and the Law* (New York: W. W. Norton & Co., Inc., 1946), p. 94.

13. Cf. United Mine Workers of America v. Coronado Coal Co., 259 U.S. 344 (1922).

14. Felix Frankfurter and Nathan Greene, *The Labor Injunction* (New York: Macmillan Co., 1930), pp. 86-89.

15. Act of March 23, 1932, 47 Stat. 70, 29 U.S.C. §§ 101-115.

16. *Ibid.*, Section 6, interpreted in United Brotherhood of Carpenters & Joiners v. United States, 330 U.S. 395 (1947).

17. The general common-law rule is that a person is responsible for any acts committed by his agent within the scope of the latter's apparent authority. For an example of the application of this rule in a case involving union violence, see International Longshoremen's Union, 79 N.L.R.B. 1487 (1948).

18. Section 301(b), Taft-Hartley Act.

19. Section 301 (E), *ibid.*

20. Section 301(b), *ibid.*

21. Cf. A. V. Dicey, *Law and Opinion in England* (2d ed.; London: Macmillan Co. Ltd., 1930), chaps. xlv ff.; Friedrich A. Hayek, *The Political Ideal of the Rule of Law* (Cairo, Egypt: 1955).

22. Section 301(a), Taft-Hartley Act. But see Assn. of Westinghouse Employees v. Westinghouse Electric Corp., 348 U.S. 437 (1955), which seems to have undone the Taft-Hartley Act in this respect.

23. Section 9, Taft-Hartley Act.

24. Section 9(c)(2) and Section 10(c), *ibid.*

25. Section 8(b)(4)(C). Cf. Oppenheim Collins & Co., 83 N.L.R.B. 355 (1949); Douds v. Knit Goods Workers Union, 27 CCH Lab. Cas. ¶ 68,802 (S.D. N.Y. 1954).

26. Authorities cited in note 9, above.

CHAPTER 14

1. Cf. Commonwealth v. Hunt, 4 Metcalf 111 (Mass. Sup. Jud. Court 1842); Vegelahn v. Guntner, 167 Mass. 92 (1896), where, speaking for the majority, Judge Allen said: "A combination among persons merely to regulate their own conduct is within allowable competition, and is lawful, although others may be indirectly affected thereby." A careful British legal scholar has said that "no case has ever been cited in which any person was, for having combined with others for the raising of wages, convicted of a conspiracy in restraint of trade at common law before the year 1825." Sir James F. Stephen, *History of the Criminal Law of England* (London: Macmillan and Co., Ltd., 1883), p. 209. This is perhaps somewhat of an overstatement, at least in terms of the implication that no such case could be found. See authorities cited in note 3, below.

2. See generally James M. Landis and Marcus Manoff, *Cases on Labor Law* (2d ed.; Chicago: The Foundation Press, Inc., 1942), pp. 1-18.

3. Landis and Manoff, *op. cit.,* p. 12, refer to two decisions: Rex v. Journeymen-Tailors of Cambridge, 8 Mod. 10 (1721) and Rex v. Eccles, Leach C.C. 274 (1783).

4. See W. A. Sanderson, *Restraints of Trade in English Law* (London: Sweet and Maxwell, 1926), pp. 11 ff. E. P. Cheyney, *An Introduction to the Industrial and Social History of England* (rev. ed.; New York: Macmillan Co., 1920), pp. 54 ff.

5. Cf. Adam Smith, *The Wealth of Nations* (Modern Library; New York: Random House, Inc.), pp. 398-490.

6. Landis and Manoff, *op. cit.,* pp. 13-14.

7. That they had some effect, however, is evident from a perusal of R. B. Morris, *Government and Labor in Early America* (New York: Columbia University Press, 1946), pp. 17 ff.

8. Cf. People v. Fisher, 14 Wend. 10 (Sup. Ct. of Judicature, New York, 1835).

9. H. A. Millis and R. E. Montgomery, *Organized Labor* (New York: McGraw-Hill Book Co., Inc., 1945), pp. 12-72.

10. Commonwealth v. Pullis, in John R. Commons *et al.* (eds.), *A Documentary History of American Industrial Society* (Cleveland: A. H. Clark Co., 1910-11), III, 60. Cf. Nelles, "The First American Labor Case," 41 *Yale Law Journal* 165 (1931).

11. Another judge of the Philadelphia Mayor's Court insisted just a few years later that labor action could be held unlawful only if criminal means were used. Commonwealth v. Moore, (1827), in Commons *et al.,* IV, 99 ff.

12. 4 Metcalf 111 (1842).

13. No purer, more succinct, or more authoritative statement of the attitude of the common law toward labor organization during the nineteenth century can be cited than that of the Massachusetts Supreme Judicial Court in Vegelahn v. Guntner, 167 Mass. 92 (1896). See note 1, above.

14. *Ibid.*

15. Injunctions always forbade coercive action taken in connection with strikes or independently thereof. They never prohibited peaceful strikes for higher wages or better working conditions. Cf. Felix Frankfurter and Nathan Greene, *The Labor Injunction* (New York: Macmillan Co., 1930), pp. 82 ff. And see Chapter 19, pages 277-78, below.

16. *Ibid.* Messrs. Frankfurter and Greene never gave any particular emphasis to this point. On the contrary, as shown in Chapter 19, pages 276-77, below, they referred frequently to injunctions restraining "strike activities," as if strikes, rather than coercive conduct, were being enjoined.

17. Great Northern Railway Co. v. Brosseau, 286 Fed. 414 (D.C. N.D. 1923).

18. The current view of labor law history in the United States has been influenced very largely by the kinds of references which have been made to the Debs case. Indeed, Mr. Debs is today considered a martyr in many respectable circles, presumably because so much has been made of the "anti-unionism" displayed, allegedly, by the federal government in the railroad controversies of the late nineteenth century. Few seem to be aware, however, of the extensive violence incited by Eugene Debs and his aides. For the facts, see *In re* Debs, 158 U.S. 564, 568 ff. (1894). Trains were derailed and wrecked, and violence was used widely in order to prevent employees from working.

19. Cf. Petro, "Effects and Purposes of Picketing," 2 *Labor Law Journal* 323-26 (1951).

20. For a recent example of what is always to be expected when picketing in numbers is allowed, see *The New York Times,* February 25, 1956, p. 1, col. 5.

21. Atchison, Topeka & Santa Fe Ry. Co. v. Gee, 139 Fed. 582, 584-85 (S.D. Iowa 1905).

22. Pierce v. Stablemen's Union, 156 Cal. 70, 103 Pac. 324 (1909).

23. Hearn Dept. Stores, Inc. v. Livingston, 124 N.Y.S.2d 552 (N.Y. Sup. Ct. 1953). On appeal, however, all picketing was enjoined. 125 N.Y.S.2d 187 (App. Div. 1953).

24. Thornhill v. Alabama, 310 U.S. 88 (1940). Cf. Charles O. Gregory, *Labor and the Law* (New York: W. W. Norton Co., Inc., 1946), pp. 334-77.

25. *Ibid.*

26. Cases tracing the retreat from the picketing–free-speech identification: Carpenters & Joiners v. Ritter's Cafe, 315 U.S. 722 (1942); Giboney v. Empire Storage & Ice Co., 336 U.S. 490 (1949); Hughes v. Superior Court, 339 U.S. 460 (1950); Int. Brotherhood of Teamsters v. Hanke, 339 U.S. 470 (1950); Building Service Employees v. Gazzam, 339 U.S. 532 (1950).

27. Section 7, Taft-Hartley Act.

28. Cf. International Longshoremen's Union, 79 N.L.R.B. 1487 (1948).

29. The definitive approach to regulation of picketing was set forth in American Steel Foundries v. Tri-City Central Trades Council, 257 U.S. 184 (1921).

30. Authorities cited in notes 19–20 to Chapter 11.

31. *Ibid.*

CHAPTER 15

1. Cf. Barr v. The Essex Trades Council, 53 N.J.Eq. 101 (1894); Pacific Typesetting Co. v. Int. Typographical Union, 125 Wash. 273, 216 Pac. 358 (1923); Quinn v. Leathem, [1901] A.C. 495 (House of Lords).

2. Cf. Empire Theatre Co. v. Cloke, 53 Mont. 183, 163 Pac. 107 (1917).

3. Compare the decisions of the New York Court of Appeals in Bossert v. Dhuy, 221 N.Y. 342, 117 N.E. 582 (1917) and Auburn Draying Co. v. Wardell, 227 N.Y. 1, 124 N.E. 97 (1919).

4. Cf. Hellerstein, "Secondary Boycotts in Labor Disputes," 47 *Yale Law Journal* 341 (1938); Sayre, "Labor and the Courts," 39 *ibid.* 682, 699 (1930).

5. Aggressive union action designed to secure the closed shop was often condemned in Massachusetts, Colonial Press, Inc. v. Ellis, 321 Mass. 495, 74 N.E.2d 1 (1947); but held privileged in New York, Williams v. Quill, 277 N.Y. 1, 12 N.E.2d 547 (1948). The difficulties of reconciling the decisions even in one jurisdiction are dwelt upon in Sayre, "Labor and the Courts," 39 *Yale Law Journal* 682 (1930).

6. W. W. Crosskey, *Politics and the Constitution in the History of the United States*, 2 vols. (Chicago: University of Chicago Press, 1953), I, 363-708.

7. *Ibid.*, II, 711-938.

8. Erie R.R. v. Tompkins, 304 U.S. 64 (1938); cf. Swift v. Tyson, 16 Pet. 1 (1842), and Crosskey, *op. cit.* pp. 865 ff.

9. As a corollary of the rule that manufacturing is a "local operation" not subject to the commerce powers of Congress; cf. United States v. E. C. Knight Co., 155 U.S. 685 (1895).

10. Act of 1890, 26 Stat. 209, 15 U.S.C. §§ 1 ff.

11. Loewe v. Lawlor, 208 U.S. 274 (1908); Duplex Printing Press Co. v. Deering, 254 U.S. 443 (1921); United States v. Brims, 272 U.S. 549 (1926).

12. Coronado Coal Co. v. United Mine Workers, 268 U.S. 295 (1925).

13. Apex Hosiery Co. v. Leader, 310 U.S. 469 (1940).

14. United States v. Hutcheson, 312 U.S. 219 (1941). Cf. Gregory, *Labor and the Law*, pp. 200–22, 253-88, and Chapter 19, pages 272-82.

15. See pages 129-30, above.

16. The Massachusetts Supreme Judicial Court, for example, gave as little as possible to the Supreme Court's theories; cf. Simon v. Swachman, 301 Mass. 573 (1939); Fashioncraft v. Halpern, 313 Mass. 385 (1943).

17. Cf. Carpenters & Joiners v. Ritter's Cafe, 315 U.S. 722 (1942), a decision by the U. S. Supreme Court reviewing an application by the Texas Supreme Court of a state antitrust statute to secondary picketing.

18. Two sections of the law should be read together: § 13 and the proviso to § 8(b)(4).

19. Cf. NLRB v. International Rice Milling Co., Inc., 341 U.S. 665 (1951); NLRB v. Denver Building & Construction Trades Council, 341 U.S. 675 (1951).

20. " 'Primary' and 'Secondary' Labor Action," 1 *Labor Law Journal* 339 (1950).

21. See note 18, above.

22. The leading cases are NLRB v. International Rice Milling Co., 341 U.S. 665 (1951); and Schultz Refrigerated Service, 87 N.L.R.B. 502 (1949). Some courts, however, agree with the view set forth in the text here. See Joliet Contractors Assn. v. NLRB, 202 F.2d 606 (7th Cir. 1953); Int. Rice Milling v. NLRB, 283 F.2d 21 (5th Cir. 1950), reversed by the Supreme Court in 341 U.S. 665 (1951).

23. I have dealt with this matter at length and in detail elsewhere; see 1 *Labor Law Journal* 1075 (1950). See also Winthrop A. Johns, "Picketing and Secondary Boycotts Under the Taft-Hartley Act," 2 *ibid.* 257 (1951), for a careful review of the authorities.

24. For a comprehensive collection of materials dealing with critical industrial disputes, see Russell A. Smith, *Labor Law Cases and Materials* (2d ed.; Indianapolis: Bobbs-Merrill Co., Inc., 1953), pp. 557-632.

25. This approach was considered and rejected by the Eightieth Congress in favor of the method used in the Taft-Hartley Act.

26. Section 206-210, Taft-Hartley Act.

27. This was the method chosen by Mr. Harry S. Truman to "settle" the steel dispute of 1951-52, although the Congress had by law directed another method. For discussion of the steel dispute and Mr. Truman's role therein, see Chapter 19, pages 256-57. As Democratic candidate for the Presidency in 1952, Mr. Adlai Stevenson also thought that seizure should be available in some disputes. *The New York Times*, September 2, 1952, p. 10.

28. Cf. Theodore R. Iserman, "The Labor Monopoly Problem," 38 *American Bar Association Journal* 743 (1952) and Kamin, "The Fiction of Labor Monopoly," *ibid.*, 748.

29. See the discussion by Milton Friedman, University of Chicago economist, in David McCord Wright (ed.), *The Impact of the Union* (New York: Harcourt, Brace and Co., Inc., 1951), pp. 204 ff.

30. The basic legal provisions are to be found in Sections 8(a)(5), 8(d), and 9(a) of the Taft-Hartley Act.

31. Cf. NLRB v. Crompton-Highland Mills, Inc., 337 U.S. 217 (1949); Bradley Washfountain Co., 192 F.2d 144 (7th Cir. 1951).

32. Cf. St. Joseph Stock Yards Co., 2 N.L.R.B. 39 (1936); American National Insurance Co., 88 N.L.R.B. 55 (1950), reversed by the United States Supreme Court in 343 U.S. 395 (1952).

33. See generally, Petro, "The Employer's Duty to Bargain," 3 *Labor Law Journal* 515 (1952) and other material cited in Chapter 18, pages 253-60.

34. NLRB v. American National Insurance Co., 343 U.S. 395 (1952).

35. 88 N.L.R.B. 55 (1950).

CHAPTER 16

1. The admirable "Report of Committee on Improvement of Administration of Union-Management Agreements on Individual Grievances," 50 *Northwestern University Law Review* 143 (1955) is marred, it seems to me, by a failure to appreciate that in a society such as ours persons must come first and institutions second. The members of this committee are Ralph E. Axley, Edward Flaherty, Robert W. Gilbert, Robert G. Howlett, William F. Lubersky, Robert E. Mathews, Plato Papps, Clyde W. Summers, *Chairman,* and Richard W. Wright.

2. See Pacific Intermountain Express Co., 107 N.L.R.B. 837 (1954) and 110 N.L.R.B. No. 14 (1954).

3. 107 N.L.R.B. 837, at 840, n. 3.

4. Sections 8(a) and 8(b)(2), NLRA, as amended.

5. 107 N.L.R.B. 837 (1954).

6. 110 N.L.R.B. No. 14 (1954).

7. Steele v. Louisville & Nashville Ry., 323 U.S. 192 (1944). See also Tunstall v. Brotherhood of Locomotive Firemen & Engineers, 323 U.S. 210; Brotherhood of Railroad Trainmen v. Howard, 343 U.S. 768 (1952).

8. Cf. Section 9(b), NLRA, as amended. Globe Machine & Stamping Co., 3 N.L.R.B. 294 (1937); American Potash & Chemical Corp., 107 N.L.R.B. 1418 (1954). It is worthy of note that in the latter decision, the Board declared that ". . . we also recognize that the equities of employees in certain other minority groups, though lacking the hallmark of craft skill, may also require that they be treated as severable units." (*Ibid.,* at 1424.)

9. While liberalizing the rules as to craft severance in the American Potash case (note 8 above), the Board gave "grave consideration to the argument of employer and union groups that fragmentation of bargaining units in highly integrated industries which are characteristic of our modern industrial system can result in loss of maximum efficiency and sometimes afford an opportunity for jurisdictional disputes as to work assignments. . . . The alternative, however, is to deny crafts separate representation, and experience has shown that this approach . . . was no less productive of labor unrest." 107 N.L.R.B. 1418, at 1422.

10. Hartley v. Brotherhood of Clerks, 283 Mich. 201, 277 N.W. 885 (1938).

11. For a similar decision, see Belanger v. Local Division No. 1128, 256 Wis. 479, 41 N.W.2d 607 (1950).

12. Wilson v. Hacker, 200 Misc. 124, 101 N.Y.S.2d 461 (N. Y. Sup. Ct. 1950).

13. Ford Motor Co. v. Huffman, 345 U.S. 330 (1953).

14. For comprehensive coverage of the cases and the literature in this field, see the article cited in note 1, above.

15. Assn. of Westinghouse Salaried Employees v. Westinghouse Electric Corp., 75 Sup. Ct. 488 (1955).

16. The ramifications of the decision are carefully analyzed in Note, 50 *Northwestern University Law Review* 289 (1955).

17. *Ibid.*

18. *Ibid.*

19. For an excellent, extended discussion of these matters, see *op. cit.*, note 1, above.

20. Ryan v. Liberty Powder Defense Corp. (W.E.R.B. Dec. No. 3895), 4 CCH Labor Law Reports ¶ 49,298 (1955).

21. E.g., Bianculli v. Brooklyn Union Gas Co., 115 N.Y.S.2d 715 (1952); cf. *In re* Julius Wile Sons & Co., 199 Misc. 654, 102 N.Y.S. 2d 862 (1951); Swinick v. Goldsmith, 28 CCH Lab. Cas. ¶ 69,349 (N. Y. Sup. Ct. 1955).

22. Parker v. Borock, 28 CCH Lab. Cas. ¶ 69,257 (N. Y. App. Div. 1955). (Murphy, J., dissenting, asserts that if the union refuses to arbitrate the aggrieved employee should be without further remedy.)

23. Anson v. Hiram Walker & Sons, 36 L.R.R.M. 2056 (7th Cir. 1955); cf. O'Brien v. Dade Bros., Inc., 28 CCH Lab. Cas. ¶ 69,258 (N. J. Sup. Ct. 1955).

24. Smithey v. St. Louis Southwestern Ry. Co., 27 CCH Lab. Cas. ¶ 69,059 (E.D. Ark. 1955).

25. *Op. cit.*, note 1, above.

CHAPTER 17

1. Chapter 11, above.

2. Chapter 7, pages 109-19, above.

3. Among other state supreme courts sharing this opinion are the high courts of Florida, Kansas, Kentucky, Maine, Michigan, Missouri, Ohio, and Wisconsin. See the decisions of those courts in Boca Raton Club v. Hotel Employees, 28 CCH Lab. Cas. ¶ 69,513 (Fla. 1955); Kaw Paving Co. v. Engineers, 178 Kan. 467 (1955); Blue Boar Cafeteria, Inc. v. Hotel & Restaurant Employees, 254 S.W.2d 335 (Ky. 1952); Pappas v. Stacey, 116 A.2d 497 (Me. 1955); Postma v. Int. Bro. Teamsters, 334 Mich. 347 (1952); Bellerive Country Club v. McVey, 28 CCH Lab. Cas. ¶ 69,278 (Mo. 1955); Chucales v. Royalty, 29 CCH Lab. Cas. ¶ 69,536 (Ohio, 1955); Vogt, Inc. v. Teamsters, 29 CCH Lab. Cas. ¶ 69,747 (Wis. 1956).

4. Garner v. Teamsters Union, 346 U.S. 485 (1953).

5. NLRB v. Capital Service, Inc., 204 F.2d 848 (9th Cir. 1953).

6. See, for example, C. O. Gregory, *Labor and the Law* (New York: W. W. Norton Co., Inc., 1946); see also the note in 20 *University of Chicago Law Review* 109 (1952), and Rothenberg, "Organizational Picketing," 5 *Labor Law Journal* 689 (1954).

7. Cf. Wood v. O'Grady, 307 N.Y. 532, 122 N.E.2d 386 (1954), discussed in *1954 Annual Survey of American Law*, 343-45.

8. Cf. Garner v. Teamsters, 373 Pa. 19, 94 A.2d 893 (1953), especially the dissenting opinion of Bell, J.

9. E.g., Kaw Paving Co. v. Engineers, 178 Kan. 467 (1955).

10. Perry Norvell Co., 80 N.L.R.B. 225 (1948). For reviews of the relevant NLRB decisions, see 20 *University of Chicago Law Review* 109 (1952) and *Washington University Law Quarterly* 183 (1955).

11. Building Service Employees v. Gazzam, 339 U.S. 532 (1950). Cf. Petro, "Free Speech and Organizational Picketing," 4 *Labor Law Journal* 3, 7-8 (1953).

12. See the compilation of state labor laws in 4 CCH Labor Law Reports at ¶ 40,351. As of 1956, the states are Alabama, Arizona, Arkansas, Colorado, Florida, Georgia, Mississippi, Nebraska, Nevada, New Mexico, North Carolina, North Dakota, South Carolina, South Dakota, Tennessee, Texas, and Virginia. A number of other states, for example Kansas and Iowa, prohibit some forms of compulsory unionism while permitting others.

13. See Chapter 11, pages 169-70.

14. *Ibid.*

15. This would take the place of present Section 8(b)(2) of the NLRA. The lengthy and complicated proviso to § 8(a)(3) should then be deleted.

16. This proposal is designed to take the place of present § 8(b)(4) of the NLRA.

17. As was the United States Court of Appeals for the Ninth Circuit in NLRB v. Capital Service, Inc., 204 F.2d 848 (9th Cir. 1953).

18. Cf. Republic Steel Corp., 9 N.L.R.B. 219 (1938); Stehli and Co., Inc., 11 N.L.R.B. 1397 (1939); Sunshine Mining Co., 7 N.L.R.B. 1252 (1938).

19. E.g., A. S. Beck Shoe Corp., 92 N.L.R.B. 1457 (1951); NLRB v. Winona Textile Mills, Inc., 160 F.2d 201 (8th Cir. 1947).

20. NLRB v. Morris Kirk & Sons, 151 F.2d 490 (9th Cir. 1945); NLRB v. Sun Tent-Luebbert Co., 151 F.2d 483 (9th Cir. 1945); Blue Ridge Shirt Mfg. Co., 70 N.L.R.B. 741 (1946).

21. Indianapolis Wire Bound Box Co., 89 N.L.R.B. 617 (1950); NLRB v. Hoppes Mfg. Co., 170 F.2d 962 (6th Cir. 1948); Winona Textile Mills, Inc., 160 F.2d 201 (8th Cir. 1947).

22. Hickory Chair Mfg. Co. v. NLRB, 131 F.2d 849 (4th Cir. 1942); Cook Auto Machine Co., 84 N.L.R.B. 688 (1949), 184 F.2d 845 (6th Cir. 1950).

23. NLRB v. Indiana Desk Co., 149 F.2d 987 (7th Cir. 1945); Grower-Shipper Vegetable Assn., 15 N.L.R.B. 322 (1939), 122 F.2d 368 (9th Cir. 1941); Waumbeck Mills, Inc., 15 N.L.R.B. 37 (1939), 114 F.2d 226 (1st Cir. 1940).

24. Section 8(c), NLRA, as amended. Cf. Pittsburgh S.S. Co. v. NLRB, 180 F.2d 731 (6th Cir. 1950).

25. As, for example, in National Licorice Co. v. NLRB, 309 U.S. 350 (1940).

26. Cf. American Potash & Chemical Corp., 107 N.L.R.B. 1418 (1954).

27. Elgin National Watch Co., 109 N.L.R.B. 273 (1954).

28. Unless the employer should refuse to bargain with the union finally certified, basing his refusal on the contention that the Board's unit determination was arbitrary, there is no way to secure court review of the unit determination, Section 9(d), NLRA, as amended. Cf. AFL v. NLRB, 308 U.S. 401 (1940); NLRB v. I.B.E.W., 308 U.S. 413 (1940).

29. United States Constitution, Art. 3, Sec. 2.

CHAPTER 18

1. Henry C. Simons, *Economic Policy for a Free Society* (Chicago: University of Chicago Press, 1948), p. 121; Charles E. Lindblom, *Unions and Capitalism* (New Haven: Yale University Press, 1949).

2. Chapter 7.

3. Cf. Ross, "Collective Bargaining and Common Sense," 2 *Labor Law Journal* 435 (1951). David McCord Wright (ed.), *The Impact of the Union,* (New York: Harcourt, Brace & Co., Inc., 1951).

4. Chapters 6 and 7.

5. Typical is a situation which arose on Long Island in connection with a strike against the Republic Aviation Co. According to a newspaper report, "when the plant opened . . . there were approximately 700 pickets at the gate attempting to stop cars from entering. They were faced by a police detail that ranged from twelve to seventy. Scuffles ensued between the police and the pickets and were followed by arrests. Most of the injured pickets were hurt when their fellows pushed them into the paths of cars during the melees. One picket was reported to have suffered a broken leg." *The New York Times,* February 21, 1956, pp. 1, 22, cols. 6 and 4. One of the union leaders accused the police of "attempting to break the strike by illegal interference with pickets." *Ibid.*

6. Chapter 10, pages 156-58; and Chapter 14.

7. *Ibid.*

8. Chapter 14.

9. Chapter 10, pages 150-56; Chapter 15, pages 202-7.

10. Cf. Cornellier v. Haverhill Shoe Manufacturers' Assn., 221 Mass. 554, 109 N.E. 643 (1915); Anderson v. Shipowners' Assn., 272 U.S. 359 (1926). See also authorities cited in note 23, Chapter 17. But see Edwin E. Witte, "Labor's Resort to Injunctions," 39 *Yale Law Journal* 374 (1930).

11. *Ibid.*, and see Petro, "The Enlightening Proviso," 1 *Labor Law Journal* 1075 (November 1950).

12. Douds v. Metropolitan Federation of Architects, 75 F. Supp. 672 (S.D. N.Y. 1948); NLRB v. Business Machine Mechanics, 29 CCH Lab. Cas. ¶ 69,649 (2d Cir. 1955).

13. Cf. Chapter 11, pages 165-69; Chapter 15, pages 202-5.

14. Cf. Chapter 15, pages 214-17.

15. NLRB v. Landis Tool Co., 193 F.2d 279 (3rd Cir. 1952); NLRB v. Montgomery Ward & Co., 133 F.2d 676 (9th Cir. 1943); Ritzwoller Co. v. NLRB, 114 F.2d 432 (7th Cir. 1940).

16. NLRB v. Truitt Mfg. Co., 30 CCH Lab. Cas. ¶ 69,932 (U.S. Sup. Ct., 1956); Yawman & Erbe Mfg. Co., 89 N.L.R.B. 881 (1950), 187 F.2d 947 (2d Cir. 1951); Ekstrom, Carlson, & Co., 114 N.L.R.B. No. 191 (1955); Taylor Forge & Pipe Works, 113 N.L.R.B. No. 65 (1955).

17. American National Insurance Co., 89 N.L.R.B. 185 (1950), reversed 187 F.2d 307 (5th Cir. 1951) and 343 U.S. 395 (1952). See also NLRB v. United Clay Mines Corp., 219 F.2d 120 (6th Cir. 1955).

18. For an excellent review of this phase of the legislative history of the Wagner Act, see Smith, "The Evolution of the 'Duty to Bargain' Concept in American Law," 39 *Michigan Law Review* 1065 (1941). See also Latham, "Legislative Purpose and Administrative Policy under the National Labor Relations Act," 4 *George Washington Law Review* 433 (1936).

19. Cf. N. W. Chamberlain, *Collective Bargaining* (New York: McGraw-Hill Book Co. Inc., 1951), pp. 335-463.

20. For a more elaborate discussion of these points, see Petro, "The Employer's Duty to Bargain," 3 *Labor Law Journal* 515 (1952).

21. This and following quotations are from Mr. Truman's memoirs as published in *The New York Times,* February 18, 1956, p. 10.

22. Section 9(c)(3), National Labor Relations Act, as amended. Cf. Theodore R. Iserman, *Changes to Make in Taft-Hartley* (New York: Dealers Digest Publishing Co., Inc., 1953), pp. 106 ff.

23. President Eisenhower has offered such an amendment to Congress each year since his accession to the presidency.

24. Rockwell Valves, Inc., 115 N.L.R.B. No. 40 (1956).

25. For a more extended analysis of this point, see Petro, "On Amending the Taft-Hartley Act," 4 *Labor Law Journal* 67, 70 (Feb. 1953).

26. Chapter 16, pages 228-32.

27. *Ibid.* The reference is to the Supreme Court's decision in Assn. of Westinghouse Employees v. Westinghouse Electric Corp., 348 U.S. 437 (1955). See the analysis of that decision in 50 *Northwestern University Law Review* 289 (1955).

28. Some federal courts now decree specific enforcement; others refuse to do so, on the ground that the Norris-LaGuardia Act precludes their exercise of equity powers. Cases granting specific performance:

United Electrical Workers v. Landers, 34 L.R.R.M. 2242 (D.C. Conn. 1954); United Textile Workers v. Goodall-Sanford, Inc., 28 CCH Lab. Cas. ¶ 69,259 (S.D. Me. 1955). For cases denying specific performance, see Mead, Inc. v. I.B.T., 217 F.2d 6 (1st Cir. 1954); Sound Lumber Co. v. Lumber & Sawmill Workers, 122 F. Supp. 925 (N.D. Calif. 1954).

29. Section 8 (d), NLRA, as amended. Cf. Lion Oil Co. v. NLRB, 221 F.2d 231 (8th Cir. 1955).

30. Cf. United Packinghouse Workers, 89 N.L.R.B. 310 (1950); Wilson & Co., Inc., 105 N.L.R.B. No. 128 (1953). But see Lion Oil Co., 109 N.L.R.B. No. 106 (1954), indicating that the Board has decided to apply the statute in accordance with its plain meaning.

CHAPTER 19

1. See pages 265-72 of this chapter.

2. F. W. Maitland, "English Law," 8 *Encyclopaedia Britannica* (1955 edition), 564, 567. See also F. W. Maitland, *Equity* (2d ed.; Cambridge: Cambridge Univerity Press, 1936), pp. 1-22, 153 ff.

3. Appreciations of Mansfield's work are legion. For one of the most penetrating of all evaluations of Mansfield's place in legal history, see W. W. Crosskey, *Politics and the Constitution in the History of the United States*, 2 vols. (Chicago: University of Chicago Press, 1953), I, 578 ff.

4. *Ibid.*

5. Maitland, works cited in note 2; A. V. Dicey, *Law and Opinion in England* (2d ed.; London: Macmillan Co., Ltd., 1930), pp. 126 ff.

6. A. T. Vanderbilt, *The Challenge of Law Reform* (Princeton: Princeton University Press, 1955), pp. 3 ff.

7. See A. T. Vanderbilt, *The Doctrine of the Separation of Powers* (Lincoln: University of Nebraska Press, 1953), especially at pp. 97 ff. The energies, activities, and accomplishments of this extraordinary jurist are already recognized. See the remarks of Judge Harold Medina in the *New York University Law Center Bulletin* 9 (Winter, 1956). But a full evaluation of his work is yet to be written.

8. Owing to the ambiguous status of unions under the common law. As to the difficulty of the common law on this score, see Sellers, "Suability of Trade Unions as a Legal Entity," 33 *California Law Review* 444 (1945).

9. General Drivers v. NLRB, 179 F.2d 492 (10th Cir. 1950); Hourihan v. NLRB, 201 F.2d 187 (D.C. Cir. 1952); Lincourt v. NLRB, 170 F.2d 306 (1st Cir. 1948).

10. Haleston Drug Stores v. NLRB, 187 F.2d 418 (9th Cir. 1948); Progressive Mine Workers v. NLRB, 189 F.2d 1 (7th Cir. 1951).

11. Amazon Cotton Mill Co. v. Textile Workers Union, 167 F.2d 183 (4th Cir. 1948).

12. *Ibid.* See note 22, below. And see International Longshoremen v. Sunset Line & Twine Co., 77 F. Supp. 119 (D.C. Calif. 1948).

13. It is almost impossible to describe adequately the confusion which prevails today concerning the jurisdiction of state courts in labor disputes. The legal literature is full of articles dealing with the problems created by the Supreme Court's pre-emption theory. See note 25, below. For a review of recent decisions, see 31 *New York University Law Review* 286-93 (Feb., 1956).

14. *Ibid.*

15. For a very recent opinion indicating the major trend, see the Missouri Supreme Court's decision in Graybar Electric Co. v. Automotive Employees, 29 CCH Lab. Cas. ¶ 69,758 (Feb. 1956).

16. Cf. Cain, Brogden & Crain v. Teamsters, 29 CCH Lab. Cas. ¶ 69,676 (Ten. Sup. Ct. 1956). But compare the decision in Holman v. Industrial Stamping & Mfg. Co., 29 CCH Lab. Cas. ¶ 69,651 (Mich. Sup. Ct. 1955).

17. Garmon v. San Diego Building Trades Council, 29 CCH Lab. Cas. ¶ 69,642 (Calif. Sup. Ct. 1955).

18. Cf. the Graybar case, *supra* note 15. And see Avon Products v. Teamsters, 29 CCH Lab. Cas. ¶ 69,578 (Del. Ch. 1955); Benton v. Painters, 29 CCH Lab. Cas. ¶ 69,643 (Calif. Sup. Ct. 1955); Holman v. Industrial Stamping Co., 29 CCH Lab. Cas. ¶ 69,651 (Mich. Sup. Ct. 1955); Kaw Paving Co. v. Engineers, 178 Kan. 467 (1955); Mississippi Valley Electric Co. v. Teamsters, 29 CCH Lab. Cas. ¶ 69,607 (La. Sup. Ct. 1955); Northern Improvement Co. v. Teamsters, 29 CCH Lab. Cas. ¶ 69,616 (N.D. Sup. Ct. 1955); Wis. Emp. Rel. Bd. v. Teamsters, 29 CCH Lab. Cas. ¶ 69,566 (Wis. 1955).

19. Cf. Garner v. Teamsters, 346 U.S. 485 (1953); General Drivers v. American Tobacco Co., 348 U.S. 978 (1955); Weber v. Anheuser-Busch, 348 U.S. 593 (1955); Teamsters v. New York, New Haven & Hartford R.R., 29 CCH Lab. Cas. ¶ 69,667 (1956).

20. NLRB v. Swift & Co., 130 F. Supp. 214, 219 (E.D. Mo. 1955).

21. Cf. 1 *Labor Law Journal* 83, 579, 995 (Nov., 1949; and May and Oct., 1950).

22. See Sections 3 and 10 of the NLRA, which, read together, give the NLRB and its General Counsel discretion in the prosecution of complaints under the NLRA. As regards the unfair practices listed in Section 8(b)(4), the NLRB is required to seek an injunction where it has reasonable cause to believe that such unfair practices exist. Section 10(1) of the NLRA.

23. The Supreme Court has recently suggested that Congress intended by the Taft-Hartley Act and the Administrative Procedure Act to give the federal courts a greater power of review than they thought

they had previously. Universal Camera Corp. v. NLRB, 340 U.S. 474 (1951). But in so holding, the Supreme Court acted as though the extent of judicial review to be allowed was up to Congress. In short, the Supreme Court perceives no constitutional issue. However that may be, the federal courts still think that their powers of review are limited. See the observations of Judge Learned Hand in NLRB v. Stow Mfg. Co., 217 F.2d 900 at 905 (2d Cir. 1955).

24. Cf. Crosskey, *op. cit.* pp. 615 ff.

25. For a few examples of the extensive literature dealing with the Supreme Court's pre-emption theories, see: George Rose, "Limitations on the Power of States to Enjoin Picketing," 41 *Virginia Law Review* 581 (1955); Martin I. Rose, "Federal-State Court Conflicts in Labor Injunction Cases," 15 *Federal Bar Journal* 17 (1955); Roumell and Schlesinger, "The Pre-emption Dilemma in Labor Relations," 18 *Univ. of Detroit Law Journal* 17, 135 (1955); Archibald Cox, "Federalism in the Law of Labor Relations," 67 *Harvard Law Review* 1297 (1954); Petro, "Participation by the States in the Enforcement and Development of National Labor Policy," 28 *Notre Dame Lawyer* 1 (1952); Russell A. Smith, "The Taft-Hartley Act and State Jurisdiction over Labor Relations," 46 *Michigan Law Review* 593 (1948).

26. *The Federalist* No. XXVII.

27. See Petro, *op. cit.* in note 25, at 36, 66 ff.

28. Cf. Garner v. Teamsters Union, 346 U.S. 485, at 499 (1953).

29. Cf. Cox and Seidman, "Federalism and Labor Relations," 64 *Harvard Law Review* 211, at 224, 226 ff.; Smith, *op. cit.* in note 25; Petro, *op. cit.* in note 25, especially note 79, and pp. 38–40.

30. See, for example, *Legislative History of the Labor Management Relations Act* (Washington D.C.: Government Printing Office, 1947), II, 1208.

31. Senate Bill 3143, 84th Cong., 2d Sess. (1956).

32. Chief Justice Stone has said, citing many cases in support of the proposition, that "Congress, in enacting legislation within its constitutional authority over interstate commerce, will not be deemed to have intended to strike down a state statute designed to protect the health and safety of the public unless its purpose to do so is clearly manifested, . . . or unless the state law, in terms or in its practical administration, conflicts with the Act of Congress, or plainly and palpably infringes its policy." Southern Pacific Co. v. Arizona, 325 U.S. 761, 766 (1945).

33. Garner v. Teamsters Union, 346 U.S. 485 (1953).

34. *Ibid.*, at 499.

35. NLRB v. Columbian Enameling & Stamping Co., 306 U.S. 292 (1939); NLRB v. Fansteel Metallurgical Corp., 306 U.S. 240 (1939); Int'l Union UAW-AFL v. WERB, 336 U.S. 245 (1949); NLRB v. Local 1229, 346 U.S. 464 (1953); NLRB v. Rockaway News Supply

Co., 345 U.S. 71 (1953); NLRB v. Sands Mfg. Co., 306 U.S. 332 (1939); Southern S.S. Co. v. NLRB, 316 U.S. 31 (1942).

36. Cf. Smith, *op. cit.* in note 25, at 613, note 44.

37. Justice Black of the United States Supreme Court has referred to the "constitutional principle that states have power to legislate against what are found to be injurious practices in their internal commercial and business affairs so long as their laws do not run afoul of some specific federal constitutional prohibition or of some valid federal law." Lincoln Federal Labor Union v. Northwestern Iron & Metal Co., 335 U.S. 525, 536 (1949). For another example of Justice Black's view of state power, see his dissenting opinion in the Arizona case, cited in note 32. For Justice Frankfurter's earlier views on state power, see his dissenting opinion in Hill v. Florida, 325 U.S. 538, 547-61 (1945). One of the minor puzzles of our time is what has induced these justices to abandon their earlier views concerning the allowable scope of state action in a field involving federal law.

38. A classic statement of the rule by the Supreme Court itself declared that "the repugnance or conflict should be direct and positive, so that the two acts could not be reconciled or consistently stand together." Sinnot v. Davenport, 22 How. 242 (1859). It will be noted that the new Senate proposal is little more than a rephrasing of the Court's formulation of the rule. Congress is, it would seem, trying only to induce the Supreme Court to follow its own rules.

39. For a general survey of legal developments in England, see Sir David Lindsay Keir, *The Constitutional History of Modern Britain, 1485-1937* (3d ed.; Princeton: D. Van Nostrand Co., Inc., 1948), especially pp. 27 ff.

40. Sir Henry Sumner Maine, *Ancient Law* (World Classics; London: Oxford University Press, 1950), chap. i.

41. *Ibid.,* chap. iii.

42. *Ibid.* And see Maitland, *Equity,* pp. 7 ff.; G. W. Keeton, *An Introduction to Equity* (London: Sir Isaac Pitman & Sons, 1938), pp. 22 ff.

43. Dill, J., in Vanderbilt v. Mitchell, 67 Atl. 97, 102 (New Jersey Court of Errors and Appeals, 1907). A suit to cancel a false paternity certificate by a man who contended that his wife was wrongfully attributing parentage to him.

44. Roscoe Pound, "Equitable Relief Against Defamation and Injuries to Personality," 29 *Harvard Law Review* 640, at 666-67 (1916).

45. "English Law," 8 *Encyclopaedia Britannica* (1955 edition), 564, 567.

46. Cf. Charles O. Gregory, *Labor and the Law* (New York: W. W. Norton & Co., Inc., 1946), p. 94.

47. This is not by any means to say that the courts all held all boycotts indiscriminately unlawful. Many courts refused to enjoin

boycotts. See, for example, Pierce v. Stablemen's Union, 156 Cal. 70 (1909); Lindsay v. Montana Federation, 37 Mont. 264 (1908).

48. Cf. Chapter 14.

49. For the history of the crusade, see Felix Frankfurter and Nathan Greene, *The Labor Injunction* (New York: Macmillan Co., 1930), pp. 134 ff., especially pp. 206-208.

50. American Steel Foundries v. Tri-City Central Trades Council, 257 U.S. 184 (1921). For an analysis of the Court's interpretation of the Clayton Act in this case, see 2 *Labor Law Journal* 483 (1951).

51. *The Labor Injunction*, p. 201.

52. Cf. Chapter 14.

53. See the samples of decrees reproduced in Appendices IV-VII of *The Labor Injunction*.

54. See the table of cases, *ibid.*, p. 291.

55. *Ibid.*, pp. 32, 33, 39, 88, 97, 171.

56. American Steel Foundries, cited in note 50.

57. See *The Labor Injunction*, pp. 47-8.

58. Gregory, *Labor and the Law*, p. 97.

59. Cf. Chapter 4, pages 39-42 and notes thereto.

60. Gregory, p. 95.

61. Sir Richard Malins, V. C., in Dixon v. Holden, L. R. 7 Eq. 488 (1869). Roscoe Pound said in 1916 that "the view taken [by Malins in that case] as to the meaning of the term property in connection with equity jurisdiction still obtains." *Op. cit.* in note 44, at 648.

62. The validity of this conclusion is, in fact, attested by the Norris-LaGuardia Act itself; for, while drastically limiting the equity jurisdiction of the federal courts, it nevertheless permits the issuance of *ex parte* restraining orders in some instances (29 U.S.C. § 107).

63. Francis B. Sayre, "Labor and the Courts," 39 *Yale Law Journal* 682 (1930).

64. See the catalogue of unenjoinable conduct in Section 4 of the Norris Act. In order to be unenjoinable, the specified conduct (including every kind of strike, picketing, or boycott, regardless of objective) has to occur in a "case involving or growing out of any labor dispute." However, the term "labor dispute" was defined broadly enough in Section 13 of the Act, to include practically every situation in which a trade union might be involved. See New Negro Alliance v. Sanitary Grocery Co., Inc., 303 U.S. 552 (1938); Matson Navigation Co. v. Seafarer's International Union, 100 F. Supp. 730 (D.C. Md. 1951).

65. Of the Norris Act, Judge Otis said: "[It] is only another of a series of acts . . . through which runs the assumption that judges, although appointed by the President by and with the advice and consent of the Senate, either at the time of their appointment or immediately thereafter (as the result of a strange metamorphosis that comes over them), really are not possessed of either impartiality or integrity. Perhaps the humiliation which this assumption would inflict is a little lessened

by the realization that such a statute is enacted not so much to enable men to escape the judges as to escape the law." Donnelly Garment Co. v. Int. Ladies' Garment Workers, 21 F. Supp. 807, 817 (D.C. Mo. 1937).

66. At p. 215. For other evidence in *The Labor Injunction* of fidelity to "the reign of law," see pp. 200, 213, 219, 220, 222-23, 226.

67. United States v. Hutcheson, 312 U.S. 219 (1941).

68. *Ibid.,* at 245. Justice Roberts' short dissenting opinion is well worth reading.

69. See, for example, Archibald Cox, "Federalism in the Law of Labor Relations," 67 *Harvard Law Review* 1297, 1302 ff. (1954).

70. See generally Bernard Schwartz, "Administrative Justice and Its Place in the Legal Order," 30 *New York University Law Review* 1390, 1397-1410 (1955).

71. *Ibid.*

72. For a detailed analysis of a fairly typical piece of NLRB "reasoning," see my articles in 3 *Labor Law Journal* 659, 739, especially at 802-803 (Oct. and Nov., 1952).

73. See the investigations, reports, statistics, and trends in the law cited by Schwartz, *op. cit.* in note 70.

74. Section 10(b) of the National Labor Relations Act so provides.

75. See the works cited in note 21, above.

76. Cf. note 23, above.

77. NLRB v. Pittsburgh S.S. Co., 337 U.S. 656 (1949); NLRB v. Geraldine Novelty Co., 173 F. 2d 14 (2d Cir. 1949).

78. See the tortuous process involved in Capital Service v. NLRB, 347 U.S. 501 (1954) and described in 4 *Labor Law Journal* 534, 659 (1953).

79. See the symposium, "Hoover Commission and Task Force Reports on Legal Services and Procedure," 30 *New York University Law Review* 1267 ff. (Nov., 1955).

80. Quoted by Schwartz, *op. cit.* in note 70, at 1415.

81. For several examples, see *op. cit.* in note 72, at 659-60.

82. *Ibid.,* at 387, 447-48.

83. Vogt, Inc. v. Teamsters, 29 CCH Lab. Cas. ¶ 69,747 (1956).

84. *Op. cit.* in note 70 above, at 1411.

85. *Ibid.* at 1413.

86. Albert Schweitzer, *Out of My Life and Thought* (New York: Henry Holt & Co., Inc., 1949); see especially the epilogue.

INDEX

to leading cases, to names, and to topics

Free trade
  domestic, in U. S., 103
  frustrated by union conduct, 116-17
  and tariffs, 60
Freedom, as basic human objective, 8;
    see also Personal freedom
Freedom of association; *see* Free association
Freedom of contract
  and coercion, 45-48
  indispensable to personal freedom, 37-39
  natural and human coercion distinguished, 46-48
  as property right, 42
  role in society, 63-65
  scope of, 44-48
Freedom of press
  and advertising revenues, 57
  and interventionism, 56-57
  private property necessary to, 56-57
Freedom of speech
  basic social right, 82
  of employers, 145-47
  and picketing, 130, 198-99, 239
  price-controls violative of, 176-79
  relationship to private property, 56
  scope of right of, 82-83
Freidman, Milton, 315

Garner v. Teamsters, 308, 317, 322, 323
General Counsel, NLRB, authority of, 265-67
General Motors Corp., 296
General welfare and property rights, 87
Giboney v. Empire Storage Co., 313
Gompers, Samuel, 275
Good-faith bargaining requirement
  as disguised interventionism, 214-17, 254-56
  proposal to abolish, 254-56
Goodwins v. Hagedorn, 307
Government; *see also* State
  and personal freedom, 36
  personnel not godlike, 61
  as social institution, 14
  waste and inefficiency, 35
"Government by Injunction," charges

considered, 194-98, 275-79; *see also* Equity; Injunctions
Government seizure; *see* Seizure in labor disputes
Great Northern Ry. v. Brosseau, 312
Gregory, Charles O., 278, 302, 304, 306, 307, 308, 311, 312, 317, 324
Grievances; *see also* Arbitration
  employee vs. union and employer, 228
  legal action by workers, 231
  prosecution of, by unions, 230

Hamilton, Alexander, 270
Hand, Judge Learned, 323
Hartley v. Brotherhood of Clerks, 223, 316
Hayek, Freidrich A., 61, 292, 295, 296, 298, 311
Health, as a human objective, 15-17
Hiring power of unions and employers compared, 110-12
Hitchman Coal & Coke Co. v. Mitchell, 49, 301, 303
Hoffer, Eric, 298
Holmes, Justice O. W., 81, 161, 308
Hoover Commission, 287
"Hot-cargo" contracts
  defined, 154-55
  status under federal law, 168
Hughes v. Superior Court, 313
Human objectives
  role of society in promoting, 3-23
  unity and harmony of, 8, 10-23
Humboldt, Baron von, 32
Hume, David, 120

Independent unions
  under interventionism, 184-86
  Taft-Hartley Act, 187
Individual action, effect of taxation on, 94
Individual employees; *see also* Workers
  common law status of, 193
  right to present grievances, 133
  right to refuse to strike, 134
Industrial unions; *see* Affiliated unions; Craft groups; Trade unions
Industry-wide bargaining, ambiguities of, 135